BIBLIOGRAPHY OF THE HISTORY

OF BRITISH METAL MINING

Books, Theses and Articles Published on the
History of Metal Mining in England, Wales
Scotland and the Isle of Man Since the
Second World War

Roger Burt

Peter Waite

The University of Exeter
in association with
The National Association of
Mining History Organisations

First Published 1988 by the University of Exeter
in association with The National Association
of Mining History Organisations

Other related publications

The Derbyshire Mineral Statistics 1845-1913
The Yorkshire Mineral Statistics 1845-1913
The Cumberland Mineral Statistics 1845-1913
*The Lancashire and Westmorland Mineral Statistics
with the Isle of Man 1845-1913*
The Durham and Northumberland Mineral Statistics 1845-1913
Devon and Somerset Mines 1845-1913
Cornish Mines 1845-1913
The Mines of Cardiganshire 1845-1913

ISBN 0 85989 319 7

Printed in Great Britain by A. Wheaton & Co. Ltd, Exeter

CONTENTS

PREFACE

This is the first publication to be sponsored by the National Association of Mining History Organisations. We hope that it will lay the foundations of a continuing series. The bibliography is designed to be part of an expanding "tool kit" of material to facilitate research into the history of metal mining in Britain and abroad and joins work previously published from the University of Exeter on *The Mineral Statistics of the United Kingdom*. It draws together a wide range of disparate literature published over five decades and for the first time gives a complete national picture of a subject which has developed on a piece–meal regional basis. It is intended both as a guide for those already working in the field and as an introduction to those approaching it for the first time. As such, it is clearly within the purview of N.A.M.H.O. which was formed in 1979, "to establish the subject of mining history as a cohesive discipline and to promote the subject in all of its various aspects." Today N.A.M.H.O. has over forty member organisations, many of whose publications are included here.

We have collected most of the material presented here and must take responsibility for its accuracy and method of presentation. However, we have received invaluable assistance from a large number of people in all parts of the country who have sent details of additional material and helped to check our lists. If we mention a few by name, we hope that the many others who are not included will not be offended. Particular thanks must be expressed to Mike Gill and Lynn Willies for their work on Derbyshire and Yorkshire respectively; Ivor Brown for material on Shropshire and other areas; David Bick, Jeremy Wilkinson, Alan and Christopher Williams for references on North and Central Wales; Paul Sowan for a large part of our limited material on the South East; Christopher Schmitz for his work on Scotland; and Andy Bowman for all sorts of interesting bits and pieces. We hope that whoever updates this collection in years to come, can call on such friendly and expert advice.

INTRODUCTION

This collection was intended as a comprehensive bibliography of all books, theses and articles on British metalliferous mining that have been published since the Second World War. It almost certainly falls short of that objective. There are undoubtedly many titles, perhaps even entire journals, that have been overlooked. We hope that we have covered the ground fairly well, however, and that there are no major omissions. Any significant material that does come to light could be included in future up–dating editions. What we think that we have achieved here is a useful collection of secondary reference works to assist new and established mining historians in checking the existing literature in the field and in helping them to shape and develop long–term research plans.

The main purpose of the study was to try to identify and pull together literature which could be principally identified as "metal mining history". In 1981, John Benson, Robert Neville and Charles Thompson produced a comprehensive *Bibliography of the British Coal Industry* for the National Coal Board, listing secondary references as well as a wide range of primary material, including Parliamentary Papers, Maps and Plans. We thought it appropriate to produce a similar, though less ambitious work, on Britain's other major extractive industries. Restricting ourselves for the moment to the modern secondary literature, and leaving quarrying aside for a separate volume, we have collected material on the mining of iron, copper, lead/silver, tin, zinc and manganese ores, together with the rarer metals such as gold and tungsten and major associated minerals, such as arsenic, barytes and fluorspar.

Unlike the coal industry, which has enjoyed the academic limelight for many years, the history of the metal mining industries has been largely ignored by the professional historians. This was mainly because of the early collapse of metal mining into relative obscurity. The industry did not provide significant twentieth century economic and social problems which could act as a focus for historical research. Its early demise also meant that it never experienced the benefits of nationalisation. Research into metal mining history has never received the flow of funding from the industry and wealthy unions that has so encouraged the coal historians. Whatever the reasons, metal mining history was left to develop randomly from the essentially peripheral interests of antiquarians, local historians, geologists and other non–specialists. From its origins among these groups around the mid–century, it gradually emerged into what could best be described as a specialist branch of industrial archaeology in the 1960s and 70s. Like that broader subject, it continued to lack any coherent methodology or central philosophy, let alone a theoretical structure. However, it has exploited that anarchy to find an energy and excitement that continues to draw the active support of thousands of enthusiasts nationwide. In many respects it can be compared with the "railway history phenomenon" that has received such widespread public interest since British Rail decided there was no future in steam!

From its earliest origins, metal mining was, and still remains, locally orientated. The great bulk of published material relates to the history of particular mines or small mining districts with very few attempts to generalise to a national or even a comparative regional picture. This is quite reasonable for a subject reliant mainly on part–time practitioners, finding their inspiration near at home and having easy access only to local record offices. The most convenient way to arrange the material that we have collected was on a regional basis: that is how it was written and that is how it will mainly be used. No doubt there will be quibbles over the allocation of certain references between regional sections—particularly the Pennine divisions, which were made very arbitrarily—but the great majority of the material is easily and directly classifiable. With the principal non–ferrous metals being fairly localised—copper mainly in the South West and North Wales; lead mainly in the Pennines and North and Central Wales; and tin only in Cornwall and Devon—the regional classification also provides a loose subject structure.

In our geographical coverage of the subject, we have restricted ourselves to mainland Britain, together with the Isle of Man. This reflects no particular prejudice against the Irish. A wide range of mining activities flourished there for centuries but we could not ourselves easily access the libraries of the north and south to list the specialist literature. Neither did we know anyone resident who would have acted reliably as our agent! From what we have seen, however, it would appear that not much recent work has been done and that it remains a fertile frontier for future research. Scotland did not present such formidable problems, largely because much of its mining history has been written by English researchers and/or published in English journals. An ex–Exeter colleague, Christopher Schmitz, now a member of the Department of Modern History at St.Andrews University, also greatly assisted us by providing additional references. Similarly, most of the important recent material on mining in the Isle of Man has been published in the major English mining history journals, as has much literature on the Welsh industry. For the latter we also received considerable help in identifying the material available in local history transactions and journals specifically devoted to the Principality, from David Bick, Alan Williams and many others.

The main problem encountered in pulling together a collection of this kind was not deciding or maintaining its main focus, nor arranging the final body of material. Rather it was in drawing the boundaries of the subject - what is metal mining history and what is not. At the outset it all seemed fairly clear, but as work progressed it increasingly appeared as though the subject was being viewed through a fish—eye lens, with the edges becoming more and more blurred as the frame widened. One of the most complex problems to resolve was what to do about material on the processing of the ores once they had left the mine: viz. reduction and refining. The solution that was adopted seemed to make sense at the time but has resulted in a rather unbalanced treatment of the ferrous and non—ferrous ores. As a working rule, it was decided to include all material on smelting where it made at least passing reference to the production or distribution of the ore. As it turned out, in terms of the overall shape of the material, this has meant that we have included virtually all of the recent work on the initial processing of *non—ferrous* ores. In general, relatively little has been written on the smelting of tin, copper and lead and that which has appeared tends to be found in the "mining literature" rather than in separate specialist studies. For *iron*, however, the situation is almost entirely reversed. Here the interests of historians have long been focused on smelting and refining and very little has been done on mining and the differing character of the ores. A situation has thus arisen where we have collected most of the material on the smelting of non—ferrous ores but very little on the smelting of iron. In some ways this is a fortunate result. There is so much information on iron processing that it would have swamped the entire volume, and overwhelmed its main purpose, had it been included. Nevertheless, the split between mining and metallurgical history, which is so apparent in the ferrous sector, is to be much regretted. By looking at only one aspect of the overall costs of producing metals, it clearly devalues the overall accuracy and usefulness of the work in both sectors.

Other blurred or ragged edges to the collection can be found in work which includes mining history as part of a wider account of regional geology, local history, industrial archaeology, transport or technological history etc. The central focus of attention in such material is no longer mining history but valuable material is often included which can be found

vii

nowhere else. Volumes like those of H.G.Dines and K.C.Dunham on the regional mining geology of South West England and the Northern Pennines, were never conceived or written specifically as exercises in mining history but they have become basic reference works for all historians working on those districts. Like the material on the iron industry, the big problem with this literature is knowing how far to go in including progressively more marginal references. Without carefully reading every potential inclusion—which was impossible in the time available for this project—the decisions were inevitably arbitrary and undoubtedly led to some mistakes. In the final analysis we will certainly have left out useful material that could have been included and put in some slight and barely relevant literature.

One solution to this problem would have been to leave out the marginal material altogether; to have kept strictly to the central brief of searching for a separate and identifiable subject of "metal mining history". To have done this, however, would have resulted in more damage than the simple loss of some important additional material. In recent years the subject has become increasingly introspective. From its early interdisciplinary origins, it has developed into a business largely concerned with writing the mine–by–mine history of every district of England, Wales and Scotland. There has certainly been a place for this and a great deal of invaluable material has been unearthed. There are still many other important mines and mining companies awaiting similar investigation. However, the time is at hand when the subject should begin to be put back into its broader context. Attempts must be made to show its inter–relationships with other aspects of local economy, society and culture; to investigate the routes and methods of transportation of ore from mines to smelters, to manufacturers and final market; to look at the general problems of the diffusion of new methods and machinery—these and other issues to be pursued not only regionally but nationally and internationally. Everywhere the subject needs to be reset in its large regional and industrial context. Without the reinvigorating effects of introducing these "external stimuli", the subject is in danger of collapsing under its own inertia. It certainly will fail to achieve its full potential and will fall short of its goal of projecting to the widest possible audience.

Some indication of the changing health and vigour of mining history can be obtained from analysing the chronological profile of the publications included in this collection. This approach was suggested to us by David Bick, ever conscious of the buoyancy of the market for mining publications, and provides an interesting view of the growth and development of the subject. Graph 1 shows the number of articles published annually between 1946 and 1986. It is based on a three year moving average to help iron out random short–term fluctuations and uses a sample of just over 1,700 articles. In the 1940s and 1950s the level of publications was low, generally between 10 and 20 per year. Most appeared in the transactions of local history societies and the trades' press. From the early 1960s, however, the subject began to grow rapidly, with the average annual number of articles published almost quadrupling during the decade. This growth was mainly based on the appearance of a new range of specialist journals, particularly those published by the Peak District Mines Historical Society and the Northern Cavern and Mine Research Society. There was some fall off in the rate of publications in the early 1970s but they recovered to an all–time peak by 1978. This continued growth was based on a further expansion of the number of specialist journals as well as a sustained high level of activity in the traditional local history journals. However, from that year through to the early 1980s there was a sharp and continuous fall in activity. The decline was checked in 1981/2 but the annual number of publications seems to have levelled off on a new low plateau, roughly equal to that of the early 1960s.

What has been happening? None of the major specialist journals has ceased publication. Indeed, their number and activities have even expanded slightly. What seems to have occurred is that the subject has become very specialised. Little now appears in the local transactions, general industrial archaeology literature or even other subject journals. Metal mining history has clearly become a discipline in its own right but in doing so has cut its links with other related areas. There may have been a consequent loss of interest and active participation as those contacts have been severed. However, that is probably not the whole story. The standards of the published work have also risen; authors have to work harder and longer to reach the standards required by the better journals. In its early years, metal mining history was essentially an amateurs'/antiquarians' interest. Even the doyens of the subject— A.K.Hamilton Jenkin, Nellie Kirkham, Arthur Raistrick and others— either had no formal academic training or were working well outside of their main areas of expertise. This has changed significantly in the last twenty years, partly because of the entry of academic historians into the subject but, more importantly, because of the "professionalisation" of many of the non–academics. A number of the pioneers of the great expansion of activity in the 1960s have now published very extensively, improved their work by practice and achieved the highest academic credentials for their work. While this has undoubtedly improved the quality of the best that is published, in terms of the rigour of the research and the depth of analysis, it has at the same time made it more difficult for the inexperienced to make their first mark. Improving standards have made it more difficult to publish. Again this could lead to a loss of vitality and a decline of new initiatives in the subject. Professionalism is all very well but enthusiasm and energy are just as important.

Finally, brief mention must be made of the overall structure and balance of the material collected here. Firstly it covers a wide range of different approaches from casual, inexpert accounts of underground exploration, through to highly complex analyses of archival sources and extensive secondary literature. The exclusion of newsletters from our survey generally had the effect of concentrating attention on the more substantive material but the quality remains very variable. Secondly, as previously noticed, the material is heavily locally orientated but the degree of local interest and publication varies considerably between the regions. These variations show little correlation with the relative historical importance of the local industry or the extent and importance of its surviving remains. For example, over 40 per cent of the material listed here relates to Derbyshire and the South West. Although the latter region was certainly in the forefront of mining activity throughout recent history, Derbyshire's best years were over by the end of the eighteenth century and it only again became a significant national producer for a few years in the twentieth century. Most of the vast amount of material that appears on Derbyshire mining relates to relatively small enterprises which had limited significance in the overall structure of the metal mining industry during the period with which they are primarily concerned. It is to the great credit of the Peak District Mines Historical Society that they have been able to engender and sustain that interest. By contrast, the very large and important lead mines of the northern Pennines have received scant attention from their local inhabitants. Much of the relatively small amount of material that has been published on the region comes from "outsiders", moving their interests northwards from the heartland of mining history in Yorkshire and Derbyshire. An even worse case of neglect can be found for the Flintshire/ Denbighshire district of north east Wales. A leading lead/silver producing district of both the eighteenth and nineteenth centuries, with important visitable remains, its history has been hardly touched by researchers in the last fifteen years. North west and mid–Wales fare better as does Shropshire/

Cheshire/Staffordshire, which has received relatively good coverage.

The regional imbalance in the material is matched by a chronological and topical imbalance. Most published material is heavily orientated towards the nineteenth century with some shading back into the eighteenth century. There is very little on the seventeenth century and earlier and even less on the twentieth century. The scarcity of records and the difficulties for the untrained in reading and interpreting them provides some explanation for the poor attention paid to the earlier period but this is hardly relevant to the twentieth century. Metal mining certainly declined sharply in the late nineteenth century but it did not entirely disappear after the First World War. All districts have seen continuing activity of one sort or another and a now lengthy period awaits investigation. It would be appropriate to start looking at twentieth century metal mining before lurching into the twenty first century! The topical imbalance has already been mentioned in terms of the relatively small amount of material on iron mining. It might also be noticed that the heavy concentration on the mining of lead, copper and tin has banished consideration of the other important non–ferrous metals, such as zinc and manganese, to a twilight zone. Still less has been done on the production, sale and uses of the associated minerals, such as barytes, fluorspar and arsenic and virtually nothing on the rarer minerals wolfram, uranium, radium etc. Some of these ores played an important part in the overall economy of the mining of the major metals and they deserve greater attention.

It is important to stress that none of these irregularities results from any general lack of interest or energy. Even the most obscure subjects have supported some investigation. Rather it is that some areas are cast into shadow by the exceptionally high level of activity elsewhere. A great deal of work has been done on all aspects of metal mining history and sound foundations have been established for a comprehensive national view of this important industry. The literature listed in this collection represents a triumph for grass–roots enterprise and initiative and reflects great credit on the large number of clubs, societies and institutions who have fostered and published it. Hopefully the subject will continue to receive the same enthusiastic support and be assisted in its future growth and development by this guide to its past achievements.

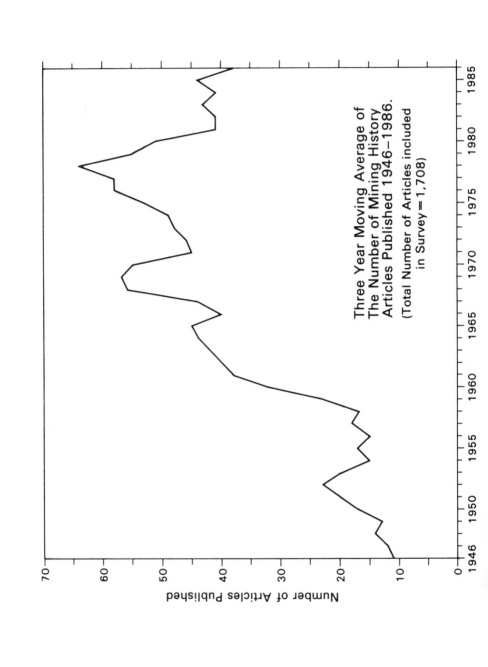

Three Year Moving Average of
The Number of Mining History
Articles Published 1946–1986.
(Total Number of Articles included
in Survey = 1,708)

BIBLIOGRAPHY OF THE HISTORY

OF BRITISH METAL MINING

Arranged in
Regional Divisions

GENERAL REFERENCES

Books

AGRICOLA, G. *De Re Metallica* (translated by H.C.& L.H. Hoover) (New York: 1950)

ALLEN, J.S. *See* ROLT, L.T.C. & ALLEN, J.S.

ANDERSON, W. *See* WHITEHEAD, T.H., ANDERSON, W., WILSON, V. & WRAY, D.A.

ANON *Metal Statistics* (Frankfurt–am–Main: Metallgesellschaft A.G., Annually since 1912)

ANON *Economic Minerals of the United Kingdom. Mineral Dossier No.9. Tin* (H.M.S.O., 1975)

ARMSTRONG, Thomas *Adam Brunskill* (Collins, 1952)

BARBEY, M.F. *Civil Engineering Heritage: Northern England* (Thomas Telford Ltd., 1981)

BARKER, Theodore C. *See* HATCHER, John & BARKER, Theodore C.

BEAVER, S.H. *See* STAMP, L.D. & BEAVER, S.H.

BIRD, Richard H. *Britain's Old Metal Mines* (Truro: Bradford Barton, 1974)

BIRD, Richard H. *Yesterday's Golcondas: Notable British Metal Mines* (Buxton: Moorland, 1977)

BRYAN, Andrew *The Evolution of Health and Safety in Mines* (Ashire, 1975)

BURT, Roger *A Short History of British Metal Mining Technology in the Eighteenth and Nineteenth Centuries* (Lelielaan: De Archaeologische Pers, 1982)

BURT, Roger *A Short History of British Ore Preparation Techniques in the Eighteenth and Nineteenth Centuries* (Lelielaan: De Archaeologische Pers, 1982)

BURT, Roger *The British Lead Mining Industry* (Redruth: Dyllansow Truran, 1984)

CARDWELL, D.S.L. *Steam Power in the Eighteenth Century* (Sheed & Ward, 1963)

1

GENERAL REFERENCES

COCKS, E.J. & WALTERS, B. *A History of the Zinc Smelting Industry in Britain* (Harrap, 1968)

COSTE, P-L. & PERDONNET, A.A. *Smelting of Lead Ores in Reverberatory Furnaces as Performed in Great Britain* (First published in *Annales des Mines* Vol.III (1830). English translation published Eindhoven: De Archaeologische Pers, 1986)

CRADDOCK, P.T.(Ed) *Scientific Studies in Early Mining and Extractive Metallurgy* (British Museum, Occassional Paper No.20, 1980)

CRADDOCK, P.T. & HUGHES, M.J. (Ed.) *Furnaces and Smelting Technology in Antiquity* (British Museum, Occasional Paper No.48, 1985)

CRAWFORD, H. (Ed.) *Subterranean Britain* (John Barker, 1979)

CROSSLEY, David W. *Medieval Industry* (Council for British Archaeology, Research Report No.40, 1981)

DAY, Joan *Bristol Brass: A History of the Industry* (Newton Abbot: David & Charles, 1973)

DONALD, M.B. *Elizabethan Copper: The History of the Company of Mines Royal* (Pergamon, 1955)

DONALD, M.B. *Elizabethan Copper: The History of the Company of the Mines Royal* (Whitehaven: Michael Moon, 1987. Reprint of 1955 Edition.)

DONALD, M.B. *Elizabethan Monopolies* (Oliver & Boyd, 1961)

DOWNS–ROSE, Geoffrey *See* HARVEY, William & DOWNS–ROSE, Geoffrey

FAREY, John *A Treatise on the Steam Engine* 2 Volumes (Newton Abbot: David & Charles, 1971. Reprint of 1827 Edition.)

FELL, James E. *See* NIEBUR, Jay E. & FELL, James E.

FOX, William *Tin: The Working of a Commodity Agreement* (Mining Journal, 1974)

FULLER, T. (With Introduction and Notes by John Freeman) *The Worthies of England* (1952. Reprint of 1662 Edition.)

GREGORY, Cedric E. *A Concise History of Mining* (Pergamon, 1980)

GROVES, A.W. *Wartime Investigations into the Haematite and Manganese Ore Resources of Great Britain and Northern Ireland* (Ministry of Supply Monographs, No.20, 1952)

HAMILTON, H. *The English Brass and Copper Industries to 1800* (Cass, 1967. Second Edition)

2

HANNAN, Norman E. *Travels and Heartaches of a Mining Family* (Romford: Private Publication, 1984)

HARVEY, William & DOWNS–ROSE, Geoffrey *William Symington: Inventor and Engine Builder* (Northgate Publishing Co., 1980)

HATCHER, John and BARKER, Theodore C. *A History of British Pewter* (Longmans, 1974)

HAYES, Geoffrey *Stationary Steam Engines: A Guide* (Buxton: Moorland, 1981)

HEALY, John F. *Mining and Metallurgy in the Greek and Roman World* (Thames & Hudson, 1978)

HEWLETT, H.B. *The Quarries, Ironstone, Limestone and Sand* (Oakham: Market Overton Industrial Railway Association, 1979. Reprint of 1935 Edition.)

HUGHES, M.J. *See* CRADDOCK, P.T. & HUGHES, M.J.

HUNT, Robert *A Historical Sketch of British Mining by Robert Hunt, F.R.S. being Book 1 and the Appendix to British Mining by Robert Hunt (1887)* (East Ardsley: E.P. Publishing Ltd., 1978)

INSTITUTION OF MINING AND METALLURGY *The Future of Non–Ferrous Mining in Great Britain and Ireland: A Symposium* (Institution of Mining and Metallurgy, 1959)

McDONALD, Donald *Percival Norton Johnson: The Biography of a Pioneer Metallurgist* (Johnson Matthey & Co. Ltd., 1951)

McNEIL, I *Hydraulic Power* (Longmans, 1972)

METCALFE, J.E. *British Mining Fields* (Institution of Mining and Metallurgy, 1969)

MINCHINTON, Walter E. *The British Tinplate Industry* (Oxford: Clarendon Press, 1957)

MOLLOY, Peter M. *The History of Metal Mining and Metallurgy: An Annotated Bibliography* Vol.12 in *Bibliographies of the History of Science and Technology* (New York: Garland, 1986)

NATIONAL COUNCIL OF ASSOCIATED IRON ORE PRODUCERS *The Iron Industry of Great Britain* (Kettering: National Council of Iron Ore Producers, 1960)

NAYLOR, Peter *Discovering Lost Mines* (Aylesbury: Shire Publications, 1981)

NEWMAN, B. *One Hundred Years of Good Company: Ruston and Hornsby Ltd* (Ruston & Hornsby Ltd., 1958)

GENERAL REFERENCES

NIEBUR, Jay E. with FELL, James E. *Arthur Redman Wilfley: Miner, Inventor and Entrepreneur* (Colorado Historical Society, 1983)

PALMER, Marilyn (Ed) *The Onset of Industrialisation: Papers Presented at a Conference at Nottingham University, December 1976* (Nottingham: University of Nottingham Department of Adult Education, 1977)

PEARSON, A. *Robert Hunt, F.R.S.* (Cornwall: Federation of Old Cornwall Societies, 1976)

PERCY, John *Metallurgy: Vol.1 Pt 1 Fuel; Fire Clays; Copper; Zinc; Brass* (Eindhoven: Der Archaeologische Pers, 1985. Reprint of 1861 Edition.)

PERCY, John *Metallurgy: Vol.1 Pt 2 Copper; Zinc; Brass* (Eindhoven: Der Archaeologische Pers, 1985. Reprint of 1861 Edition.)

PERCY, John *Metallurgy: Vol.2 Pt 1 Properties of Iron; Iron Ores; Direct Production Process* (Eindhoven: Der Archaeologische Pers, 1985. Reprint of 1864 Edition.)

PERCY, John *Metallurgy: Vol.2 Pt 2 Indirect Reduction Process* (Eindhoven: Der Archaeologische Pers, 1985. Reprint of 1864 Edition.)

PERCY, John *Metallurgy: Vol.2 Pt 3 Wrought Iron; Steel* (Eindhoven: Der Archaeologische Pers, 1985. Reprint of 1864 Edition.)

PERCY, John *Metallurgy: Vol.3 Pt 1 Properties of Lead; Lead Desilverization* (Eindhoven: Der Archaeologische Pers, 1986. Reprint of 1870 Edition.)

PERCY, John *Metallurgy: Vol.3 Pt 2 Lead* (Eindhoven: Der Archaeologische Pers, 1986. Reprint of 1870 Edition.)

PERDONNET, A.A. *See* COSTE, P–L. & PERDONNET, A.A.

PETTUS, J. *Fodinae Regales* (Institution of Mining and Metallurgy, 1980. Reprint of 1639 Edition.)

PIKE, J.R. *Britain's Metal Mines: A Complete Guide to Their Laws, Usages, Localities and Statistics* (Sheffield: Mining Facsimiles, 1987. Reprint of 1860 Edition.)

PLATTES, G. *A Discovery of Subterranean Treasure* (Institution of Mining and Metallurgy, 1980. Reprint of 1639 Edition.)

RAISTRICK, Arthur *Silver and Lead. The Story of a Quaker Mining Experiment* (Friends Home Service Committee, 1948)

RAISTRICK, Arthur *Quakers in Science and Industry: Being an Account of the Quaker Contributions to Science and Industry During the*

4

17th and 18th Centuries (Bannisdale Press, 1950)

RAISTRICK, Arthur *Quakers in Science and Industry: Being an Account of the Quaker Contributions to Science and Industry During the 17th and 18th Centuries* (Newton Abbot: David & Charles, 1968. Reprint of 1950 Edition.)

RAISTRICK, Arthur *Dynasty of Iron Founders: The Darbys and Coalbrookdale* (Longmans, 1953)

RAISTRICK, Arthur (Ed.) *The Hatchett Diary: A Tour Through the Counties of England and Scotland in 1796 Visiting their Mines and Manufactories* (Truro: Bradford Barton, 1967)

REES, W. *Industry before the Industrial Revolution* (Cardiff, 1968)

RICHARDSON, J.B. *Metal Mining* (Allen Lane, 1974)

ROLT, L.T.C. & ALLEN, J.S. *The Steam Engine of Thomas Newcomen* (Buxton: Moorland, 1977)

ROWE, David J. *Lead Manufacturing in Britain: A History* (Beckenham: Croom Helm, 1983)

SCHMITZ, Christopher J. *World Metal Production and Prices* (Frank Cass, 1979)

SCOTT, W.R. *The Constitution and Finance of English, Scottish and Irish Joint Stock Companies to 1720* (Cambridge: Cambridge University Press, 1951. Reprint of 1910–12 Edition.)

SHEPHERD, R. *Prehistoric Mining and Allied Industries* (Academic Press, 1980)

SPOONER, Derek *Mining and Regional Development* (Oxford: Oxford University Press, 1981)

STAMP, L.D. & BEAVER, S.H. *The British Isles: A Geographic and Economic Survey* (1954)

SUTCLIFFE, E.D. *See* SUTCLIFFE, R. & SUTCLIFFE, E.D.

SUTCLIFFE, R. & SUTCLIFFE, E.D. *Richard Sutcliffe. The Pioneer of Underground Belt Conveying* (Edinburgh: Private Publication, 1956)

TAYLOR, John *Records of Mining* (Sheffield: Mining Facsimiles, 1986. Reprint of 1829 Edition)

TUNZELMAN, G. Nicholas von *Steam Power and British Industrialisation to 1860* (Oxford: Clarendon Press, 1978)

TYLECOTE, R.F. *A History of Metallurgy* (Metals Society, 1976)

TYLECOTE, R.F. *Pre-History of Metallurgy in the British Isles* (Institute of Metals, 1986)

5

WALTERS, B. *See* COCKS, E.J. & WALTERS, B.

WHITEHEAD, T.H., ANDERSON, W., WILSON, V. & WRAY, D.A. *The Mesozoic Ironstones of England: The Liassic Ironstones* (Memoirs of the Geological Survey, H.M.S.O., 1952)

WILLIES, Lynn *Lead and Lead Mining* (Shire Books, 1982)

WILSON, V. *See* WHITEHEAD, T.H., ANDERSON, W., WILSON, V. & WRAY, D.A.

WOODALL, Frank D. *Steam Engines and Waterwheels: A Pictorial Study of Some Early Mining Machines* (Buxton: Moorland, 1975)

WRAY, D.A. *See* WHITEHEAD, T.H., ANDERSON, W., WILSON, V. & WRAY, D.A.

Theses

ALOND, J.K. *Factors Influencing Education in Metallurgy in England and Wales 1851–1950* (University of Durham MEd Thesis, 1983)

ATKINSON, Michael *Iron Ore Mining in Mainland Britain in the Nineteenth and Early Twentieth Centuries and its Links with the Iron and Steel Industry, with Particular Reference to Cleveland, Cumbria and the South Western Counties of England* (University of Exeter PhD Thesis, 1981)

BIRCH, A. *The Development and Organisation of the British Iron Industry 1815–1867* (University of Manchester MPhil Thesis, 1951)

BIRCH, A. *The Economic History of the British Iron and Steel Industry 1784–1897* (University of Manchester PhD Thesis, 1953)

BLAKE–COLEMAN, B.C. *The Rise of Copper Wire, its Manufacture and Use to 1900: A Case of Industrial Circumspection* (Open University MPhil Thesis, 1981)

BRADBEER, J.B. *Some Aspects of the Economic Geography of the Non-Ferrous Metal Mining Industry* (Council for Academic Awards MPhil Thesis, 1981)

BRAND, J.D. *The English Coinage 1180–1247: Money, Mints, and Exchange* (University of Kent MA Thesis, 1981)

BROWN, E.G. *The History of Metallic Magnesium 1808-1890* (University of Salford MSc Thesis, 1972)

BURT, Roger *The Lead Industry of England and Wales 1700-1880* (University of London PhD Thesis, 1971)

BUSH, R.C. *The Development of Geological Mapping in Britain between 1790 and 1825* (University of London PhD Thesis, 1974)

CHILD, H.S. *Explosives in the United Kingdom during the Middle Part of the Nineteenth Century, with Special Reference to Civilian Explosives* (University of Durham MSc Thesis, 1982)

CLEERE, H.F. *The Iron Industry of Roman Britain* (University of London PhD Thesis, 1981)

COSTELLO, Lynette M. *Profits A Prendre to Mineral Rights: The Evolution of Remedies in English Law* (University of Exeter MPhil Thesis, 1984)

DAVEY, P.C. *Studies in the History of Mining and Metallurgy to the Middle of the Seventeenth Century, Considered in Relation to the Progress of Scientific Knowledge and with Some Reference to Mining in Cornwall* (University of London PhD Thesis, 1954)

ELLIS, H.L. *The Marketing of Non–Ferrous Metals* (University of Birmingham MComm Thesis, 1926)

FLINN, M.W. *British Overseas Investment in Iron Ore Mining 1870-1914* (University of Manchester MA Thesis, 1952)

FOX, E.S. *A Review of the Contribution Made to the Development of the Steam Engine by the Employees, Associates and Customers of Matthew Boulton and James Watt, 1769-1800* (University of Leicester MPhil Thesis, 1982)

FREEMAN, W.A.D. *The Mints and Moneyers of Edward the Confessor* (University of Reading PhD Thesis, 1983)

GUDGIN, A. *The Marketing of Lead* (University of Wales MA Thesis, 1973)

HAMILTON, B.M. *The Development of Hard Rock Geology in Britain 1840-1900* (University of Lancaster PhD Thesis, 1979)

HARVEY, C.E. *The Rio Tinto Company 1873-1954: An Economic History of a Leading International Mining Concern* (University of Bristol PhD Thesis, 1981)

HETHERINGTON, R.J. *The Characterisation of Archaeological Slags, with Special Reference to those Derived from Lead Smelting* (University of Newcastle–upon–Tyne PhD Thesis, 1978)

GENERAL REFERENCES

HOPKINS, T.G.L. *The Development and Location of the Aluminium Industry in the U.K.* (University of Oxford BLitt Thesis, 1958)

McINTYRE, J.B. *The Role of the Wet Process in the Growth of the Pyrite Industry* (University of Nottingham PhD Thesis, 1975)

PORTER, Jeffery H. *Industrial Conciliation and Arbitration 1860–1914* (University of Leeds PhD Thesis, 1968)

PORTER, R.S. *The Making of the Science of Geology in Britain 1660–1815* (University of Cambridge PhD Thesis, 1975)

RIDEN, P. *The Growth of the British Iron Industry 1700–1880* (University of Oxford MLitt Thesis, 1979)

ROBERTS, Peter K. *British Canal Tunnels: A Geographical Study* (University of Salford PhD Thesis, 1977)

ROWE, D.J. *A History of the Lead Manufacturing Industry in Great Britain 1778–1980, with Special Reference to the Constituent Companies of Associated Lead Manufacturers Ltd.* (University of Newcastle–upon–Tyne PhD Thesis, 1982)

TAYLOR, J.J. *Prehistoric Gold–Working in the British Isles and its Relationship with Contemporary Gold–Working in Western Europe* (University of Cambridge PhD Thesis, 1970/1)

TYLER, W.A. *Prehistoric and Roman Mining for Metals in England and Wales* (University of Wales, Cardiff, PhD Thesis, 1983)

WILLIAMS, A.R. *Studies in the History of Gunpowder in the Middle Ages* (University of Manchester Institute of Science and Technology MSc Thesis, 1971/2)

Articles

ALLEN, G.Keith "A Half Century of Progress in Metal Mining: Part 1" *Mining Magazine*, Vol.101 No.4 (October 1959), pp.153–169

ALLEN, G.Keith "A Half Century of Progress in Metal Mining: Part 2" *Mining Magazine*, Vol.101 No.5 (November 1959), pp.232–246

ANON "The Ancient Art of Fire Setting" *Mine and Quarry Engineering*, Vol.15 (September 1949), pp.283–288

ANON "Domestic Haematite and Manganese" *Mining Magazine*, Vol.88 No.2 (February 1953), pp.66–67

ANON "British Mining" *Mine and Quarry Engineering*, Vol.28 (August 1962), p.337

BARKER, J.Lawrence "To the Poor Miner and to every Nobleman, Gentleman and Tradesman in the Country who feels interested in the Miner's Fate" *Memoirs of the Northern Cavern and Mine Research Society*, (December 1967), pp.17–24

BATCHELOR, L.B. "The Development of Statutory Duties in Relation to the Mining Industry in the United Kingdom" *Camborne School of Mines Journal*, (1973), pp.57–59

BICK, David E. "Exploring Derelict Metal Mines" *Dowty Group Journal*, (Autumn 1957), pp.6–7

BIRD, Richard H. "Notes on Subterranean Temperatures in Metal Mines" *British Mining*, No.3 (1976), pp.16–20

BIRD, Richard H. "A Note on the Application of Photography to Mining" *British Mining*, No.11 (1979), pp.48–49

BIRD, Richard H. "Surviving Miscellany" *British Mining*, No.19 (1982), pp.48–54

BLANCE, B. "Early Copper Working in Europe" *Antiquity*, Vol.33 (1959), pp.61–63

BLANCHARD, I.S.W. "The Miner and the Agricultural Community in Late Medieval England" *Agricultural History Review*, Second Series Vol.20 No.2 (1972), pp.93–106

BLANCHARD, I.S.W. "Labour Productivity and Work Psychology in the English Mining Industry 1400–1600" *Economic History Review*, Vol.XXXI No.1 (February 1978), pp.1–24

BLEZARD, M. "Some Aspects of Ore Flotation" *Shropshire Mining Club Journal*, (1971–2), pp.26–30

BOGGS, W.B. "The Copper Reverberatory" *Mining Magazine*, Vol.79 No.4 (October 1948), pp.201–207

BOR, L. "Mineral Resources of the British Jurassic" *Mine and Quarry Engineering*, Vol.17 (March 1951), pp.87–90

BREARS, Peter C.D. "Mines, Smelt Mills: Descriptions by an Edwardian Traveller" *British Mining*, No.23 (1983), pp.5–19

BRIGGS, C.S. "Bronze Age Mining" *Current Archaeology*, Vol.101 (1986), p191

BRITTON, G.C. & JOHNSON, C.H. "Strontium Pt.1: History, Mineralogy and Extraction" *School Science Review*, Vol.68 No.243 (1986), pp.236–244

BROOKE, Justin "The Bubble Company" *British Mining*, No.5 (1977), pp.6–9

BROWN, Ivor J. "Historical Outline of Mining" *Shropshire Mining Club*, Yearbook (1963–4), pp.40–45

BROWN, Ivor J. "The End of an Era" *Bulletin of the Peak District Mines Historical Society*, Vol.3 No.2 (December 1966), pp.75–84

BROWN, Ivor J. "Underground Iron Mining in Britain 1960–1975" *Shropshire Mining Club Journal*, (1974–5), pp.30–34

BROWN, Ivor J. "Mining History in the Making" *Bulletin of the Peak District Mines Historical Society*, Vol.8 No.3 (Summer 1982), pp.181–184

BUGLER, Jeremy *See* THOMAS, Richard & BUGLER, Jeremy

BURNETT, J.M. "Peat as an Industrial Fuel" *Memoirs of the Northern Cavern and Mine Research Society*, (October 1969), pp.22–24

BURT, Roger "Lead Production in England and Wales, 1700–1772" *Economic History Review*, Second Series Vol.XXII No.2 (1969), pp.249–268

BURT, Roger "The London Mining Exchange 1850–1900" *Business History*, Vol.XIV No.1 (1972), pp.124–143

BURT, Roger "The Mineral Statistics of the United Kingdom: An Analysis of the Accuracy of the Copper and Tin Returns for Cornwall and Devon" *Journal of the Trevithick Society*, No.8 (1981), pp.31–46

BURT, Roger "The Use of Some Minor Elements and Minerals Since the 18th Century" *Geology Teaching*, Vol.9 No.4 (December 1984), pp.119–124

BURT, Roger & WAITE, Peter "An Introduction to the Mineral Statistics of the United Kingdom, 1845–1913" *British Mining*, No.23 (1983), pp.40–58

CAW, J.M. "Mining in Great Britain and Ireland. Part 1" *Mine and Quarry Engineering*, Vol.25 (January 1959), pp.22–30

CAW, J.M. "Mining in Great Britain and Ireland. Part 2" *Mine and Quarry Engineering*, Vol.25 (February 1959), pp.62–73

CAW, J.M. "Mining in Great Britain and Ireland. Part 3" *Mine and Quarry Engineering*, Vol.25 (March 1959), pp.122–132

CHADWICK, R. "Copper: The British Contribution" *Canadian Mining and Metallurgical Bulletin*, Vol.76 No.858 (October 1983), pp.84–88

CHADWICK, R. "Trading in Ores 1600–1900" *Tamar Journal*, No.5 (1983), pp.18–29

CHALMERS, W.R. *See* CUMMINGS, A.D., CHALMERS, W.R. & MATTINGLY, H.B.

CHATBURN, Axel "Some Notes on Underground Photography" *Bulletin of the Peak District Mines Historical Society*, Vol.4 No.6 (December 1971), pp.451–462

CHEVALIER, J. "La Mission de Gabriel Jars dans les Mines et les Usines Britaniques en 1764" (English Translation) *Transactions of the Newcomen Society*, Vol.26 (1947–8), pp.57–69

CHILD, W.R. "England's Iron Trade in the Fifteenth Century" *Economic History Review*, Second Series Vol.XXXIV No.1 (February 1981), pp.25–47

CLAUGHTON, Peter F. "Historical Research" *Plymouth Mineral and Mining Club Journal*, Vol.5 No.3 (January 1975), pp.8–9

COCKERTON, R.W.P. "Notes on Roman Lead Mining" *Journal of the Derbyshire Archaeological and Natural History Society*, Vol.LXXXII (1962), p.106

CORBYN, D.B. "Underground Gases" *Shropshire Mining Club*, Yearbook (1963–4), pp.57–60

CROSSLEY, David W. "The Management of a Sixteenth Century Iron Works" *Economic History Review*, Second Series Vol.XIX No.2 (1966), pp.273–288

CURRY, David "Bats in Mines" *Plymouth Mineral and Mining Club Journal*, Vol.8 No.1 (Spring 1977), pp.6–7

CUMMINGS, A.D., CHALMERS, W.R. & MATTINGLY, H.B. "A Roman Mining Document" *Mine and Quarry Engineering*, Vol.22 (August 1956), pp.339–342

DAVIS, T.J. "Mining Novels" *Shropshire Mining Club Journal*, (1977), pp.7–10

DENNIS, W.H. "Milestones in the Non–Ferrous Metallurgical Industry" *Mine and Quarry Engineering*, Vol.16 (September 1950), pp.292–295

DENNISON, J.B. & VARVILL, W.W. "Prospecting with the Diamond Drill for Lead and Zinc Ores in the British Isles" *Transactions of the Institution of Mining and Metallurgy*, Vol.62 (1952–53), pp.1–21

DICKINSON, J.M. "N.C. & M.R.S., Standards of Cave Surveying" *Transactions of the Northern Cavern and Mine Research Society*, Vol.1 No.1 (June 1961), pp.7–11

DICKINSON, John Michael "Old Mine Timbers" *Memoirs of the Northern Cavern and Mine Research Society*, (December 1966), p.34

DOBIE, J.M. "Recent Developments in Wire Rope Manufacture and Application" *Mine and Quarry Engineering*, Vol.28 (August 1962), pp.356–362

DOWNS-ROSE, Geoffrey *See* HARVEY, William S & DOWNS-ROSE, Geoffrey

ENERGLYN, Lord "Retapping Britain's Minerals" *Geographical Magazine*, (December 1971)

FIRMAN, R.J. "Some British Ideas about Ore Genesis from Hooke to Whitehurst 1688–1786" *Bulletin of the Peak District Mines Historical Society*, Vol.9 No.6 (Winter 1986), pp.404–412

FORD, Trevor D. *See* WORLEY, Noel E. & FORD, Trevor D.

FREEMAN, J.E. "And Things that go Bump in the Night" *Memoirs of the Northern Cavern and Mine Research Society*, No.3 (November 1964), pp.9–11

GILL, Michael C. "The Northern Mine Research Society" *Industrial Archaeology*, Vol.15 No.2 (1980), pp.168–179

GILL, Michael C. "An Assessment of the Lead Smelting Processes and the Use of XRF for the Analysis of the Resulting Slags" *Journal of the Historical Metallurgy Society*, Vol.20 No.2 (1986)

GLANVILL, J. "On Lead Smelting in England in the 17th Century" *Memoirs of the Northern Cavern and Mine Research Society*, (August 1965), p.26

GRICE, P.W. "The United Kingdom and Australia: A History of Co-operation in Trade and Investment in the Mining Industry" in Newbold, D.M.(Ed),*Jobson's Mining Yearbook 1984–1985* (Dun & Bradstreet, 1984), pp.92–93; 96–97

GUTHRIE, Robert G. "Lead Value in 1536 and 1537" *Memoirs of the Northern Cavern and Mine Research Society*, (August 1965), pp.24–25

HALL, George W. "Preparation of Plans of Old Workings" *Shropshire Mining Club*, Yearbook (1964–5), p.60

HAMMERSLEY, George "Technique or Economy? The Rise and Decline of the Early English Copper Industry ca.1550–1660" *Business History*, Vol.XV No.1 (1973), pp.1–31

HARLEY, J.B. "A Guide to Ordnance Survey Maps as Historical Sources. Part 1" *The Amateur Historian*, Vol.5 No.5 (Autumn 1962), pp.130–140

HARLEY, J.B. "A Guide to Ordnance Survey Maps as Historical Sources. Part 3" *The Amateur Historian*, Vol.5 No.7 (Spring 1963), pp.202–211

HARLEY, J.B. "A Guide to Ordnance Survey Maps as Historical Sources. Part 4" *The Amateur Historian*, Vol.5 No.8 (Summer 1963), pp.251–259

HARLEY, J.B. "Maps for the Local Historian: A Guide to British Sources. No.6 County Maps" *The Amateur Historian*, Vol.8 No.5 (1968), pp.167–179

HARRIS, John R. "Copper and Shipping in the Eighteenth Century" *Economic History Review*, Second Series Vol.XIX No.3 (1966), pp.550–568

HARVEY, Charles E. & PRESS, Jonathan P. "Origins and Early History of the Institution of Mining and Metallurgy" *Transactions of the Institution of Mining and Metallurgy*, Vol.95 (October 1986), pp.A171–A175

HARVEY, William S. & DOWNS–ROSE, Geoffrey "Miners' Bargains" *British Mining*, No.34 (1987), pp.5–9

HEATHCOTE, J.A. "The Identification of Minerals" *Shropshire Mining Club Journal*, (1979), pp.45–61

HODGSON, Victor "British Non–Ferrous Metalliferous Mining" *Mine and Quarry Engineering*, Vol.10 (March 1945), pp.70–71

HOLLAND, J.Anthony "Mineral Rights" *Plymouth Mineral and Mining Club Journal*, Vol.11 No.3 (1980), pp.9–10

HOLMAN, A.T. "The Development of the Rock Drill with Notes on the Impact of Disease on Design" *Transactions of the Cornish Institute of Engineers*, Vol.V (1949–50), pp.40–50

HOLMAN, Treve "Historical Relationship of Mining, Silicosis and Rock Removal" *Mine and Quarry Engineering*, Vol.13 (November 1947), pp.331–333

HUGHES, S.J.S. "George Green, Engineer and Entrepreneur 1824–1895" *British Mining*, No.34 (1987), pp.10–14

JEFFERSON, D.P. "A Short Survey of the Problem of Ore Genesis through the Ages" *Bulletin of the Peak District Mines Historical Society*, Vol.1 No.4 (April 1961), pp.5–9

13

JENKIN, R "The Zinc Industry in England: The Early Years up to about 1850" *Transactions of the Newcomen Society*, Vol.25 (1946–7), pp.41–53

JOHNSON, C.H. *See* BRITTON, G.C. & JOHNSON, C.H.

JOHNSON, K.H. "Folklore and Superstition in the Mines" *Bulletin of the Peak District Mines Historical Society*, Vol.5 No.3 (May 1973), pp.156–158

JONES, Bari & LEWIS, Peter "Ancient Mining and the Environment" in Ratitz, P.A.(ed) *Rescue Archaeology* (Penguin, 1974)

KANEFSKY, John & ROBEY, John A. "Steam Engines in Eighteenth Century Britain: A Quantitative Assessment" *Technology and Culture*, Vol.XXI No.2 (1980)

LEBETER, F. "Historical Survey of Crushing and Grinding. Part 1" *Mine and Quarry Engineering*, Vol.15 (September 1949), pp.271–277

LEBETER, F. "Historical Survey of Crushing and Grinding. Part 2" *Mine and Quarry Engineering*, Vol.15 (October 1949), pp.307–311

LEBETER, F. "Historical Survey of Crushing and Grinding. Part 3" *Mine and Quarry Engineering*, Vol.15 (November 1949), pp.345–353

LEBETER, F. "Historical Survey of Crushing and Grinding. Part 4" *Mine and Quarry Engineering*, Vol.15 (December 1949), pp.385–393

LEBETER, F. "The Man Engine" *Mine and Quarry Engineering*, Vol.16 (February 1950), pp.53–57

LEWIS, Peter *See* JONES, Bari & LEWIS, Peter

LYNCH, A.J. "The Evolution of Mineral Processing" *Camborne School of Mines Journal*, (1979), pp.39–40

MATTINGLY, H.B. *See* CUMMING, A.D., CHALMERS, W.R. & MATTINGLY, H.B.

MAYNE, L.Bruce "A Select Bibliography of Tours in Great Britain. Part 1" *The Amateur Historian*, Vol.3 No.1 (Autumn 1956), pp.26–31

MAYNE, L.Bruce "A Select Bibliography of Tours in Great Britain. Part 2" *The Amateur Historian*, Vol.3 No.2 (Winter 1956–7), pp.63–66

METCALFE, J.E. "Base Metals in Britain: A Brief Review" *Mine and Quarry Engineering*, Vol.13 (Jully 1947), pp.211–212

MICHELL, F.B. "The Dressing of Iron Ore" *Mine and Quarry Engineering*, Vol.13 (February 1947), pp.45–53

MICHELL, F.B. "The Introduction of the Plunger Pole or Force Pump" *Journal of the Trevithick Society*, No,7 (1979–1980), pp.34–36

MITCHELL, M. "Safety in Disused Metal Mines" *The Mine Explorer*, Vol.2 (1986), pp.5–6

MORTIMER, R.S. "The Archives of the Society of Friends" *The Amateur Historian*, Vol.3 No.2 (Winter 1956–7), pp.55–61

MUIR, W.L.G. "Problems of Mine Finance" *Mining Magazine*, (June 1965), pp.382–391

NAYLOR, Peter J. "Origins and History of Fire Setting" *Bulletin of the Peak District Mines Historical Society*, Vol.5 No.2 (October 1972), pp.90–92

NAYLOR, Peter J. *See* STRANGE, P., NAYLOR, Peter J. & WILLIES, Lynn

NELSON, A. "The Maintenance of Discipline" *Mine and Quarry Engineering*, Vol.10 (August 1945), pp.193–195

NELSON, A. "The Divining Rod in Fable and Fact" *Mine and Quarry Engineering*, Vol.14 (July 1948), pp.205–207

NICHOLLS, Bryan "The Importance of Mineral Resources in the Growth of British Industry in the Nineteenth Century: Part 1" *Plymouth Mineral and Mining Club Journal*, Vol.7 No.1 (Spring 1976), pp.9–11

NICHOLLS, Bryan "The Importance of Mineral Resources in the Growth of British Industry in the Nineteenth Century: Part 2" *Plymouth Mineral and Mining Club Journal*, Vol.7 No.2 (Autumn 1976), pp.9–11

O'NEILL, H.O. "Monastic Mining and Metallurgy in the British Isles" *Met.Mat.*, Vol.1 (June 1967), pp.182–190

PORTER, Jeffery H. "Wage Determination by Selling Price Sliding Scales, 1870–1914" *Manchester School*, Vol.39 (1971), pp.13–21

PRESS, Jonathan P. *See* HARVEY, Charles E. & PRESS, Jonathan P.

PRYOR, E.J. "Mineral Dressing: Old and New" *Mining Magazine*, Vol.101 No.6 (December 1959), pp.297–308

RIEUWERTS, James H. "Connections between the Pioneers of Civil Engineering and Mining Practice" *Bulletin of the Peak District Mines Historical Society*, Vol.1 No.4 (April 1961), pp.10–12

ROBERTS, A. "University Mining Schools and the Mining Industry" *Mining Magazine*, Vol.110 (1964), pp.84–87

ROBERTS, Peter K. "Canal Tunnels Associated with Mineral Exploitation" *Industrial Archaeology Review*, Vol.V (1980–81), pp.5–14

ROBERTS, Peter K. "Boat Levels Associated with Mining. Pt.II. Metal Mines." *Industrial Archaeology Review*, Vol.V (1981), pp.203–216

ROBERTS, R.O. "The Smelting of Non–Ferrous Metals Since 1750" in John, Arthur H. & Williams, G.,*Glamorgan County History* Vol.5 (Cardiff: University of Wales, 1980) pp.47–95

ROBEY, John A. "Britain's Mines and Manufactures: Celia Fiennes Observations in 1697–1698" *Bulletin of the Peak District Mines Historical Society*, Vol.5 No.6 (October 1974), pp.341–348

ROBEY, John A. *See* KANEFSKY, John & ROBEY, John A.

ROSS, H.U. "Iron Ore for Great Britain" *Mine and Quarry Engineering*, Vol.16 (March 1950), pp.80–84

SAVORY, M.J. "Mining and Metallurgy: A New Source of Research Material" *Journal of the Gloucester Society for Industrial Archaeology*, (1972)

SCHMITZ, Christopher J. "The Rise of Big Business in the World Copper Industry 1870–1930" *Economic History Review*, Second Series Vol.XXXIX No.3 (August 1986), pp.392–410

SCHNELLMANN, G.A. "Reviving Britain's Metal Mining Industry" *Mining Magazine*, Vol.LXXXVI No.6 (June 1952), pp.329–333

SCHOFIELD, M. "Centenaries in Aluminium History" *Mining Magazine*, Vol.XCIX No.3 (September 1958), pp.145-147

SCHOFIELD, M. "Lithium: Its History and Growing Importance" *Mining Magazine*, Vol.XCIX No.4 (October 1958), pp.201–202

SCHOFIELD, M. "Vanadium in Industry" *Mining Magazine*, Vol.C No.6 (June 1959), pp.329–331

SCHUBERT, H.R. "The First Stamp Mills in English History" *Journal of the Iron and Steel Institute*, Vol.159 (1947), pp.343–344

SCOTT, James W. "Technological and Economic Changes in the Metalliferous Mining and Smelting Industries in Tudor England" *Albion*, Vol.4 (1972), pp.94–110

SCOTT, James W. "Theory and Practice in Early Metalliferous Mining in the British Isles: Some Comments on the State of Geological Knowledge in Tudor and Stuart Times" *Albion*, Vol.5 (1973), pp.211–225

SHAW, Gareth "The Content and Reliability of Nineteenth Century Trade Directories" *The Local Historian*, Vol.13 No.4 (November 1978), pp.205–222

SKELTON, R.H. "The Future for Base Metal Mining in Great Britain" *Mining Magazine*, Vol.LXXXVI No.3 (March 1952), pp.137–144

SKELTON, R.H. "The Appraisal of Domestic Non–Ferrous Mineral Resources" *Mining Magazine*, Vol.LXXXVI No.4 (April 1952), pp.201–205

STANDERLINE, G.V. "The Drill Carriage" *Mine and Quarry Engineering*, Vol.14 (September 1948), pp.265–271

STRANGE, P., NAYLOR, Peter J. & WILLIES, Lynn "Preservation of Mining Relics: Notes for Guidance" *Bulletin of the Peak District Mines Historical Society*, Vol.5 No.5 (April 1974), pp.312–314

TAYLOR, A. "Water and the Miner" *Shropshire Mining Club Journal*, (1974–5), pp.35–52

THACKRAY, J.C. "Source Materials for the History of British Mining in the Archives of the Institute of Geological Sciences" *British Mining*, No.8 (1978), pp.10–13

THOMAS, Richard & BUGLER, Jeremy "Quiet Mineral Rush Covering Britain" *The Observer* 3rd October 1971

TROUNSON, John H. "British Non–Ferrous Metalliferous Mining. Part 1" *Mine and Quarry Engineering*, Vol.10 (April 1945), pp.90–91

TROUNSON, John H. "British Non–Ferrous Metalliferous Mining. Part 2" *Mine and Quarry Engineering*, Vol.10 (August 1945), pp.189–190

TUCKER, D.Gordon "Fumes, Flues, Condensers and Chimneys in Lead Smelting" *Bulletin of the Historical Metallurgy Group*, Vol.6 No.2 (1972), pp.1–6

TUCKER, D.Gordon *See* TUCKER, Mary & TUCKER, D.Gordon

TUCKER, Mary & TUCKER, D.Gordon "The Sacking of the Francises by John Taylor, 1841–1842" *British Mining*, No.5 (1977), pp.14–17

TYLECOTE, R.F. "Lead Smelting and Refining during the Industrial Revolution" *Industrial Archaeology*, Vol.12 No.2 (1977), pp.102–110

VARVILL, W.W. "Lead Mining in the British Isles: Can it be revived. Part 1" *Mine and Quarry Engineering*, Vol.20 (August 1954), pp.352–361

VARVILL, W.W. "Lead Mining in the British Isles: Can it be revived. Part 2" *Mine and Quarry Engineering*, Vol.20 (September 1954), pp.398–406

VARVILL, W.W. "Lead Mining in the British Isles: Can it be revived.

Part 3" *Mine and Quarry Engineering*, Vol.20 (October 1954), pp.436–443

VARVILL, W.W. "Lead Mining in the British Isles: Can it be revived. Part 4" *Mine and Quarry Engineering*, Vol.20 (November 1954), pp.488–493

VARVILL, W.W. "Lead Mining in the British Isles: Can it be revived. Part 5" *Mine and Quarry Engineering*, Vol.20 (December 1954), pp.532–538

VARVILL, W.W. *See* DENNISON, J.B. & VARVILL, W.W.

WADE, John Caleb "Divining" *Transactions of the Northern Cavern and Mine Research Society*, Vol.1 No.1 (June 1961), pp.12–22

WAITE, Peter *See* BURT, Roger & WAITE, Peter

WALTHAM, A.C. "The Study of Underground Features from Aerial Photography" *Memoirs of the Northern Cavern and Mine Research Society*, (October 1969), pp.93–98

WARRINGTON, G. "The British Copper Company Ltd. 1864–1882" *Shropshire Mining Club Journal*, (1980), pp.9–10

WATKINS, George M. "The Development of the Steam Winding Engine" *Transactions of the Newcomen Society*, Vol.50 (1978–9), pp.11–25

WHELAN,P.F. "Trends in the Major Non–Ferrous Metals" *Mine and Quarry Engineering*, Vol.23 (October 1957), pp.440–442

WHITTICK, G.Clement "The Casting Technique of Romano–British Lead Ingots" *Journal of Roman Studies*, Vol.51 (1961), pp.105–111

WILLIAMS, R.A. "The High Mortality of British Metal and Slate Miners and Beliefs about Causes 1556–1904" *British Mining*, No.34 (1987), pp.18–33

WILLIES, Lynn "A Note on the Price of Lead, 1730–1900" *Bulletin of the Peak District Mines Historical Society*, Vol.4 No.2 (November 1969), pp.179–191

WILLIES, Lynn "Eighteenth Century Lead Ingots from the Hollandia" *Bulletin of the Peak District Mines Historical Society*, Vol.9 No.4 (Winter 1985), pp.233–249

WILLIES, Lynn *See* STRANGE, P., NAYLOR, Peter J. & WILLIES, Lynn

WILSON, P. "Forgotten Mines" *Country Life*, Vol.115 (6th May 1954), pp.1388–90

WORLEY, Noel E. & FORD, Trevor D. "Mississippi Valley Type Ore-fields in Britain" *Bulletin of the Peak District Mines Historical Society*, Vol.6 No.5 (May 1977), pp.201–208

SCOTLAND

Books

BUTT, John *The Industrial Archaeology of Scotland* (Newton Abbot: David & Charles, 1967)

CALLENDER, R.M. *The Ancient Lead Mining Industry of Islay* (Islay: Islay Museums Trust, ca.1981)

CALLENDER, R.M. & MACAULAY, J. *The Ancient Metal Mines of the Isle of Islay, Argyll* (Sheffield: Northern Mine Research Society, British Mining No.24, 1984)

CRAWFORD, John C. *Wanlockhead Miners Library* (Wanlockhead: Wanlockhead Museum Trust, 1978)

DICKIE, D.M. & FORSTER, C.W. (Eds.) *Mines and Minerals of Ochils* (Clackmannanshire Field Studies Society, 1986)

DONNACHIE, Ian *The Industrial Archaeology of Galloway* (Newton Abbot: David & Charles, 1971)

DONNACHIE, Ian, HUME, John R. & MOSS, M. *Historic Industrial Scenes: Scotland* (Hartington: Moorland, 1977)

DOWNS–ROSE, Geoffrey *See* HARVEY, William & DOWNS–ROSE, Geoffrey

FLETT, J. *Special Reports on the Mineral Resources of the G.B. Vol.27: The Lead, Zinc, Copper and Nickel Ores of Scotland* (Sheffield: Mining Facsimiles, 1986. Reprint of Geological Survey 1921 Edition.)

FORSTER, C.W. *See* DICKIE, D.M. & FORSTER, C.W.

FOSTER–SMITH, J.R. *The Non–Ferrous Metal Mines of South West Scotland* (Sheffield: Northern Cavern and Mine Research Society, Occasional Paper No.2, 1967)

GOODLET, G.A. *See* GREIG, D.C., GOODLET, G.A., LUMSDEN, G.I. & TULLOCH, W.

GREIG, D.C., GOODLET, G.A., LUMSDEN, G.I. & TULLOCH, W. *British Regional Geology. The South of Scotland* (Institute of Geological Sciences, H.M.S.O., 1971)

HAMILTON, H. *An Economic History of Scotland in the Eighteenth Century* (Oxford: Clarendon Press, 1963)

HARVEY, William & DOWNS–ROSE, Geoffrey *The Bay Mine, Wanlockhead, Scotland* (Sheffield: Northern Mine Research Society, British Mining No.2, 1976)

HARVEY, William & DOWNS–ROSE, Geoffrey *William Symington: Inventor and Engine Builder* (Northgate Publishing Co., 1980)

HAY, G.D. *See* STELL, G.P. & HAY, G.D.

HUME, John R. *The Industrial Archaeology of Scotland: I. The Lowlands and Borders* (Batsford, 1976)

HUME, John R. *The Industrial Archaeology of Scotland: II. Highlands and Islands* (Batsford, 1977)

HUME, John R. *See* DONNACHIE, Ian, HUME, John R. & MOSS, M.

LANDLESS, Jeremy G. *A Gazetteer of the Metal Mines of Scotland* (Wanlockhead: Wanlockhead Museum Trust, Occassional Paper No.1, 1985)

LUMSDEN, G.I. *See* GREIG, D.C., GOODLET, G.A., LUMSDEN, G.I. & TULLOCH, W.

LYTHE, S.G.Edgar *The Economy of Scotland in its European Setting 1550–1625* (Edinburgh: Oliver & Boyd, 1960)

MACAULAY, J. *See* CALLENDER, R.M. & MACAULAY, J.

MOSS, M. *See* DONNACHIE, Ian, HUME, John R. & MOSS, M.

PAYNE, P.L. (Ed) *Studies in Scottish Business History* (Frank Cass, 1967)

ROW, Goldscaur *The Wanlockhead Museum Trust. No.1 All About Wanlockhead* (Wanlockhead: Wanlockhead Museum Trust, 1980)

SMITH, David L. *The Dalmellington Iron Company: Its Engines and Men* (Newton Abbot: David & Charles, 1967)

STELL, G.P. & HAY, G.D. *Bonawe Iron Furnace* (Edinburgh: H.M.S.O., 1984)

THOMS, Lisbeth M. *The Archaeology of Industrial Scotland* (Edinburgh: Scottish Archaeology Forum No.8, 1976)

TULLOCH, W. *See* GREIG, D.C., GOODLET, G.A., LUMSDEN, G.I. & TULLOCH, W.

Theses

Articles

ANON "Wanlockhead Lead Mine" *Mine and Quarry Engineering*, Vol.22 (August 1956), p.317

ANON "Perthshire Mine Means North Sea Benefit" *Dundee Courier and Advertiser* 9th July 1979, p.6

ANON "Report on the Mines of Ochills" *Clackmannan Field Studies Centre*

ATKINSON, Michael *See* BURT, Roger, WAITE, Peter & ATKINSON, Michael

BAINBRIDGE, John W. "A Nineteenth Century Copper Working: Tomnadashan, Lochtayside" *Industrial Archaeology*, Vol.7 No.1 (1970) pp.60–74

BAINBRIDGE, John W. "Lord Breadalbane's Mines" *Scots Magazine*, CXIV (1980), pp.38–45

BROWN, E.M. & WILLIAMS, James "A Leadhills Diary for 1745" *Transactions of the Dumfries and Galloway Natural History and Archaeology Society*, LIV (1979), pp.105–131

BURT, Roger, WAITE, Peter & ATKINSON, Michael "Scottish Metalliferous Mining 1845–1913: Detailed Returns from the Mineral Statistics. Part 1" *Industrial Archaeology*, Vol.16 No.1 (1981), pp.4–19

BURT, Roger, WAITE, Peter & ATKINSON, Michael "Scottish Metalliferous Mining 1845–1913: Detailed Returns from the Mineral Statistics. Part 2" *Industrial Archaeology*, Vol.16 No.2 (1981), pp.140–157

CALLENDER, R.M. "The Strontian Connection" *Industrial and Commercial Photographer*, XIX, No.3, (March 1979), pp.48–53

CAMPBELL, Marion & SANDEMAN, Mary "Mid–Argyll: An Archaeological Survey. Mines in Mid–Argyll" *Proceedings of the Society of Antiquaries of Scotland*, Vol.XCV (1961-2), pp.1–125

CANNELL, Alfred E. & CANNELL, M. "The Mines of South–West Scotland" *Memoirs of the Northern Cavern and Mine Research Society*, (January 1969), pp.71–75

CANNELL, Alfred E. & CANNELL, M. "Underground in Arran, Bute, Scotland" *Memoirs of the Northern Cavern and Mine Research Society*, (January 1969), pp.75–76

CANNELL, M. *See* CANNELL, Alfred E. & CANNELL, M.

CRAWFORD, John C. & JAMES, Stuart "Wanlockhead Miners' Library, 1756–1979" *Transactions of the Dumfries and Galloway Natural History and Archaeology Society*, LIV, (1979), pp.97–104

DONNACHIE, Ian "Sources for Industrial Archaeology and Local History in Scotland" *The Local Historian*, Vol.12 No.6 (May 1977), pp.296–303

DOWNS–ROSE, Geoffrey "Waterwheel Pumping Engines on the Straitsteps Vein at Wanlockhead" *Memoirs of the Northern Cavern and Mines Research Society*, Vol.2 No.2 (May 1972), pp.80–88

DOWNS–ROSE, Geoffrey "God's Treasure House in Scotland. The Wanlockhead Museum Trust. Museum of the Scottish Lead Mining Industry" *Industrial Past*, Vol.5 No.2 (1978), pp.4–6

DOWNS–ROSE, Geoffrey "A Note on Housing at Wanlockhead" *Transactions of the Dumfries and Galloway Natural History and Archaeology Society*, LIV, (1979), pp.174–176

DOWNS–ROSE, Geoffrey & HARVEY, William S. "Water–bucket Pumps and the Wanlockhead Engine" *Industrial Archaeology*, Vol.10 No.2 (1973), pp.129–147

DOWNS–ROSE, Geoffrey & HARVEY, William S. "Lead Smelting Sites at Wanlockhead, 1682–1934" *Transactions of the Dumfries and Galloway Natural History and Archaeology Society*, LIV, (1979), pp.75–84

DOWNS–ROSE, Geoffrey *See* HARVEY, William S. & DOWNS–ROSE, Geoffrey

FLOYD, James D. "Some Unrecorded Mineral Trials in Kirkcudbrightshire" *Transactions of the Dumfries and Galloway Natural History and Archaeology Society*, LIV, (1979), pp.149–152

HARVEY, William S. "Lead Mining in 1768: Old Records of a Scottish Mining Company" *Industrial Archaeology*, Vol.7 No.3 (1970), pp.310–318

HARVEY, William S. "Miners' Bargains at Leadhills during the Eighteenth Century" *Glasgow Spelaeological Society Journal*, Vol.2 No.1 (February 1970), pp.1–21

HARVEY, William S. "The Wanlockhead Beam Engine" *Glasgow Spelaeological Society Journal*, Vol.2 No.1 (February 1970), pp.23–37

HARVEY, William S. "The Rules of the Leadhills Mining Company" *Memoirs of the Northern Cavern and Mine Research Society*, Vol.2 No.2 (May 1972), pp.60–66

HARVEY, William S. "Weights and Measures Used at the Mines of Leadhills and Wanlockhead in the late Eighteenth Century" *Memoirs of the Northern Cavern and Mine Research Society*, Vol.2 No.3 (September 1973), pp.139–144

HARVEY, William S. "Pumping Engines at the Leadhills Mines" *British Mining*, No.19 (1982), pp.5–14

HARVEY, William S. "An Examination of Bolts found at Wanlockhead Mines" *Industrial Archaeology*, Vol.17 No.1–4 (Not Dated), pp.130–151

HARVEY, William S. "The Strike at Leadhills Mine, 1836" *The Local Historian*, Vol.17 No.2 (May 1986), pp.101–106

HARVEY, William S. & DOWNS–ROSE, Geoffrey "Lead and Leases" *British Mining*, No.3 (1976), pp.21–28

HARVEY, William S. & DOWNS–ROSE, Geoffrey "A Report on Excavations at the Site of the Eighteenth Century Lead Smelter at Pate's Knowes, Wanlockhead" *British Mining*, No.8 (1978), pp.1–9

HARVEY, William S. & DOWNS–ROSE, Geoffrey "The Rebuilding of Two Smelting Hearths at Wanlockhead" *British Mining*, No.11 (1979), pp.82–86

HARVEY, William S. & DOWNS–ROSE, Geoffrey "A View of the Leadmines at Wanlockhead, 1775" *Transactions of the Dumfries and Galloway Natural History and Archaeology Society*, LIV, (1979), pp.90–96

HARVEY, William S. & DOWNS–ROSE, Geoffrey "The Lead Mining Museum at Wanlockhead" *Industrial Archaeology*, Vol.15 No.1 (1980), pp.11–29

HARVEY, William S. *See* DOWNS–ROSE, Geoffrey & HARVEY, William S.

JACKSON, R. *See* JACKSON, S.H. & JACKSON, R.

JACKSON, S.H. & JACKSON, R. "Some Notes on Scottish Mines" *Memoirs of the Northern Cavern and Mine Research Society*, (January 1969), pp.22–26

JAMES, Stuart *See* CRAWFORD, John C. & JAMES, Stuart

JEFFREYS, Alan L. "Tunnel at Vicar's Bridge, Clackmannanshire" *Bulletin of the Grampian Spelaeological Group*, Vol.4 No.3 (1964), p.19

SCOTLAND

LANDLESS, Jeremy "Strontian Lead Mines" *British Mining*, No.1 (1975), pp.51–54

McCRACKEN, A.M. "Westwater Lead Mine" *Transactions of the Dumfries and Galloway Natural History and Antiquarian Society*, Vol.XLVII (1970)

PALMER, Joan "Britain's Oldest Library (Leadhills)" *The Lady*, Vol.201 No.5204 (1985), pp.554–556

PREVOST, W.A.J. "Lord Hopetoun's Mine at Leadhills: Illustrated by David Allan and Paul Sandby" *Transactions of the Dumfries and Galloway Natural History and Archaeology Society*, LIV, (1979), pp.85–89

RIVINGTON, J.B. "Recent Chromite Exploration in Shetland" *Mining Magazine*, Vol.89, (1953), pp.329–337

ROBERTSON, James "Wanlockhead Roads" *Transactions of the Dumfries and Galloway Natural History and Archaeology Society*, LIV, (1979), pp.161–164

SALVONA, James "A Visit to Strontian Lead Mines" *Bulletin of the Grampian Spelaeological Group*, 2nd Series Vol.3 No.1 (1980), pp.41–44

SANDEMAN, Mary *See* CAMPBELL, Marion & SANDEMAN, Mary

SASSOON, J. "Leadmining at Woodhead, Carsphairn" *Transactions of the Dumfries and Galloway Natural History and Antiquarian Society*, Vol.XLVI (1969)

SCHOFIELD, M. "Birth of a Scottish Industry (Iron)" *Mining Magazine*, Vol.103 No.1 (July 1960), pp.18–20

SCHOFIELD, M. "Notes on Strontium" *Mining Magazine*, Vol.103 No.3 (September 1960), pp.147–149

SHAW, Richard P. "Arran Barytes Mine, Glen Sannox, Isle of Arran" *Bulletin of the Peak District Mines Historical Society*, Vol.6 No.5 (May 1977), pp.209–217

SHAW, W.T. "The Mines of Auchencairn" *Memoirs of the Northern Cavern and Mine Research Society*, Vol.2 No.4 (June 1974), pp.163–174

SMOUT, T.C. "The Lead Mines at Wanlockhead" *Transactions of the Dumfries and Galloway Natural History and Archaeology Society*, 39, (1962), pp.144–158

SWINBANK, Peter "Wanlockhead: The Maps, the Documents, the Relics and the Confusion" *Scottish Archaeological Forum*, Vol.VIII (1976), pp.23–36

SWINBANK, Peter "Wanlockhead: An Introduction" *Journal of the Historical Metallurgy Society*, Vol.11 No.1 (1977), pp.39–43

TEMPLE, A.K. "The Leadhills–Wanlockhead Lead and Zinc Deposits" *Transactions of the Royal Society of Edinburgh*, Vol.LXIII Pt.1 (1955–56), pp.85–113

WAITE, Peter *See* BURT, Roger, WAITE, Peter & ATKINSON, Michael

WILLIAMS, James "The Minerals of South West Scotland" *Bulletin of the Historical Metallurgy Group*, Vol.10 No.1 (1976), pp.36–40

WILLIAMS, James "Eighteenth Century Property Lists from Wanlockhead Testaments" *Transactions of the Dumfries and Galloway Natural History and Archaeology Society*, Vol.LIV (1979), pp.132–146

WILLIAMS, James The Day Book (1742–50) of William Hendry, a Wanlockhead and Leadhills Merchant" *Transactions of the Dumfries and Galloway Natural History and Archaeology Society*, Vol.LIV (1979), pp.167–172

WILLIAMS, James *See* BROWN, E.M. & WILLIAMS, James

YOUNG, Ivan & YUILL, Jackie "Vicar's Bridge and Melloch Ironstone Mines" *Bulletin of the Grampian Spelaeological Group*, Vol.4 No.4 (1985), pp.31–33

YUILL, Jackie *See* YOUNG, Ivan & YUILL, Jackie

ZIEMBA, T.Garth P. "The Mineral Veins of Bannerdale Crags" *British Mining*, No.1 (1975), pp.41–49

NORTHERN PENNINES

Books

ATKINSON, Frank *The Industrial Archaeology of North East England* 2 Volumes (Newton Abbot: David & Charles, 1974)

ATKINSON, Frank *Life and Tradition in Northumberland and Durham* (Dent, 1977)

ATKINSON, Frank *North East England: People at Work 1860–1950* (Ashbourne: Moorland, 1980)

BEADLE, Harold L. *Mining and Smelting in Teesdale* (Redcar: Cleveland Industrial Archaeology Society, Research Report No.3, 1980)

BURNLEY, Raymond *See* BURT, Roger, WAITE, Peter & BURNLEY, Raymond

BURGESS, I.C. *See* TAYLOR, B.J., BURGESS, I.C., LAND, D.H., MILLS, D.A.C., SMITH, D.B. & WARREN, P.T.

BURT, Roger, WAITE, Peter & BURNLEY, Raymond *The Cumberland Mineral Statistics 1845–1913* (Exeter: Department of Economic History, University of Exeter, 1982)

BURT, Roger, WAITE, Peter & BURNLEY, Raymond *The Durham and Northumberland Mineral Statistics 1845–1913* (Exeter: Department of Economic History, University of Exeter, 1983)

CARRUTHERS, R.G. & STRAHAN, A. *Special Reports on the Mineral Resources of G.B. Vol.26; Lead and Zinc Ores of Durham, Yorkshire, Derbyshire and Notes on the Isle of Man* (Sheffield: Mining Facsimiles, 1986. Reprint of Geological Survey 1923 Edition.)

DIXON, H. *An Allendale Miscellany* (Frank Graham, 1974)

DUNHAM, Kingsley C. *Geology of the North Pennine Orefield. Vol.1 Tyne to Stainmore.* (Memoirs of the Geological Survey, H.M.S.O., 1967)

DUNHAM, Kingsley C. & WILSON, A.A. *Geology of the Northern Pennine Orefield. Vol.2 Stainmore to Craven* (Memoirs of the Geological Survey, H.M.S.O., 1985)

EDWARDS, K.H.R. *The Chronology of the Development of the Iron and Steel Industries of Tees-side* (Wigan: Private Publication, 1955)

EDWARDS, W. & TROTTER, F.M. *British Regional Geology. The Pennines and Adjacent Areas* (Institute of Geological Sciences, H.M.S.O., 1978)

FLINN, Michael W. *Men of Iron: The Crowleys in the Early Iron Industry* (Edinburgh, 1962)

FORSTER, Westergarth *A Treatise on a Section of the Strata from Newcastle–upon–Tyne to Cross Fell* (Newcastle–upon–Tyne: Davis Books, 1985. Reprint of 1883 Edition.)

GREENWOOD, John *The Industrial Archaeology and Industrial History of Northern England: A Bibliography* (Open University, 1985)

HUGHES, E. *North Country Life in the Eighteenth Century* 2 Volumes (Oxford, Oxford University Press, 1952)

HUNT, Christopher J. *The Lead Miners of the Northern Pennines in the Eighteenth and Nineteenth Centuries* (Manchester: Manchester University Press, 1970)

JENNINGS, Bernard *See* RAISTRICK, Arthur & JENNINGS, Bernard

KIRBY, M.W. *Men of Business and Politics. The Rise and Fall of the Quaker Pease Dynasty of North East England 1700–1943* (Allen & Unwin, 1984)

LAND, D.H. *See* TAYLOR, B.J., BURGESS, I.C., LAND, D.H., MILLS, D.A.C., SMITH, D.B. & WARREN, P.T.

LILLIE, W. *The History of Middlesbrough: An Illustration of the Evolution of English Industry* (Middlesbrough: 1968)

MCCORD, N. *North East England: An Economic and Social History* (Batsford, 1979)

MILLS, D.A.C. *See* TAYLOR, B.J., BURGESS, I.C., LAND, D.H., MILLS, D.A.C., SMITH, D.B. & WARREN, P.T.

MITCHELL, William R. *Pennine Lead Miner: Eric Richardson of Nenthead* (Clapham: Dalesman, 1979)

RAISTRICK, Arthur & JENNINGS, Bernard *A History of Lead Mining in the Pennines* (Longmans, 1965)

RAISTRICK, Arthur & ROBERTS, Arthur *Life and Work of the Northern Lead Miner* (Beamish: North of England Open Air Museum & Northern Mine Research Society, 1984)

RIDLEY, Viscount *The Development of the Iron and Steel Industry in North West Durham* (Tyneside Geographical Society, 1961)

ROBERTS, Arthur *See* RAISTRICK, Arthur & ROBERTS, Arthur

ROWE, David J. *The Economy of the North East in the Nineteenth Century* (Beamish: North of England Open Air Museum, 1973)

SMITH, D.B. *See* TAYLOR, B.J., BURGESS, I.C., LAND, D.H., MILLS, D.A.C., SMITH, D.B. & WARREN, P.T.

SMITH, S. *Special Reports on the Mineral Resources of G.B. Vol.25. Lead and Zinc Ores of Northumberland and Alston Moor* (Sheffield: Mining Facsimiles, 1986. Reprint of Geological Survey 1923 Edition.)

SOPWITH, Thomas *The Mining District of Alston Moor, Weardale and Teesdale* (Newcastle–upon–Tyne: Davis Books, 1984. Reprint of 1833 Edition)

STRAHAN, A. *See* CARRUTHERS, R.G. & STRAHAN, A.

TAYLOR, B.J., BURGESS, I.C., LAND, D.H., MILLS, D.A.C., SMITH, D.B. & WARREN, P.T. *British Regional Geology. Northern England* (Institute of Geological Sciences, H.M.S.O., 1979)

TROTTER, F.M. *See* EDWARDS, W. & TROTTER, F.M.

TURNBULL, Les *The History of Lead Mining in the North East of England* (Newcastle–upon–Tyne: Harold Hill & Son, 1975)

WAITE, Peter *See* BURT, Roger, WAITE, Peter & BURNLEY, Raymond

WALLACE, W. *Alston Moor: Its Pastoral People: Its Mines and Miners* (Newcastle–upon–Tyne: Davis Books, 1986. Reprint of 1890 Edition.)

WARREN, P.T. *See* TAYLOR, B.J., BURGESS, I.C., LAND, D.H., MILLS, D.A.C., SMITH, D.B. & WARREN, P.T.

WILSON, A.A. *See* DUNHAM, Kingsley C. & WILSON, A.A.

WOODROW, A. *A History of the Conlig and Whitespots Lead Mines* (Sheffield: Northern Mine Research Society, British Mining No.7, 1978)

Theses

BOWES, P.L. *Settlement and Economy in the Forest and Park of Weardale, Co. Durham, 1100–1800: A Study in Historical Geography* (University of Durham MA Thesis, 1979)

DODDS, W.G. *The Turnpike Trusts of Northumberland* (University of Durham MA Thesis, 1966)

HUGHES, M. *Lead, Land and Coal as Sources of Landlord Income in Northumberland between 1700 and 1850* (University of Durham PhD Thesis, 1963)

HUNT, C.J. *The Economic and Social Condition of the Lead Miners in the Northern Pennines in the Eighteenth and Nineteenth Centuries* (University of Durham MLitt Thesis, 1968)

WILLIAMS, L.A. *The Development of Road Transport in Cumberland, Westmorland and the Furness District of Lancashire 1800-1885* (University of Leicester PhD Thesis, 1967)

WILSON, A.S. *The Consett Iron Company Ltd: A Case Study in Victorian Business History* (University of Durham MPhil Thesis, 1972/3)

Articles

ADAMS, D.R. "Mining Areas of Northern England" *Shropshire Mining Club*, Yearbook (1964/5), pp.55–59

ALMOND, Jake K. "A Fluorspar Producer in County Durham" *Mine and Quarry Engineering*, Vol.19 (April 1953), pp.109–115

ALMOND, Jake K. "Nenthead and Tynedale Lead and Zinc Company Ltd., 1882–1896" *British Mining*, No.5 (1977), pp.22–40

ALMOND, Jake K. "Tindale Fell Spelter Works, East Cumbria and its Closure in 1895" *Transactions of the Cumberland and Westmorland Antiquarian and Archaeology Society*, Vol.LXXVIII (1978), pp.177–185

ANON "An Ancient Cavern near Darlington, Co. Durham, Ancient Prophecy" *Transactions of the Northern Cavern and Mine Research Society*, Vol.1 No.2 (April 1964), pp.52–53

ANON "History of Cow Green Mines" *Bulletin of the Durham County Local History Society*, No.9 (1968)

ANON "A Contemporary Description of the Flats at Hudgillburn Mine, Alston" *Memoirs of the Northern Cavern and Mine Research Society*, (October 1969), pp.66–68

ANON "Survey of a Water Wheel at Killhope Lead Mines" *North East Industrial Archaeology Society.* Bulletin No.7

ATKINSON, Michael *See* BURT, Roger, WAITE, Peter & ATKINSON, Michael

BARNBY, R.A. "The Influence of the London Lead Company upon the Development of Middleton–in–Teesdale" *Bulletin of the Durham City Local History Society*, Vol.XV (1972), pp.19–32

BEADLE, Harold L. "The History of the Cow Green Mines" *Bulletin of Durham City Local History Society*, No.9 (1968), pp.1–10

BEADLE, Harold L. "Killhope Lead Crushing Mill, Weardale. Part 1" *Bulletin of the North East Industrial Archaeology Society*, No.6 (1968), pp.9–18

BEADLE, Harold L. "Killhope Lead Crushing Mill, Weardale. Part 2" *Bulletin of the North East Industrial Archaeology Society*, No.7 (1968), pp.6–8

BEADLE, Harold L. "The Lead Smelting Mills of Teesdale and District" *Bulletin of the Durham City Local History Society*, No.11 (1969), pp.2–10

BEADLE, Harold L. "Sir John's Mine, Tynehead, Garrigill, NY762378" *Cleveland Industrial Archaeologist*, No.5 (1976), pp.35–42

BEADLE, Harold L. "Lady's Rake Lead Mine, Harwood–in–Teesdale" *Cleveland Industrial Archaeologist*, No.7 (1977), pp.17–23

BEADLE, Harold L. "Teesdale Mining Company 1821–1842" *Cleveland Industrial Archaeologist*, No.13 (1981), pp.1–14

BEAVIS, H. *See* CHARLTON, L.G. & BEAVIS, H.

BLANCHARD, I.S.W. "Commercial Crisis and Change: the Trade and the Industrial Economy of the North East 1509–1532" *Northern History*, Vol.VIII (1973), pp.64–85

BLANCHARD, I.S.W. "Seigneurial Entrepreneurship: the Bishops of Durham and the Weardale Lead Industry 1406–1529" *Business History*, Vol.XV (1973), pp.97–111

BROOK, Frank "Fallowfield Lead and Witherite Mines" *Industrial Archaeology*, Vol.4 No.4 (1967), pp.311–322

BROOK, Frank "Settlingstone: The World's Last Witherite Mine" *Bulletin of the Peak District Mines Historical Society*, Vol.4 No.2 (November 1969), pp.171–176

BROOK, Frank "Settlingstones, the World's Last Witherite Mine" *Memoirs of the Northern Cavern and Mine Research Society*, Vol.2 No.1 (April 1971), pp.22–24

BURT, Roger, WAITE, Peter & ATKINSON, Michael "The Mineral Statistics and Lead and Zinc Mining on Alston Moor, Cumberland" *British Mining*, No.11 (1979), pp.6–10

CANNELL, Alfred E. "A Further Report on the Nenthead Area" *Memoirs of the Northern Cavern and Mine Research Society*, No.3 (November 1964), pp.14–16

CHARLTON, L.G. & BEAVIS, H. "Settlingstones Mine" *Bulletin of the Industrial Archaeology Society of the North East*, No.9 (1969), pp.19–20

COOMBES, L.C. "Lead Mining in East and West Allendale" *Archaeologia Aeliana*, 4th Series Vol.XXXVI (1958), pp.245–270

CRANSTONE, David "The Washing Floor at Killhope Lead Mine, Co. Durham: An Interim Report" *Bulletin of the Peak District Mines Historical Society*, Vol.9 No.5 (Summer 1986), pp.283–305

CRITCHLEY, Martin F. "The History and Workings of the Nenthead Mines, Cumbria" *Bulletin of the Peak District Mines Historical Society*, Vol.9 No.1 (Summer 1984), pp.1–50

DAWSON, E.W.O. "Wartime Treatment of Lead–Zinc Dumps Situated at Nenthead, Cumberland" *Bulletin of the Institution of Mining and Metallurgy*, No.485 (1947), p.15f

DENT-YOUNG, D.M. "Barytes Production in the U.K.: With Particular Reference to Cow Green Mine, Co. Durham" *Camborne School of Mines Journal*, (1951), pp.27–37

DRURY, J.L. "Note on Weardale Lead Mining in the Eighteenth Century" *Bulletin of the Durham City Local History Society*, No.19 (1976), pp.53–55

DRURY, J.L. "Lead Works in Weardale, County Durham 1425–1431" *Durham County Local History Society Bulletin* No.38 (May 1987), pp.3–10

DUNHAM, Kingsley C. "The Production of Galena and Associated Minerals in the Northern Pennines: With Comparative Statistics for Great Britain" *Transactions of the Institution of Mining and Metallurgy*, Vol.LIII (1944)

DUNHAM, R.K. & HOBBS, R.J. "Burtree Pasture Lead Mine, Weardale" *Industrial Archaeology Review*, Vol.1 No.1 (1976), pp.7–17

DURHAM COUNTY COUNCIL PLANNING DEPARTMENT "Killhope Wheel Lead Mining Centre" *Industrial Heritage*, Vol.3 No.3 (1985), pp.2–12

FAIRBAIRN, R.A. "An Account of a Small Nineteenth Century Lead Mining Company on Alston Moor" *Industrial Archaeology Review*, Vol.IV No.3 (1980), pp.245–256

FOSTER–SMITH, J.R. "The North Pennine Metalliferous Mining Fields: Glossary" *Transactions of the Northern Cavern and Mine Research Society*, Vol.1 No.2 (April 1964), pp.5–22

GILL, Michael C. (Ed.) "Thomas Sopwith's Geological Sections of Holyfield, Hudgill Cross Vein and Silver Bank Mines" *British Mining*, No.19 (1982), pp.20–26

GORMAN, John "The Beamish Collection and Photographic Archive" *History Workshop*, Vol.16 (Autumn 1978), pp.195–206

HARRISON, J.K. "Killhope Lead Crushing Mill" *Bulletin of the Industrial Archaeology Society of the North East*, No.7 (1968), pp.5–7

HEMINGWAY, J. "The Redesdale Ironstone Beds" *Bulletin of the Historical Metallurgy Group*, Vol.6 No.2 (1972), pp.12–14

HOBBS, R.J. *See* DUNHAM, R.K. & HOBBS, R.J.

HOUSTON, William J. "Rampgill Mine" *Mine and Quarry Engineering*, Vol.29 (February 1963), pp.75–78

HOUSTON, William J. "Weardale Lead" *Mine and Quarry Engineering*, Vol.30 (March 1964), pp.98–107

INESON, P.R. "Review of the Mining Potentialities in the Alston Block of the Northern Pennine Orefield" *Bulletin of the Peak District Mines Historical Society*, Vol.6 No.3 (April 1976), pp.117–128

JACKSON, Peter "The Mine Buildings of the Upper Nent Valley. Part 1. Buildings Extant" *Memoirs of the Northern Cavern and Mine Research Society*, (October 1969), pp.39–41

JACKSON, Peter "Some Preliminary Notes on the Mining Region of Alston Moor" *Memoirs of the Northern Cavern and Mine Research Society*, (October 1969), pp.41–53

JACKSON, Peter "Two Small Mine Buildings of Alston Moor" *Memoirs of the Northern Cavern and Mine Research Society*, Vol.2 No.1 (April 1971), pp.29–30

JACKSON, Peter "Two Mine Wagons from Alston Moor" *Bulletin of the Peak District Mines Historical Society*, Vol.4 No.5 (June 1971), pp.357–361

JACKSON, Peter "Surface Remains at East End Shaft" *Memoirs of the Northern Cavern and Mines Research Society*, Vol.2 No.4 (June 1974), pp.205–206

JACKSON, Peter "Hudgillburn Mine and its Cavern" *Moldywarps Spelaeological Group Journal*, No.9 (1976), pp.23–24

JONES, Alison "Brewery Shaft, Nenthead" *The Mine Explorer*, Vol.1 (1984), pp.46–47

JOY, David "Mine Railways: An Introduction to their History and Development in the North of England" *Memoirs of the Northern Cavern and Mine Research Society*, (October 1969), pp.77–84

LANDLESS, Jeremy "Nenthead Lead Mines and Works of the Vieille Montagne Zinc Company, 1913" *British Mining*, No.5 (1977), pp.41–45

LAWSON, J. *See* LAWSON, John & LAWSON, J.

LAWSON, John "The Mineral Production Figures of Alston Moor" *British Mining*, No.8 (1978), pp.23–37

LAWSON, John & LAWSON, J. "Working the Alston Moor Mines" *Memoirs of the Northern Cavern and Mine Research Society*, (January 1969), pp.27–31

MAHER, Martin "Cumbria Amenity Trust Investigations on the Nentforce Level" *The Mine Explorer*, Vol.1 (1984), pp.43–45

MULCASTER, James "An Account of the Method of Smelting Lead Ore as it is Practiced in the Northern Part of England" *Bulletin of the Historical Metallurgy Group*, Vol.5 No.2 (1971), pp.45–62

MYERS, J.O. "The Caverns of Silverband Mine" *Journal of the Northern Pennine Club*, Vol.3 No.1 (Summer 1967), pp.34–40

N.C.M.R.S. RECORDS "Epitome of Evidence, North of England Lead Mines. Merryfield Mines" *Memoirs of the Northern Cavern and Mine Research Society*, No.2 (August 1964), pp.6–8

N.C.M.R.S. RECORDS "General Report on the Lead Mines in the Coalcleugh District, Northumberland, for the Month Ending August 31st, 1860" *Memoirs of the Northern Cavern and Mine Research Society*, (August 1965), pp.21–22

N.C.M.R.S. RECORDS "Reports of Coalcleugh Mine, 1861" *Memoirs of the Northern Cavern and Mine Research Society*, (August 1965), pp.22–24

NICHOLSON, G. "The Lead Road" *Bulletin of the Durham City Local History Society*, No.18 (April 1975), pp.32–41

PEARCE, J.L. "The Allendale Bargain Books" *Memoirs of the Northern Cavern and Mine Research Society*, Vol.2 N0.1 (April 1971), pp.24–27

POLLITT, David T. "A Visit to Stanhopeburn Mine, Weardale" *Bulletin of the Peak District Mines Historical Society*, Vol.3 No.4 (December 1967), pp.239–242

RAYNES, F. "Morrison Witherite Mine" *Camborne School of Mines Journal*, (1949), pp.34–40

ROBINSON, H.Y. "Fluorspar–Galena Ore Concentration" *Mine and Quarry Engineering*, Vol.22 (November 1956), pp.462–470

SALMON. L.B. "Coalpithole Rake" *Cave Science*, Vol.5 No.33 (April 1963), pp.36–52

SCHOFIELD, M. "Eminent Metallurgist and Chemist (Sir Isaac Lowthian Bell) *Metallurgia*, Vol.73 (February 1966), pp.64–66

SMITH, F.W. "The Weardale Lead Company Ltd." *British Mining*, No.5 (1977), pp.9–13

WAITE, Peter *See* BURT, Roger, WAITE, Peter, ATKINSON, Michael

WALTON, Joseph "The Medieval Mines of Alston" *Transactions of the Cumberland and Westmorland Antiquarian and Archaeological Society*, Vol.XLV New Series (1945), pp.22–33

WILDRIDGE, Joseph D.J. "The Smallcleugh Fan" *Industrial Archaeology*, Vol.4 No.3 (1967), pp.265–268

WILDRIDGE, Joseph D.J. "The Smallcleugh Fan" *Memoirs of the Northern Cavern and Mine Research Society*, (January 1969), pp.31–34

WILDRIDGE, Joseph D.J. "The Mines of Windy Hill, Woodend and Barf" *Memoirs of the Northern Cavern and Mine Research Society*, Vol.2 No.3 (September 1973), pp.123–126

WILSON, Paul N. "The Nent Force Level" *Transactions of the Cumberland and Westmorland Antiquarian and Archaeological Society*, Vol.63 New Series (1963), pp.253–280

THE LAKE DISTRICT AND FURNESS

Books

ASHMEAD, P. *See* MOSELEY, C.M., ASHMEAD, P. & CUMPSTY, P.

ATKINSON, Michael *See* BURT, Roger, WAITE, Peter, ATKINSON, Michael & BURNLEY, Raymond

BARBER, R. *Iron Ore and After: Boom Time, Depression and Survival in a West Cumbrian Town, Cleator Moor 1840–1960* (York: University of York for Cleator Moor Local Studies Group, 1976)

BURNLEY, Raymond *See* BURT, Roger, WAITE, Peter & BURNLEY, Raymond

BURNLEY, Raymond *See* BURT, Roger, WAITE, Peter, ATKINSON, Michael & BURNLEY, Raymond

BURT, Roger, WAITE, Peter & BURNLEY, Raymond *The Cumberland Mineral Statistics 1845–1913* (Exeter: Department of Economic History, University of Exeter, 1982)

BURT, Roger, WAITE, Peter, ATKINSON, Michael & BURNLEY, Raymond *The Lancashire and Westmorland Mineral Statistics with the Isle of Man 1845–1913* (Exeter: Department of Economic History, University of Exeter, 1983)

CAINE, C. *Cleator and Cleator Moor, Past and Present* (Beckermet: Michael Moon, 1973)

COLLINGWOOD, W.G. *Elizabethan Keswick* (Whitehaven: Michael Moon, 1986. Reprint of 1912 Edition.)

CUMPSTY, P. *See* MOSELEY, C.M., ASHMEAD, P. & CUMPSTY, P.

DAVIES–SHIEL, Michael & MARSHALL, John D. *Industrial Archaeology in the Lake Counties* (Newton Abbot: David & Charles, 1969)

DAVIES–SHIEL, Michael *See* MARSHALL, John D. & DAVIES–SHIEL, Michael

DEWEY, H. & EASTWOOD, T. *Special Reports on the Mineral Resources of G.B. Vol.30: Copper Ores of the Midlands, Wales, the Lake District and the Isle of Man* (Sheffield: Mining Facsimiles, 1986. Reprint of the Geological Survey 1925 Edition)

EASTWOOD, T. *Special Reports on the Mineral Resources of G.B. Vol.22: Lead and Zinc Ores of the Lake District* (Sheffield: Mining Facsimiles, 1986. Reprint of Geological Survey 1921 Edition.)

EASTWOOD, T. *See* DEWEY, H. & EASTWOOD, T.

FELL, Alfred *The Early Iron Industry of Furness and District* (Frank Cass, 1968. Reprint of 1908 Edition.)

HARRIS, A. *Cumberland Iron: The Story of Hodbarrow Mine 1855–1968* (Truro: Bradford Barton, 1970)

HOLLAND, Eric G. *Coniston Copper Mines: A Field Guide to the Mines in the Copper Ore Field at Coniston in the English Lake District* (Milnthorpe: Cicerone Press, 1981)

HOLLAND, Eric G. *Coniston Copper: A History* (Milnthorpe: Cicerone Press, 1987)

LANCASHIRE AND MERSEYSIDE INDUSTRIAL DEVELOPMENT ASSOCIATION *The Furness Area* (LMIDA, Industrial Surveys No.1, 1948)

MARSHALL, John D. *Furness and the Industrial Revolution: An Economic History of Furness (1711–1900) and the Town of Barrow (1757–1897) with an Epilogue* (Beckermet: Michael Moon, 1958)

MARSHALL, John D. *Old Lakeland* (Newton Abbot: David & Charles, 1972)

MARSHALL, John D. & DAVIES–SHIEL, Michael *The Lake District at Work: Past and Present* (Newton Abbot: David & Charles, 1970)

MARSHALL, John D. & DAVIES–SHIEL, Michael *Industrial Archaeology of the Lake Counties* (Beckermet: Michael Moon, 1977. Second Edition)

MARSHALL, John D. & WALTON, J.K. *The Lake Counties from 1830 to the Mid–Twentieth Century: A Study in Regional Change* (Manchester: Manchester University Press, 1981)

MARSHALL, John D. *See* DAVIES–SHIEL, Michael & MARSHALL, John D.

McFADZEAN, Alen *Wythburn Mine and the Lead Miners of Helvellyn* (Ulverston: Red Earth Publications, 1987)

MILLWARD, D. *See* YOUNG, B. & MILLWARD, D.

MOSELEY, C.M., ASHMEAD, P. & CUMPSTY, P. *The Metalliferous Mines of the Arnside–Carnforth Districts of Lancashire and Westmor-*

land (Skipton: Northern Cavern & Mine Research Society, Individual Survey Series No.3, 1969)

POSTLETHWAITE, John *Mines and Mining in the English Lake District* (Beckermet: Michael Moon, 1976. Reprint of 1877 Edition.)

ROLLINSON, W. *Life and Tradition in the Lake District* (Dent, 1974)

SHAW, W.T. *Mining in the Lake Counties* (Clapham: Dalesman, 1970)

SHAW, W.T. *Mining in the Lake Counties* (Clapham: Dalesman, 1972. Second Edition.)

SHAW, W.T. *Mining in the Lake Counties* (Clapham: Dalesman, 1975. Third Edition.)

WAITE, Peter *See* BURT, Roger, WAITE, Peter & BURNLEY, Raymond

WAITE, Peter *See* BURT, Roger, WAITE, Peter & ATKINSON, Michael & BURNLEY, Raymond

WALTON, J.K. *See* MARSHALL, John D. & WALTON, J.K.

WILSON, K.(Ed.) *The History of Lothersdale* (Cross Hills: Lothersdale Parish Council, 1972)

YOUNG, B. & MILLWARD, D. *Catalogue of Mining Information (other than coal, fireclay and slate) for the Lake District and South Cumbria held by the Northern England Office of the British Geological Survey* (British Geological Survey, Lake District Regional Survey, 1984)

Theses

BARBER, R.J. *The Iron Ore Mines of West Cumberland 1840–1914* (University of Newcastle–upon–Tyne MA Thesis, 1980)

BERRY, D. *The Social and Economic Development and Organisation of the Lake District, 1750–1814* (University of Manchester MA Thesis, 1962–3)

MARSHALL, J.D. *The Economic and Social History of the Furness Area from 1711 to 1875* (University of London PhD Thesis, 1956)

WILLIAMS, L.A. *The Development of Road Transport in Cumberland, Westmorland and the Furness District of Lancashire 1800–1885* (University of Leicester PhD Thesis, 1967)

WOOD, O *The Development of the Coal, Iron and Shipbuilding Industries of West Cumberland, 1750-1914* (University of London PhD Thesis, 1952)

Articles

ANON "Beckermet Mine. Part 1" *Mine and Quarry Engineering*, Vol.20 (April 1954), pp.148–158

ANON "Beckermet Mine. Part 2" *Mine and Quarry Engineering*, Vol.20 (May 1954), pp.204–214

ANON "Mechanised Mining of Haematite (Beckermet and Haile Moore)" *Mining Magazine*, (April 1968), pp.250–251

ANON "Carrock Fell: United Kingdom Tungsten Mine with an Interesting History is Again Producing Concentrates" *Mining Magazine*, (March 1977), pp.169–175

ANON "Florence Mine. The Last Working Iron Mine" *Industrial Heritage*, Vol.2 No.4 (1984), pp.2–3

ANON "Glossary of Terms" *The Mine Explorer*, Vol.1 (1984), p.88

ANON "Mine Plans (Coniston, Helvellyn, Tilberthwaite, Ding Dong)" *The Mine Explorer*, Vol.1 (1984)

ARX, R. Von "Caldbeck Fells Stationery" *British Mining*, No.34 (1987), p.34

ASHMORE, O. "The Industrial Archaeology of North West England" *Chetham Society*, Vol.XXIX (1982)

AUSTIN, A. "Early Mining in Eskdale and Wasdale" *The Mine Explorer*, Vol.2 (1986), pp.36–40

AUSTIN, A. & HEWER, Richard E. "The Mines of Eskdale and Mitredale, Cumberland" *The Mine Explorer*, Vol.1 (1984), pp.63–71

BELL, Michael R. "Lindal Moor Iron Mines, Cumberland" *Bulletin of the Peak District Mines Historical Society*, Vol.1 No.6 (May 1962), pp.39–42

BLUNDELL, D. "Carrock Mine: A Short History" *The Mine Explorer*, Vol.2 (1986), pp.95–101

BROWN, Ivor J. "Mines of the Lake District" *Shropshire Mining Club*, Yearbook (1962-3), pp.36–38

BURR, P. "Mining (Goldscope and Scar Crag Mines)" *University of Leeds Spelaeological Association*, Review No.5 (Summer 1969), pp.17–19

CANNELL, Alfred E. & CANNELL, M. "The Iron Mines of Tongue Gill" *Memoirs of the Northern Cavern and Mine Research Society*, (January 1969), pp.65–66

CANNELL, Alfred E. & CANNELL, M. "Greenhead Gill Trial, Westmorland" *Memoirs of the Northern Cavern and Mine Research Society*, (January 1969), p.66

CANNELL, Alfred E. & CANNELL, M. "Hartsop Hall Mines, Westmorland" *Memoirs of the Northern Cavern and Mine Research Society*, (January 1969), p67–68

CANNELL, Alfred E. & CANNELL, M. "Lowthwaite Mines, Cumberland" *Memoirs of the Northern Cavern and Mine Research Society*, (January 1969), pp.68–69

CANNELL, Alfred E. & CANNELL, M. "Grisedale Lead Mines, Patterdale, Westmorland" *Memoirs of the Northern Cavern and Mine Research Society*, (January 1969), pp.69–70

CANNELL, M. *See* CANNELL, Alfred & CANNELL, M.

CHALLIS, Peter J. "Greenside Mine: Ore Dressing Circa 1900: The Dam Disaster 1927" *British Mining*, No.11 (1979), pp.75–81

CHERRY, J. "Eskmeal and Sand–dunes Occupation Sites. Phase II Iron Manufacture" *Transactions of the Cumberland and Westmorland Antiquarian and Archaeology Society*, Vol.LXVI New Series (1966), pp.46–56

CONNOR, C. "Greenside Mine: Mining and Milling Practice. Part 1" *Mine and Quarry Engineering*, Vol.17 (November 1951), pp.367–372

CONNOR, C. "Greenside Mine: Mining and Milling Practice. Part 2" *Mine and Quarry Engineering*, Vol.17 (December 1951), pp.387–390

DAVEY, R.A. "Hydraulic Sand Filling at Hodbarrow (Haematite) Mine, South Cumberland" *Camborne School of Mines Journal*, (1964), pp.65–67

DAVIES–SHIEL, Michael *See* MARSHALL, John D. & DAVIES–SHIEL, Michael

DAVIS, Ronald B. *See* HARRIS, Alan & DAVIS, Ronald B.

FLEMING, Peter "Coniston Copper Mines Rediscovered. Part 1" *The Mine Explorer*, Vol.1 (1984), pp.2–15

FLEMING, Peter "Coniston Copper Mines Rediscovered. Part 2" *The Mine Explorer*, Vol.2 (1986), pp.7–25

GALGANO, M.J. "Iron–mining in Restoration Furness: the case of Sir Thomas Preston" *Recusant History*, Vol.XIII (1976), pp.212–218

GEORGE, A.D. "The Industrial Archaeology of West Cumberland" *Industrial Archaeology*, Vol.7 No.2 (1970), pp.145–164

GILCHRIST, D.G. "Waterblain Iron Mines, Underhill, Millom" *The Mine Explorer*, Vol.2 (1986), pp.90–94

GILCHRIST, D.G. & MOORE, C. "Whicham Mines, Kirksanton, Millom" *The Mine Explorer*, Vol.2 (1986), pp.66–71

HARKER, Roger S. "Copper Mines of the Lake District" *Memoirs of the Northern Cavern and Mine Research Society*, (December 1966), pp.35–40

HARRIS, Alan "Askam Iron: the Development of Askam–in–Furness, 1850–1920" *Transactions of the Cumberland and Westmorland Antiquarian and Archaeological Society*, Vol.LXV New Series (1965), pp.381–407

HARRIS, Alan "Millom: a Victorian New Town" *Transactions of the Cumberland and Westmorland Antiquarian and Archaeological Society*, Vol.LXVI (1966), pp.449–467

HARRIS, Alan & DAVIS, Ronald B. "The Hodbarrow Iron Mines" *Transactions of the Cumberland and Westmorland Antiquarian and Archaeological Society*, Vol.LXVIII (1968), pp.151–168

HEWER, Richard E. "Hartsop Hall Mine, 1980" *British Mining*, No.19 (1982), pp.34–36

HEWER, Richard E. "Survey of 'Wood Level' at Brandlehow, Cumbria" *British Mining*, No.19 (1982), pp.43–45

HEWER, Richard E. "Bannerdale Lead Mine" *The Mine Explorer*, Vol.1 (1984), pp.36–37

HEWER, Richard E. *See* AUSTIN, A. & HEWER, Richard E.

HOLLAND, Eric G. "Hodbarrow Mines, Cumberland. Part 1" *Mine and Quarry Engineering*, Vol.28 (May 1962), pp.220–227

HOLLAND, Eric G. "Hodbarrow Mines, Cumberland. Part 2" *Mine and Quarry Engineering*, Vol.28 (June 1962), pp.266–274

HOLLAND, Eric G. "A Brief History of the Coniston Copper Mines" *The Mine Explorer*, Vol.2 (1986), pp.31–35

HOLMES, P. "The Skylark: An Unusual Furness Winding Engine" *The Mine Explorer*, Vol.2 (1986), pp.26–29

HOLMES, P. "Electric Traction at Greenside" *The Mine Explorer*, Vol.2 (1986), pp.102f

JACKSON, P. "The Mines of Coniston" *Journal of the Sheffield University Spelaeological Society*, Vol.1 No.4 (1969), pp.155–159

JONES, Christopher D. "Goldscope Mine: A Short History" *The Mine Explorer*, Vol.1 (1984), pp.29–35

JONES, Christopher D. "Exploration in Tilberthwaite Mine, Near Coniston" *The Mine Explorer*, Vol.1 (1984), pp.38–39

JONES, Christopher D. "Hartside Mines" *The Mine Explorer*, Vol.1 (1984), p.58

LANDLESS, Vaughan "Force Crag Today: October, 1976" *British Mining*, No.5 (1977), pp.18–20

LANDLESS, Vaughan "Greenside Explored" *British Mining*, No.11 (1979), pp.66–74

LAWSON, John "Statistics of the Mineral Production of the Pennines: Part 2 Westmorland and the Lake District" *Memoirs of the Northern Cavern and Mine Research Society*, Vol.2 No.2 (May 1972), pp.44–59

LINGS, A.S. "Dent Copper Mine" *The Mine Explorer*, Vol.2 (1986), p.30

MAJOR, J.K. "An Inventory of Water Power Sites on the Coniston Massif, Lancashire" *Memoirs of the Northern Cavern and Mine Research Society*, (October 1969), pp.54–59

MARSHALL, John D. "Some Aspects of the Furness Charcoal Iron Industry" *Bulletin of the Historical Metallurgy Group*, Vol.3 No.1 (1969), pp.4–5

MARSHALL, John D. "Some Aspects of the Social History of Nineteenth Century Cumbria: (I) Migration and Literacy" *Transactions of the Cumberland and Westmorland Antiquarian and Archaeological Society*, Vol.LXIX (1969), pp.280–307

MARSHALL, John D. "Some Aspects of the Social History of Nineteenth Century Cumbria: (II) Crime, Police, Morals and the Countryman" *Transactions of the Cumberland and Westmorland Antiquarian and Archaeological Society*, Vol.LXX (1970), pp.221–246

MARSHALL, John D. & DAVIES–SHIEL, Michael "Industrial Archaeology in the Lake Counties and Furness" *Northern History*, Vol.II (1967), pp.112–133

MARSHALL, John D. *See* POLLARD, Sidney & MARSHALL, John D.

MATHESON, I. "Coniston Mines in 1849" *The Mine Explorer*, Vol.2 (1986), pp.41–44

MATHESON, I. "John Barrett of Coniston" *The Mine Explorer*, Vol.2 (1986), pp.72–80

McFADZEAN, Alan "Up and Above the City: A Glimpse into the History of Helvellyn Mine" *The Mine Explorer*, Vol.1 (1984), pp.17–24

MOON, John "Iron Ores of the Lake District and Furness" *Memoirs of the Northern Cavern and Mine Research Society*, No.3 (November 1964), pp.11–14

MOON, John & WILDRIDGE, Joseph D.J. "Embleton Lead Mine, Embleton, Cumbria" *Memoirs of the Northern Cavern and Mine Research Society*, No.2 (August 1964), pp.14–15

MOON, John & WILDRIDGE, Joseph D.J. "The Geology and Non-ferrous Mines of Buttermere and Loweswater Valleys" *Memoirs of the Northern Cavern and Mine Research Society*, (January 1969), pp.38–52

MOORE, C. *See* GILCHRIST, D.G. & MOORE, C.

MORTON, G.R. "Technical Aspects of the Early Iron Industry of Furness and District" *Bulletin of the Historical Metallurgy Group*, Vol.3 No.1 (1969), pp.6–11

PHILLIPS, C.B. "Iron–mining in Restoration Furness: the Case of Sir Thomas Preston: a Comment" *Recusant History*, Vol.XIV (1977), p.39

POLLARD, Sydney "Barrow-in-Furness and the Seventh Duke of Devonshire" *Economic History Review*, 2nd Series Vol.VIII (1955–56), pp.213–221

POLLARD, Sydney & MARSHALL, John D. "The Furness Railway and the Growth of Barrow" *Journal of Transport History*, Vol.1 No.2 (November 1953), pp.109–126

SCHNELLMANN, G.A. "The West Coast Haematite Bodies" *Mining Magazine*, Vol.LXXVI No.3 (March 1947), pp.137–151

SYKES, T. "The Rediscovery and Exploration of the Crag Foot Mine System" *British Caving*, Vol.43 (1966), pp.36–39

TYLER, Ian "Castlenook Mine" *The Mine Explorer*, Vol.1 (1984), p.40

TYLER, Ian "Black Howe Mine" *The Mine Explorer*, Vol.1 (1984), p.40

TYLER, Ian "Hazelholme Mine" *The Mine Explorer*, Vol.1 (1984), p.48

TYLER, Ian "Kinniside Mine" *The Mine Explorer*, Vol.1 (1984), p.59

WARD, J.T. "Some West Cumberland Landowners and Industry" *Industrial Archaeology*, Vol.9 No.4 (1972), pp.341–362

WICKENDEN, Mark "The Ding Dong" *The Mine Explorer*, Vol.1 (1984), pp.77–87

WILDRIDGE, Joseph D.J. "Dale Head Copper Mine, near Newlands, Keswick" *Memoirs of the Northern Cavern and Mine Research Society*, No.1 (April 1964), pp.23–24

WILDRIDGE, Joseph D.J. "Plumbago Mines, Seathwaite, Cumberland" *Memoirs of the Northern Cavern and Mine Research Society*, No.2 (August 1964), pp.27–29

WILDRIDGE, Joseph D.J. "Mines of the Buttermere and Loweswater Valleys" *Memoirs of the Northern Cavern and Mine Research Society*, Vol.2 N0.3 (September 1973), pp.145–147

WILDRIDGE, Joseph D.J. "The Instructions Given by the Company of Mines Royal to George Bowes and Francis Needham" *British Mining*, No.1 (1975), pp.25–40

WILDRIDGE, Joseph D.J. *See* MOON, John & WILDRIDGE, Joseph D.J.

LANCASHIRE AND YORKSHIRE

Books

ALMOND, J.K. *See* SHAYLER, A.E., ALMOND, J.K. & BEADLE, Harold L.

ARMSTRONG, Thomas *Adam Brunskill* (Collins, 1952)

ASHMORE, Owen *The Industrial Archaeology of Lancashire* (Newton Abbot: David & Charles, 1969)

ATKINSON, Michael *See* BURT, Roger, WAITE, Peter, ATKINSON, Michael & BURNLEY, Raymond

BAUGHAN, P.E. *The Railways of Wharfdale* (Newton Abbot: David & Charles, 1969)

BEADLE, Harold L. *See* SHAYLER, A.E., ALMOND, J.K. & BEADLE, Harold L.

BIRD, Richard H. (ed.) *The Mines of Grassington Moor and Wharfdale* (Sheffield: Northern Mine Research Society, British Mining No.13, 1980)

BROCK, J.R. *The History of the Greenhow–Grassington Lead Mining Field* (Harrogate, 1958)

BRUMHEAD, Derek *Geology Explained in the Yorkshire Dales and the Yorkshire Coast* (Newton Abbot: David & Charles, 1979)

BURNLEY, Raymond *See* BURT, Roger, WAITE, Peter, ATKINSON, Michael & BURNLEY, Raymond

BURT, Roger, WAITE, Peter, ATKINSON, Michael & BURNLEY, Raymond *The Yorkshire Mineral Statistics 1845–1913* (Exeter: Department of Economic History, University of Exeter, 1982)

BURT, Roger, WAITE, Peter, ATKINSON, Michael & BURNLEY, Raymond *The Lancashire and Westmorland Mineral Statistics with the Isle of Man 1845–1913* (Exeter: Department of Economic History, University of Exeter, 1983)

CARRUTHERS, R.G. & STRAHAN, A. *Special Reports on the Mineral Resources of G.B. Vol.26: Lead and Zinc Ores of Durham, Yorkshire, Derbyshire and Notes on the Isle of Man* (Sheffield: Mining Facsimiles, 1986. Reprint of Geological Survey 1923 Edition)

CHAPMAN, S.Keith *Cleveland Ironstone* (Clapham: Dalesman Books, 1973)

CHAPMAN, S.Keith *Gazetteer of Cleveland Ironstone Mines* (Guisborough: Loughborough Museum Service Research Series, 1976. Second Edition)

CLOUGH, Robert T. *The Lead Smelting Mills of the Yorkshire Dales and Northern Pennines: Their Architectural Character, Construction and Place in the European Tradition* (Keighley: Robert T. Clough, 1980. Reprinted with Additional Material.)

COOPER, E. *Men of Swaledale: An Account of Yorkshire Farmers and Miners* (Clapham, Dalesman, 1960)

DAWSON, Peter & DAWSON, Ruth *Rescue of the Kettlewell Providence Mine Water Wheel and Crusher* (Earby Mine Research Group, 1971)

DAWSON, Ruth *See* DAWSON, Peter & DAWSON, Ruth

DICKINSON, John Michael *The Greenhow Lead Mining Field (A Historical Survey)* (Keighley: Northern Cavern & Mine Research Society, Individual Survey Series No.4, 1970)

DICKINSON, John Michael *Mines and T'Miners: A History of Lead Mining in Airdale, Wharfdale and Nidderdale* (Keighley: Private Publication, 1972)

DICKINSON, John Michael *Mines and T'Miners* (Keighley: Bingstead, 1985)

DICKINSON, John Michael & GILL, Michael C. *The Greenhow Lead Mining Field: A Historical Survey* (Sheffield: Northern Mine Research Society, British Mining No.21, 1983)

FAWCETT, Edward R. (Ed. by Brian Lee) *Lead Mining in Swaledale: From the Manuscript of Edward R. Fawcett* (Roughlee: Faust, 1985)

FIELDHOUSE, Roger & JENNINGS, Bernard *A History of Richmond and Swaledale* (Phillimore, 1978)

FRANCE, R.S. *The Thieveley Lead Mines, 1629–1635* (Lancashire and Cheshire Record Society, 1959)

GILL, Michael C. *The Yorkshire and Lancashire Lead Mines: A Study in Lead Mining in the South Craven and Rossendale District* (Sheffield: Northern Mine Research Society, British Mining No.33, 1987)

GILL, Michael C. *See* DICKINSON, John Michael & GILL, Michael C.

HAYES, R.H. and RUTTER, J.G. *Rosedale Mines and Railway* (Scarborough: Scarborough and District Archaeology Society, Research

Reprint No.9, 1974)

HEMPSTEAD, C.A. (Ed.) *Cleveland Iron and Steel: Background and Nineteenth Century History* (Redcar: British Steel Corporation, 1979)

HORNSHAW, T.R. *Copper Mining in Middleton Tyas* (Northallerton: North Yorkshire County Council, 1975)

HORTON, M.C. *The Story of Cleveland* (Middlesbrough: Cleveland County Libraries, 1979)

ILLINGWORTH, John Lawson *See* RAISTRICK, Arthur & ILLINGWORTH, John Lawson

JENNINGS, Bernard *See* FIELDHOUSE, Roger & JENNINGS, Bernard

JENNINGS, Bernard *See* RAISTRICK, Arthur & JENNINGS, Bernard

LEE, B. *Lead Mining in Swaledale* (Roughlee: Raust, 1985)

N.M.R.S. RECORDS *The Mines of Grassington Moor and Wharfedale* (Sheffield: Northern Mine Research Society, British Mining No.13, 1980)

OWEN, John S. *Cleveland Ironstone Mining* (Redcar: C. Books, 1986)

POMEROY, P.I. *All O'er T'Parish: A Second Stroll Around Cliviger* (Lancashire County Council, Library and Leisure Committee, 1985)

RAISTRICK, Arthur *Malhamdale* (Clapham: Dalesman, 1946)

RAISTRICK, Arthur *Malham and Malham Moor* (Clapham: Dalesman, 1947)

RAISTRICK, Arthur *Grassington and Upper Wharfdale* (Clapham: Dalesman, 1948)

RAISTRICK, Arthur *Mines and Miners of Swaledale* (Clapham: Dalesman, 1955)

RAISTRICK, Arthur *The Romans in Yorkshire* (Clapham: Dalesman, 1960)

RAISTRICK, Arthur *Yorkshire and the North East* (Oliver & Boyd, 1963)

RAISTRICK, Arthur *Prehistoric Yorkshire* (Clapham: Dalesman, 1964)

RAISTRICK, Arthur (Ed.) *Old Yorkshire Dales* (Newton Abbot: David & Charles, 1967)

RAISTRICK, Arthur *The Pennine Dales* (Eyre & Spottiswoode, 1968)

RAISTRICK, Arthur *The West Riding of Yorkshire* (Hodder & Stoughton, 1970)

RAISTRICK, Arthur *Lead Mining in the Yorkshire Dales* (Clapham: Dalesman, 1972)

RAISTRICK, Arthur *Lead Mining in the Mid–Pennines: The Mines of Nidderdale, Wharfedale, Airedale, Ribblesdale and Bowland* (Truro: Bradford Barton, 1973)

RAISTRICK, Arthur *The Lead Industry of Wensleydale and Swaledale: Volume 1 The Mines* (Hartington: Moorland, 1975)

RAISTRICK, Arthur *The Lead Industry of Wensleydale and Swaledale: Volume 2 The Smelting Mills* (Hartington: Moorland, 1975)

RAISTRICK, Arthur *Two Centuries of Industrial Welfare: The London (Quaker) Lead Company, 1692–1905* (Hartington: Moorland, 1977. Second Edition Revised.)

RAISTRICK, Arthur *Lead Mining in the Yorkshire Dales* (Lancaster: Dalesman, 1981)

RAISTRICK, Arthur *The Wharton Mines in Swaledale in the Seventeenth Century* (Northallerton: North Yorkshire County Council, 1982)

RAISTRICK, Arthur *Mines and Miners on Malham Moor* (Littleborough: Kelsall, 1983)

RAISTRICK, Arthur & ILLINGWORTH, John Lawson *The Face of North West Yorkshire* (Clapham: Dalesman, 1965)

RAISTRICK, Arthur & JENNINGS, Bernard *A History of Lead Mining in the Pennines* (Longmans, 1965)

RICHARDSON, D.T. (Ed.) *Springs Wood Level, Starbotton, Kettlewell, Yorkshire* (Skipton: Northern Cavern & Mine Research Society, Individual Survey Series No.1, 1966)

RUTTER, J.G. *See* HAYES, R.H. & RUTTER, J.G.

SHAYLER, A.E., ALMOND, J.K. & BEADLE, H.L. *A Guide to the Past Lead Industry in Swaledale and Teesdale: Mining and Smelting in Swaledale and Teesdale* (Redcar: Cleveland Industrial Archaeology Society, 1979)

TYSON, Leslie Owen *A History of the Manor and Lead Mines of Arkengarthdale, Yorkshire* (Sheffield: Northern Mine Research Society, British Mining No.29, 1986)

STRAHAN, A. *See* CARRUTHERS, R.G. & STRAHAN, A.

WAITE, Peter *See* BURT, Roger, WAITE, Peter, ATKINSON, Michael & BURNLEY, Raymond

WILSON, R.E. *Two Hundred Precious Metal Years: A History of the Sheffield Smelting Company Ltd 1760–1960* (Benn, 1960)

Theses

BAINBRIDGE, J.W. *A Comparative Study of the Growth and Decline of Two Iron Ore Mining Districts (Cleveland and West Cumberland)* (University of Durham MSc Thesis, 1964)

FOSTER, J. *Elementary Education in Skipton during the Nineteenth Century* (University of Leeds MEd Thesis, 1973/4)

HARRIS, J.R. *The Copper Industry in Lancashire and North Wales, 1760–1815* (University of Manchester PhD Thesis, 1952)

HORNSHAW, T.R. *Copper Mining in Richmondshire in the Eighteenth and Nineteenth Centuries* (University of Durham MA Thesis, 1971/2)

JENNINGS, Bernard *The Leadmining Industry in Swaledale* (University of Leeds MA Thesis, 1959)

ROBERTSON, J.G. *Some Aspects of Mineral Production in Modern Britain, with Particular Reference to Yorkshire Potash and Merioneth Copper* (University of Hull PhD Thesis, 1973/4)

SHUTT, G. *Wharfdale Watermills* (University of Leeds MPhil Thesis, 1979)

Articles

ANON "New Mill at Greenhow Hill" *Mine and Quarry Engineering,* Vol.30 (May 1964), p.221

ANON "Lead Mining and Smelting in Swaledale and Yorkshire" *Cleveland Industrial Archaeology Society Research Report,* No.2 (1979)

BALDERTONE, J. "Kettlewell Lead Smelting Mill. Part I" *Cave Science,* No.13 (1950), pp.225–229

BALDERTONE, J. "Kettlewell Lead Smelting Mill. Part II" *Cave Science,* No.14 (1950), pp.263–274

BARKER, J.Lawrence "Warrant against Adam Barker, 2nd May 1692" *Memoirs of the Northern Cavern and Mine Research Society,* (December 1967), p.16

BARKER, J.Lawrence "Letter from John Renshaw to Philip Lord Wharton. Lord of the Muker and Healaugh Manors, 10th July 1685" *Memoirs of the Northern Cavern and Mine Research Society*, (December 1967), pp.24–25

BARKER, J.Lawrence "Document Relating to a Dispute over Ownership of Grinton Manor" *Memoirs of the Northern Cavern and Mine Research Society*, (December 1967), pp.26–30

BARKER, J.Lawrence "Document Relating to the Beldi Hill Dispute" *Memoirs of the Northern Cavern and Mine Research Society*, (January 1969), pp.79–84

BARKER, J.Lawrence "Extract from one of the Law Cases Re Beldi Hill Dispute" *Memoirs of the Northern Cavern and Mine Research Society*, (January 1969), pp.84–89

BARKER, J.Lawrence "Portion of a Letter and Plan Re Beldi Hill, Flooding of Mine etc." *Memoirs of the Northern Cavern and Mine Research Society*, (January 1969), pp.89–92

BARKER, J.Lawrence "Details Relating to Grinton and Harkside Mine, Grinton" *Memoirs of the Northern Cavern and Mine Research Society*, (January 1969), p.92

BARKER, J.Lawrence "The Lead Miners of Swaledale and Arkengarthdale in 1851" *Memoirs of the Northern Cavern and Mine Research Society*, Vol.2 No.2 (May 1972), pp.89–97

BARKER, J.Lawrence "Bale Hills in Swaledale and Arkengarthdale" *British Mining*, No.8 (1978), pp.49–54

BARTLETT, J.M. "A Pig of Lead from Broomfleet, East Yorkshire" *Journal of the Derbyshire Archaeological and Natural History Society*, Vol.LXXXVII (1967), pp.167–8

BIRD, Richard H. "Notes on the Rockley Mine" *Memoirs of the Northern Cavern and Mine Research Society*, Vol.2 No.4 (June 1974), pp.175–178

BIRD, Richard H. "The Inundation of the Spitalwell Mine" *Memoirs of the Northern Cavern and Mine Research Society*, Vol.2 No.4 (June 1974), pp.189–192

BRETTON, R. "Copperas Works, Siddal" *Transactions of the Halifax Antiquarian Society*, (1961), pp.93–99

BROOK, E.S. "The Story of Old Sal, the Passing of a Notable Sheffield Landmark" *Bulletin of the Peak District Mines Historical Society*, Vol.2 No.2 (1963), pp.68–69

CANNELL, Alfred E. "A Mine near Dinkling Green, Yorkshire" *Transactions of the Northern Cavern and Mine Research Society*, Vol.1 No.2 (April 1964), pp.54–55

CANNELL, Alfred E. "A Report on a Mine at Sykes, Bowland Forest" *Memoirs of the Northern Cavern and Mine Research Society*, No.3 (November 1964), pp.15–18

CANNELL, Alfred E. & CANNELL, M. "St.Hubert Mine, near Holden, Bowland" *Transactions of the Northern Cavern and Mine Research Society*, Vol.1 No.3 (September 1963), p.23

CANNELL, Alfred E. & CANNELL, M. "Victoria Mine, near Holden, Bowland" *Memoirs of the Northern Cavern and Mine Research Society*, No.1 (April 1964), pp.22–23

CANNELL, Alfred E. & CANNELL, M. "Ashnott Mine, near Newton, Bowland, Lancashire" *Memoirs of the Northern Cavern and Mine Research Society*, (December 1966), pp.46–48

CANNELL, Alfred E. & CANNELL, M. "Mineral Occurance in Marl Clough Beck, Nr. Newton, Bowland, Lancashire" *Memoirs of the Northern Cavern and Mine Research Society*, (December 1966), pp.48–49

CANNELL, Alfred E. & CANNELL, M. "On Further Visits to Mineral Occurances in the Forest of Bowland, Lancashire" *Memoirs of the Northern Cavern and Mine Research Society*, (January 1969), pp.62–65

CANNELL, M. *See* CANNELL, Alfred E. & CANNELL, M.

CHAPMAN, Nigel A. *See* CHAPMAN, Simon A. & CHAPMAN, Nigel A.

CHAPMAN, Simon A. "Description of the Waddle Ventilation Fan, Lumpsey Ironstone Mine, NGR NZ686188" *Cleveland Industrial Archaeologist*, No.9 (1978), pp.1–5

CHAPMAN, Simon A. "Ventilating Furnace at Ayton Ironstone Mine NGR NZ585102" *Cleveland Industrial Archaeologist*, No.9 (1979), pp.25–26

CHAPMAN, Simon A. "The Ventilating Machines of M.Guibal in Cleveland" *Cleveland Industrial Archaeologist*, No.13 (1981), pp.15–21

CHAPMAN, Simon A. & CHAPMAN, Nigel A. "Lumpsey Ironstone Mine" *Bulletin of the North East Industrial Archaeology Society*, Vol.12 (December 1970), pp.2–24

CHAPMAN, S.K. "An Historical Survey of the Cleveland Ironstone Industry" *Transactions of the Teesside Industrial Archaeology Group*, Vol.I No.1 (1967), pp.1–15

CHAPMAN, S.K. "Port Mulgrave Ironstone Workings" *Bulletin of the Industrial Archaeology Society of the North East*, No.5 (1968), pp.3–7

CHAPMAN, S.K. "Gazetteer of Cleveland Ironstone Mines" *Loughborough Museum Service*. Research Series. No.1 (1976)

CLARK, H. "Water Wheels and Mills in Mid–Wharfedale" *The Dalesman*, Vol.32 No.3 (June 1970), pp.223–7

CLOUGH, Robert T. "The Lead Smelting Mills of Yorkshire, with Special Reference to their Construction and Architectural Features. Preliminary Survey and Details, Merryfield Mill, Nidderdale" *Cave Science*, Vol.1 No.1 (1947), p.24

CLOUGH, Robert T. "Preliminary Survey, Kettlewell Mill" *Cave Science*, Vol.1 No.2 (1947), p.61

CLOUGH, Robert T. "Preliminary Survey, Cockhill Mill, Greenhow Hill. Part 1" *Cave Science*, Vol.1 No.3 (1948), p.96

CLOUGH, Robert T. "Preliminary Survey, Cockhill Mill, Greenhow Hill. Part 2" *Cave Science*, Vol.1 No.4 (1948), p.124

CLOUGH, Robert T. "The Lead Smelting Mills of Yorkshire. Part I. Airedale, Wharfedale, Greenhow Hill and Nidderdale" *Cave Science*, Vol.1 No.5 (1948), pp.165–177

CLOUGH, Robert T. "Cobscar Mill" *Cave Science*, Vol.1 No.7 (1949), p.285

CLOUGH, Robert T. "The Lead Smelting Mills of Yorkshire. Part II. Wensleydale" *Cave Science*, Vol.1 No.8 (1949), pp.324–333

CLOUGH, Robert T. "The Lead Smelting Mills of Yorkshire. Part III. Swaledale and Arkengarthdale. Part 1" *Cave Science*, Vol.2 No.9 (1949), pp.31–43

CLOUGH, Robert T. "The Lead Smelting Mills of Yorkshire. Part III. Swaledale and Arkengarthdale. Part 2" *Cave Science* Vol.2 No.10 (1949), pp79–87

CLOUGH, Robert T. "The Lead Smelting Mills of Yorkshire. Part III. Swaledale and Arkengarthdale. Part 3" *Cave Science*, Vol.2 No.11 (1950), pp.133–135

CLOUGH, Robert T "A Lead Crushing Plant, Kettlewell" *Cave Science*, Vol.3 No.18 (1951), pp.83–84

CLOUGH, Robert T. "The Old Laws and Customs of the Grassington Lead Mines, Yorkshire" *British Caver*, Vol.XXIII (1952), pp.1–5

CLOUGH, Robert T. "Lead Miners' Tools and Equipment Illustrated from Examples in the Backhouse Collection of Photographs, Central Library, Leeds" *Transactions of the Northern Cavern and Mine Research Society*, Vol.1 No.1 (June 1961), pp.28–39

CLOUGH, Robert T. "Lead Mines and Mining at Cononley, near Skipton" *Transactions of the Northern Cavern and Mine Research Society*, Vol.1 No.1 (June 1961), pp.40–43

CLOUGH, Robert T. "Catalogue of a Collection of Yorkshire Mine Plans Relative to the Greenhow Area" *Memoirs of the Northern Cavern and Mine Research Society*, (December 1967), pp.11–15

CLOUGH, Robert T. "Lead Miners' Tools and Equipment, Illustrated from Examples in the Backhouse Collection of Photographs, Central Library, Leeds" *Industrial Archaeology*, Vol.5 No.3 (1968), pp.241–261

CRABTREE, Peter W. "The Kisdon Mining Company, Swaledale, Yorkshire, Part I: Sir George's Level" *Bulletin of the Peak District Mines Historical Society*, Vol.2 No.6 (December 1965), pp.303–306

CRABTREE, Peter W. "The Kisdon Mining Company, Swaledale, Yorkshire, Part II: Myton Level" *Bulletin of the Peak District Mines Historical Society*, Vol.3 No.1 (July 1966), pp.63–67

CRABTREE, Peter W. "The Kisdon Mining Company, Swaledale, Yorkshire, Part III: The Boundary of the Company and Guy's Level" *Bulletin of the Peak District Mines Historical Society*, Vol.3 No.2 (December 1966), pp.119–124

CRABTREE, Peter W. "The Kisdon Mining Company, Swaledale, Yorkshire Part IV: The Kisdon Shaft and Alton's Level" *Bulletin of the Peak District Mines Historical Society*, Vol.3 No.3 (May 1967), pp.155–158

CRABTREE, Peter W. "The Kisdon Mining Company, Swaledale, Yorkshire. Part V: Acre Walls Vein" *Bulletin of the Peak District Mines Historical Society*, Vol.3 No.4 (December 1967), pp.233–238

CRABTREE, Peter W. "The Kisdon Mining Company, Swaledale, Yorkshire. Part VI: Morsgill Level, Alderson's Vein and General Remarks" *Bulletin of the Peak District Mines Historical Society*, Vol.3 No.5 (May 1968), pp.299–304

CRABTREE, Peter W. & FOSTER, R. "Sir Francis Mine" *Cave Science*, Vol.5 No.33 (April 1963), pp.1–24

CRAIG, W.J. "The Keld Literary Institute" *British Mining*, No.3 (1976), pp.1–4

DAVIES, Martin "Valentine Hole, Greenhow Hill" *Yorkshire Underground Research Team Report*, No.1 (June 1968), pp.1–7

DAVIES, Martin "Pendleton Pipe" *Yorkshire Underground Research Team Review*, No.2 (September 1970), pp.25–27

DAVIS, R.V. & DICKINSON, John Michael "The Effects of Lead Mining on the Population of Villages in the Wharfedale Mining Field 1853–1880" *Memoirs of the Northern Cavern and Mine Research Society*, No.1 (1964), pp.8–9

DICKINSON, John Michael "Clough Head Level, Sutton–in–Craven" *Transactions of the Northern Cavern and Mine Research Society*, Vol.1 No.1 (June 1961), pp.58–59

DICKINSON, John Michael "Some Notes on the Lead Mines of Greenhow Hill, Yorkshire" *Transactions of the Northern Cavern and Mine Research Society*, Vol.1 No.2 (April 1963), pp.34–47

DICKINSON, John Michael "Sarah Lead Mine, Grassington Moor. Cavendish Vein 4O Fm. Level" *Transactions of the Northern Cavern and Mine Research Society*, Vol.1 No.3 (September 1963), pp.17–18

DICKINSON, John Michael "The Appletreewick Lead Mining Company 1870–1872: Part 1 Mining and Miners" *Memoirs of the Northern Cavern and Mine Research Society*, No.1 (April 1964), pp.1–5

DICKINSON, John Michael "The Appletreewick Lead Mining Company 1870–1872: Part 2 Engines, Dressing and Smelting of Ore" *Memoirs of the Northern Cavern and Mine Research Society*, No.2 (August 1964), pp.1–7

DICKINSON, John Michael "The Appletreewick Lead Mining Company 1870–1872: Part 3 Sundry Works, Mine Management, Stores" *Memoirs of the Northern Cavern and Mine Research Society*, No.3 (November 1964), pp.1–4

DICKINSON, John Michael "Eagle Level, Pateley Bridge, Yorkshire" *Memoirs of the Northern Cavern and Mine Research Society*, No.3 (November 1964), pp.4–8

DICKINSON, John Michael "The Dales Chemical Company" *Memoirs of the Northern Cavern and Mine Research Society*, (August 1965), pp.1–10

DICKINSON, John Michael "Burhill Mine" *Memoirs of the Northern Cavern and Mine Research Society*, (December 1966), pp.1–9

DICKINSON, John Michael "The Grimwith Lead Mining Company Ltd." *Memoirs of the Northern Cavern and Mine Research Society*, (1966), pp.1–21

DICKINSON, John Michael "The Rimmington Lead and Silver Mines" *Memoirs of the Northern Cavern and Mine Research Society*, (1968), pp.21–22

DICKINSON, John Michael "Compressed Air Drilling in the Yorkshire Dales Lead Mines" *Memoirs of the Northern Cavern and Mine Research Society*, (1969), pp.31–33

DICKINSON, John Michael "The Greenhow Lead Mining Field" *Memoirs of the Northern Cavern and Mine Research Society*, (October 1969), pp.25–31

DICKINSON, John Michael "Lead Mining with Steam in the Craven Dales" *Memoirs of the Northern Cavern and Mine Research Society*, Vol.2 No.2 (May 1972), pp.71–73

DICKINSON, John Michael "The Mineral Veins of Swinden Knoll" *Memoirs of the Northern Cavern and Mine Research Society*, Vol.2 No.2 (May 1972), pp.98–100

DICKINSON, John Michael "Old Providence Lead Mine" *Memoirs of the Northern Cavern and Mine Research Society*, Vol.2 No.3 (September 1973), pp.101–104

DICKINSON, John Michael "A Prototype Aerial Ropeway at Hebden" *British Mining*, No.1 (1975), pp.11–16

DICKINSON, John Michael "Buckden Out Moor Lead Smelting Mill" *British Mining*, No.8 (1978), pp.38–39

DICKINSON, John Michael & GILL, Michael C. "Wharfedale Mine" *Memoirs of the Northern Cavern and Mine Research Society*, (December 1966), p.34

DICKINSON, John Michael, GILL, Michael C. & MARTELL, Hazel "Lumb Clough Lead Smelting Mill" *British Mining*, No.1 (1975), pp.1–10

DICKINSON, John Michael & HOLDING, John E. "Coal and Iron Working in Upper Airedale" *Memoirs of the Northern Cavern and Mine Research Society*, (August 1965), pp.42–46

DICKINSON, John Michael *See* DAVIS, R.V. & DICKINSON, John MIchael

DICKINSON, John Michael *See* WADE, John Caleb & DICKINSON, John Michael

DIXON, Jean M. & RICHARDSON, Douglas T. "Starbotton Moor End Mine, Starbotton, Near Kettlewell, Yorkshire. Preliminary Biological Report and Analysis of Water Samples" *Memoirs of the Northern Cavern and Mine Research Society*, (August 1965), pp.54–57

ERRINGTON, D. "Flushhembar Mine and Bropery Gill Level" *Moldywarps Spelaeological Group Journal*, No.9 (1976), pp.19–22

FINCH, Adrian "An Account of the N.M.R.S. Exploration at Sunside, Coldstones Hill, Pateley Bridge" *British Mining*, No.8 (1978), p.22

FIRTH, Gary "The Origins of the Low Moor Iron Works, Bradford 1788–1800" *Yorkshire Archaeological Journal*, Vol.49 (1977), pp.127–139

FOSTER, R. *See* CRABTREE, Peter W. & FOSTER, R.

FOSTER–SMITH, J.R. "Extracts from the Mining Journal: Mines in the Yorkshire Dales" *Memoirs of the Northern Cavern and Mine Research Society*, (August 1965), pp.10–21

FOSTER–SMITH, J.R. "Notes on Lead Mines on the East Side of Wharfedale between Buckden and Kettlewell" *Memoirs of the Northern Cavern and Mine Research Society*, (January 1969), pp.14–21

FROST, Leslie R. "Early Traffic Developments on the Cleveland Railways" *Transport History*, Vol.6 No.1 (1973)

GILL, Michael C. "Buckden Gavel Lead Mine" *Memoirs of the Northern Cavern and Mine Research Society*, Vol.2 No.4 (June 1974), pp.179–182

GILL, Michael C. "Lolly Scar and Blayshaw Gill Lead Mines" *Memoirs of the Northern Cavern and Mine Research Society*, Vol.2 No.4 (June 1974), pp.203–204

GILL, Michael C. "North Mossdale Mine" *British Mining*, No.1 (1975), pp.17–18

GILL, Michael C. "Mire Shaft, Grassington Moor" *British Mining*, No.3 (1976), p.5

GILL, Michael C. "A History of the Hebden Moor Lead Mines in the Nineteenth Century" *British Mining*, No.3 (1976), pp.29–33

GILL, Michael C. "Blubberhouse Moor Lead Mine" *British Mining*, No.11 (1979), p.63

GILL, Michael C. "The Mines of Littondale" *British Mining*, No.11 (1979). pp.87–89

GILL, Michael C. "The Dukes Level, Grassington. A Comment on John Taylor's Views" *British Mining*, No.23 (1983), pp.59–60

GILL, Michael C. "The Mechanisation of the Grassington Mines, Yorkshire" *British Mining*, No.25 (1984), pp.45–50

GILL, Michael C. & McNEIL, John H. "A Report on the Excavations at the Chimney Shaft, Cockhill Mine" *British Mining*, No.5 (1977), pp.54–56

GILL, Michael C. *See* DICKINSON, John Michael & GILL, Michael C.

GILL, Michael C. *See* DICKINSON, John Michael, GILL, Michael C. & MARTELL, Hazel

GUTHRIE, Robert G. "Some Extracts from Poor Law Records: Arkengarthdale Select Vestry" *Memoirs of the Northern Cavern and Mine Research Society*, (August 1965), p.25

GUTHRIE, Robert G. "Jane Pedley's Stories" *Memoirs of the Northern Cavern and Mine Research Society*, (August 1965), p.31

GUTHRIE, Robert G. "Hurst Lead Mine, Swaledale" *Memoirs of the Northern Cavern and Mine Research Society*, (December 1966), pp.44–45

HARKER, Roger S. "Wharfedale and Airedale Lead Mines Selling Ore in the County of York in 1868" *Memoirs of the Northern Cavern and Mine Research Society*, (December 1966), p.33

HARRIS, John R. "Michael Highes of Sutton: the Influence of Welsh Copper on Lancashire Business, 1780–1815" *Transactions of the Historic Society of Lancashire and Cheshire*, Vol.CI (1949), pp.139–167

HARRISON, B.J.D. "The Farndale Ironstone Mine 1873–1897" *Bulletin of the Cleveland and Teesside Local History Society*, No.4 (1969), pp.3–6

HARRISON, B.J.D. "The Origins of East Cleveland and Rosedale Ironstone Miners from the 1871 Census" *Bulletin of the Cleveland and Teesside Local History Society*, No.19 (1972–3), pp.1–9

HAYES, R.H. & RUTTER, J.G. "The Rosedale Ironstone Industry and Railway" *Transactions of the Scarborough and District Archaeology Society*, Vol.2 No.11 (1968), pp.7–28

HAYES, R.H. & RUTTER, J.G. "The Rosedale Ironstone Industry and Railway" *Scarborough and District Archaeological Society*. Research Report. No.9 (1974)

HEWER, Richard E. *See* TYSON, Leslie & HEWER, Richard E.

HOLDING, John E. *See* DICKINSON, John Michael & HOLDING, John E.

HORNSHAW, T.R. "The Richmond Copper Mine" *North Yorkshire County Record Office Journal*, No.3 (April 1976), pp.77–85

HOUSTON, William J. "Fluorspar Production in Derbyshire and Yorkshire" *Quarry Managers Journal*, (April 1964), pp.149–161

INESON, P.R. "Belland Ground in the South Pennines: Causes and Alleviations" *Bulletin of the Peak District Mines Historical Society*, Vol.8 No.3 (Summer 1982), pp.193–200

JOY, David "Treasures of Dales Mining" *The Dalesman*, Vol.30 No.7 (October 1968), pp.539–543

LAWSON, John "Grassington Mines: Accounts 1796" *Memoirs of the Northern Cavern and Mine Research Society*, (October 1969), pp.33–34

LAWSON, John "Statistics of the Mineral Production of the Pennines: Part 1 The Central Pennine Orefield" *Memoirs of the Northern Cavern and Mine Research Society*, Vol.2 No.1 (April 1971), pp.1–18

LAWSON, John "Mines and Mine Owners in the Central Pennines: Part 1 Swaledale and Wensleydale" *Memoirs of the Northern Cavern and Mine Research Society*, Vol.2 No.3 (September 1973), pp.151–160

LAWSON, John "Mines and Mine Owners in the Central Pennines: Part 2 Wharfedale and Nidderdale, with Airedale" *Memoirs of the Northern Cavern and Mine Research Society*, Vol.2 No.4 (June 1974), pp.193–202

LOCH, Charles W. "Forgotten Mines in Lancashire" *Mining Magazine*, Vol.LXXIV (May 1946), pp.290–297

LODGE, P.D. "Hydraulic Pumping and Winding Machinery, Sir Francis Level, Swaledale" *Memoirs of the Northern Cavern and Mine Research Society*, (December 1966), pp.21–26

LOMBOLLE, L.J. "The Origins of the Cleveland Ironstone Miners from the 1861 Census" *Bulletin of the Cleveland and Teesside Local History Society*, No.7 (1970), pp.15–16

MACPHERSON, John "Valuation of Plant at Sir Francis Level, Swaledale" *Memoirs of the Northern Cavern and Mine Research Society*, Vol.2 No.1 (April 1971), pp. 28–29

MARSDEN, K.E. "Wealth in Yorkshire Minerals" *The Dalesman*, Vol.38 No.2 (May 1976), pp.131–132

MARTELL, Hazel *See* DICKINSON, John Michael, GILL, Michael C. & MARTELL, Hazel

McDONNELL, Jerry G. "An Account of the Iron Industry in Upper Ryedale and Bilsdale c.1150–1650" *Ryedale Historian*, No.6 (1972), pp.23–52

McNEIL, John H. "West Stonesdale Mine" *British Mining*, No.19 (1982), pp.15–19

McNEIL, John H. *See* GILL, Michael C. & McNEIL, John H.

METCALFE, J.E. "The Lead Mines of the Northern Dales. Part 1" *Mine and Quarry Engineering*, Vol.18 (January 1952), pp.5–12

METCALFE, J.E. "The Lead Mines of the Northern Dales. Part 2" *Mine and Quarry Engineering*, Vol.18 (February 1952), pp.43–48

MITCHELL, William R. "Greenhow Hill: Village on the Skyline" *The Dalesman*, Vol.17 No.3 (June 1955), pp.134–137

MITCHELL, William R. "Dawn to Dusk with a Dales' Lead Miner" *The Dalesman*, Vol.18 No.7 (October 1956), pp.355–356

MITCHELL, William R. "A Walk up Gunnerside Gill" *The Dalesman*, Vol.37 No.10 (January 1976), pp.776–780

MITCHELL, William R. "Destination Swinnergill" *The Dalesman*, Vol.38 No.8 (November 1976), pp.617–619

MITCHELL, William R. "Old Gang and Beyond" *The Dalesman*, Vol.38 No.10 (January 1977), pp.114–116

MITCHELL, William R. "Oade Will, Aint Hannah and Fred" *The Dalesman*, Vol.38 No.12 (March 1977)

MOORHOUSE, J.W. "When the Boom was on: Reminiscences of Mining Days at Cononley" *Transactions of the Northern Cavern and Mine Research Society*, Vol.1 No.1 (June 1961), pp.49–57

N.C.M.R.S. RECORDS "Lead Returns of the A.D. Mining Company, Swaledale" *Memoirs of the Northern Cavern and Mine Research Society*, No.3 (November 1964), p.9

N.C.M.R.S. RECORDS "Thomas Blackah: Bibliography" *Memoirs of the Northern Cavern and Mine Research Society*, (August 1965), pp.6–10

N.C.M.R.S. RECORDS "Ore Hearth of Keld Mining Company Smelter, Wensleydale" *Memoirs of the Northern Cavern and Mine Research Society*, (August 1965), pp.27–30

N.C.M.R.S. RECORDS "Grassington Moor Cavern" *Memoirs of the Northern Cavern and Mine Research Society*, (August 1965), p.47

N.C.M.R.S. RECORDS "How Gill Mine Fissure" *Memoirs of the Northern Cavern and Mine Research Society*, (August 1965), pp.47–48

NICHOLS, A.R. "The Discovery of a Human Skeleton in Buckden Gavel Mine" *Memoirs of the Northern Cavern and Mine Research Society*, No.2 (August 1964), pp.15–17

NICHOLS, A.R. "Dry Gill Mill" *Memoirs of the Northern Cavern and Mine Research Society*, Vol.2 No.1 (April 1971), pp.31–36

OKEY, S. "Ironstone in Cleveland" *Cleveland Industrial Archaeologist*, No.8 (1978), pp.31–32

OWEN, John S. "Geological Background to Ironstone Mining in Cleveland" *Transactions of the Teesside Local History Group*, Vol.1 No.1 (1967), pp.1–8

OWEN, John S. "Some Legal Aspects of Ironstone Mining in Cleveland" *Bulletin of the Cleveland and Teesside Local History Society*, No.3 (1968), pp.2–8

OWEN, John S. "Some Further Remarks on the Farndale Ironstone Mines" *Bulletin of the Cleveland and Teesside Local History Society*, No.5 (1969), pp.15–16

OWEN, John S. "Mining Failure in Cleveland. No.3 The Kildale Mines Part 1" *Bulletin of the Cleveland and Teesside Local History Society*, No.14 (Not Dated), pp.18–26

OWEN, John S. "Mining Failure in Cleveland. No.3 The Kildale Mines Part 2" *Bulletin of the Cleveland and Teesside Local History Society*, No.17 (Not Dated), pp.12–17

OWEN, John S. "Mining Failure in Cleveland. No.3 The Kildale Mines Part 3" *Bulletin of the Cleveland and Teesside Local History Society*, No.18 (Not Dated), pp.15–21

OWEN, John S. "Mining Failure in Cleveland. No.3 The Kildale Mines Part 4" *Bulletin of the Cleveland and Teesside Local History Society*, No.19 (Not Dated), pp.10–14

OWEN, John S. "Mining Failure in Cleveland. No.5 Tocketts Mine" *Bulletin of the Cleveland and Teesside Local History Society*, No.24 (1974), pp.10–27

OWEN, John S. "Early Days at the Rosedale Mines" *Bulletin of the Cleveland and Teesside Local History Society*, No.28 (1975), pp.1–11

OWEN, John S. "The Esk Valley Ironstone Mine: Part 1, Documented History" *Cleveland Industrial Archaeologist*, No.7 (1977), pp.1–10

OWEN, John S. "Pre–1865 Ironstone Mining Development at Skinningrove" *Cleveland Industrial Archaeologist*, No.8 (1978), pp.1–8

OWEN, John S. "The Esk Valley Ironstone Mine: Part 3, Excavations Completed" *Cleveland Industrial Archaeologist*, No.11 (1979), pp.13–24

OWEN, John S. "Excavation of the Esk Valley Ironstone Mine, North Yorkshire" *Industrial Archaeology Review*, Vol.IV No.1 (1979–80), pp.103–107

OWEN, John S. "Warren Moor Ironstone Mine, Kildale" *Cleveland Industrial Archaeologist*, No.13 (1981), pp.33–53

OWEN, John S. "Warren Moor Mine, North Yorkshire" *Industrial Archaeology Review*, Vol.V No.3 (1981), pp.260–263

OWEN, John S. "Lonsdale Ironstone Mines, Kildale" *Cleveland Industrial Archaeologist*, No.15 (1983), pp.31–48

OWEN, John S. & TUFFS, P. "The Esk Valley Ironstone Mine: Part 2, Some Site Details" *Cleveland Industrial Archaeologist*, No.7 (1977), pp.11–15

PORRITT, R.N. "The Early Years of the Cleveland Mines Association" *Bulletin of the Cleveland and Teesside Local History Society*, Vol.13 (Not Dated), pp.8–11

PRIESTLEY, J. "Charles Woodward Seeks Barytes" *The Dalesman*, Vol.18 No.11 (February 1957), p.558

RAISTRICK, Arthur "The Malham Moor Mines, Yorkshire 1790–1830" *Transactions of the Newcomen Society*, Vol.26 (1947–8), pp.69–79

RAISTRICK, Arthur "Lead from the Grey Hills" *The Dalesman*, Vol.12 No.10 (January 1951), pp.391–395

RAISTRICK, Arthur "The Lead Mines of Upper Wharfedale" *Yorkshire Bulletin of Economic and Social Research*, Vol.V (1953), pp.1–16

RAISTRICK, Arthur "The Mechanisation of the Grassington Moor Mines, Yorkshire" *Transactions of the Newcomen Society*, Vol.29 (1953–55), pp.179–195

RAISTRICK, Arthur "Water Power in the Dales: Pt.III. Waterwheels at the Mines" *The Dalesman*, Vol.23 No.2 (May 1961), pp.99–103

RAISTRICK, Arthur "The Founders' Meer" *Transactions of the Northern Cavern and Mine Research Society*, Vol.1 No.2 (April 1964), pp.1–4

RAISTRICK, Arthur "Conistone Moor Mines, Wharfedale, Yorkshire" *Memoirs of the Northern Cavern and Mine Research Society*, (December 1966), pp.27–32

RAISTRICK, Arthur "Fourteen and Ten Meers Mines and Other Eighteenth Century Mine Disputes on Grassington Moor" *Memoirs of the Northern Cavern and Mine Research Society*, (January 1969), pp.1–7

RAISTRICK, Arthur "The Routine at Berks Smelt Mill, Buckden, in the Eighteenth Century" *Memoirs of the Northern Cavern and Mine Research Society*, (October 1969), pp.8–15

RAISTRICK, Arthur "Notes on Wharfedale Smelt Mills" *Memoirs of the Northern Cavern and Mine Research Society*, (October 1969), pp.15–22

RAISTRICK, Arthur "The London (Quaker) Lead Company Mines in Yorkshire" *Memoirs of the Northern Cavern and Mine Research Society*, Vol.2 No.3 (September 1973), pp.127–132

RAISTRICK, Arthur "The Wharton Mines in Swaledale" *North Yorkshire Record Office Publication*, Vol.31 (1982)

RICHARDSON, Douglas T. *See* DIXON, Jean M. & RICHARDSON, Douglas T.

ROBINSON, P.C. "A Geological Guide to the Iron Deposits of the Scarborough District" *Transactions of the Scarborough and District Archaeological Society*, Vol.1 No.6 (1963), pp.30–34

RUTTER, J.G. "Industrial Archaeology in North East Yorkshire. Part 1.Scarborough" *Transactions of the Scarborough and District Archaeological Society*, Vol.2 No.12 (1969), pp.16–33

RUTTER, J.G. "Industrial Archaeology of North East Yorkshire. Part 2.Ryedale and Hombletons" *Transactions of the Scarborough and District Archaeological Society*, Vol.2 No.13 (1970), pp.23–51

RUTTER, J.G. "Industrial Archaeology in North East Yorkshire. Part 3 Whitby and Eskdale" *Transactions of the Scarborough and District Archaeological Society*, Vol.2 No.14 (1971), pp.17–49

RUTTER, J.G. *See* HAYES, R.H. & RUTTER, J.G.

SMITH, Michael E. "Informal Excursion to Ewden Valley" *Bulletin of the Peak District Mines Historical Society*, Vol.1 No.2 (May 1960), pp.12–13

STEVENS, G. & WOMACK, G. "Richmond Copper Mine. A Survey" *Moldywarps Spelaeological Group Journal*, No.8 (1975), pp.66–68

TUFFS, P. "North Skelton Ironstone Mine, Cleveland" *Cleveland Industrial Archaeologist*, No.3 (1975), pp.23–30

TUFFS, P. "Kilton Ironstone Mine" *Cleveland Industrial Archaeologist*, No.5 (1976), pp.21–34

TUFFS, P. "Lingdale Ironstone Mine" *Cleveland Industrial Archaeologist*, No.9 (1978), pp.11–22

TUFFS, P. *See* OWEN, John & TUFFS,P.

TYSON, Leslie O. "The Hurst Mining Field, Swaledale, Yorkshire" *British Mining*, No.23 (1983), pp.61–77

TYSON, Leslie O. & HEWER, Richard E. "Prys Mine" *British Mining*, No.19 (1982), pp.37–42

UPTON, M.J.G. "The Appleby Ironstone Mine" *Lincolnshire Industrial Archaeology Group*, Vol.6 No.4 (1971)

WADE, John Caleb & DICKINSON, John Michael "Mongo Gill Hole, Greenhow Hill" *Transactions of the Northern Cavern and Mine Research Society*, Vol.1 No.1 (June 1961), pp.60–66

WAITES, B. "Medieval Iron–working in North East Yorkshire" *Geography*, Vol.XLIX (1964), pp.33–43

WALLER, Martin "A Brief History of Lead Mining on Melbecks Moor, Swaledale, North Yorkshire" *Camborne School of Mines Journal*, (1977), pp.30–37

WATTON, W.J. "Sir Francis Mine, Swaledale, North Yorkshire" *Camborne School of Mines Journal*, (1986), pp.40–51

WILDRIDGE, Joseph D.J. "Ironstone" *Memoirs of the Northern Cavern and Mine Research Society*, No.1 (April 1964), pp.25–26

WILLIAMSON, Iain A. "The Thievely Lead Mines, an Ill–ending Adventure" *University of Nottingham Survey* No.7 (1957), pp.24–28

WILLIAMSON, Iain A. "The Skeleron or York and Lancaster Lead Mines" *The Journal of Past and Present Mining Studies Association*, Vol.I (1959), pp.46–50

WILLIAMSON, Iain A. "The Anglezarke Lead Mines: a Note on the History of a Field which was the Original Source of Witherite" *Mining Magazine*, Vol.CVIII (1963), pp.133–139

WOMACK, G. *See* STEVENS, G. & WOMACK, G.

WRIGHT, G.N. "Mines in Wensleydale" *Country Life*, Vol.180 No.4637 (1986), pp.30–31

DERBYSHIRE

Books

AMNER, R.(Ed.) *Good Luck Mine, Via Gellia, Near Cromford, Derbyshire* (Private Publication, 1978)

ANDREWS, M. *Long Ago in Peakland* (Nottingham: Milward, 1948)

ATKINSON, Michael *See* BURT, Roger, WAITE, Peter, ATKINSON, Michael & BURNLEY, Raymond

BREARLEY, G.H. *Lead Mining in the Peak District* (Clapham: Dalesman, 1977)

BROWN, Ivor J., ROCHE, V.S. & FORD, Trevor D. *Magpie Mine, Sheldon, near Bakewell: A Chronology. The Magpie Mine Engine House of 1864. The Geology of the Magpie Mine* (Matlock: Peak District Mines Historical Society, Special Publication No.3, 1971)

BURNLEY, Raymond *See* BURT, Roger, WAITE, Peter, ATKINSON, Michael & BURNLEY, Raymond

BURT, Roger, WAITE, Peter, ATKINSON, Michael & BURNLEY, Raymond *The Derbyshire Mineral Statistics 1845–1913* (Exeter: Department of Economic History, University of Exeter, 1981)

CAMERON, Kenneth *The Place Names of Derbyshire* 3 Volumes (Cambridge: Cambridge University Press, 1959)

CARRUTHERS, R.G. & STRAHAN, A. *Special Reports on the Mineral Resources of G.B. Vol.26: Lead and Zinc Ores of Durham, Yorkshire, Derbyshire and Notes on the Isle of Man* (Sheffield: Mining Facsimiles, 1986. Reprint of Geological Survey 1923 Edition)

ENTHOVEN, H.J. & Sons Ltd. *A Brief Historical Note on the Great Barmote Courts, Wirksworth, Derbyshire, in the Duchy of Lancaster* (Wirksworth: Private Publication, 1953)

FLINDALL, Roger B. & HAYES, A. *The Caverns and Mines of Matlock Bath* (Buxton: Moorland, 1976)

FORD, Trevor D. *The Story of the Speedwell Cavern* (Castleton: R.J. & D.Harrison, 1962))

FORD, Trevor D. & RIEUWERTS, James H. *Lead Mining in the Peak District* (Bakewell: Peak Park Joint Planning Board, 1968)

FORD, Trevor D. & RIEUWERTS, James H. *Lead Mining in the Peak District* (Bakewell: Peak Park Joint Planning Board, 1970. Reprint of 1968 Edition with Revisions)

FORD, Trevor D. & RIEUWERTS, James H. *Lead Mining in the Peak District* (Bakewell: Peak Park Joint Planning Board, 1975. Second Edition)

FORD, Trevor D. & RIEUWERTS, James H. *Lead Mining in the Peak District* (Bakewell: Peak Park Joint Planning Board, 1983. Third Edition)

FORD, Trevor D. *See* BROWN, Ivor J., ROCHE, V.S. & FORD, Trevor D.

HARRIS, Helen *The Industrial Archaeology of the Peak District* (Newton Abbot: David & Charles, 1972)

HARRISON, D. *See* OLLERENSHAW, Arthur E., OLLERENSHAW, R.J. & HARRISON, D.

HAYES, A. *See* FLINDALL, Roger B. & HAYES, A.

HOOSON, William *The Miners' Dictionary* (Ilkley: Scolar Press for the Institute of Mining and Metallurgy, 1979. Reprint of 1747 Edition.)

HOPKINSON, G *The Laws and Customs of the Mines within the Wapentake of Wirksworth* (Nottingham: Foreman, 1948. Reprint of 1644 Edition.)

JENNINGS, Bernard *See* RAISTRICK, Arthur & JENNINGS, Bernard

KIRKHAM, Nellie *Derbyshire* (Paul Elek, 1947)

KIRKHAM, Nellie *Derbyshire Lead Mining Glossary* (Leamington Spa: Cave Research Group, Publication No.2, 1949)

KIRKHAM, Nellie *Caverns in Mines* (British Caving, 1953)

KIRKHAM, Nellie *The Draining of the Wirksworth Lead Mines* (Derbyshire Archaeological Society, Local History Section, 1963)

KIRKHAM, Nellie *Derbyshire Lead Mining Through the Centuries* (Truro: Bradford Barton, 1968)

NIXON, Frank *The Industrial Archaeology of Derbyshire* (Newton Abbot: David & Charles, 1969)

OLLERENSHAW, Arthur E., OLLERENSHAW, R.J. & HARRISON, D. *The Histroy of Blue John Stone. Methods of Mining and Working, Ancient and Modern* (Castleton: Private Publication, Not Dated)

OLLERENSHAW, R.J. *See* OLLERENSHAW, Arthur E., OLLERENSHAW, R.J. & HARRISON, D.

O'NEAL, R.A.H. *Derbyshire Lead and Lead Mining: A Bibliography* (Matlock: Derbyshire County Library, 1960)

PARKER, H.M. & WILLIES, Lynn *Peakland Lead Mines and Miners* (Ashbourne: Moorland, 1979)

PORTEOUS, C. *Derbyshire* (Hale, 1950)

RAISTRICK, Arthur & JENNINGS, Bernard *A History of Lead Mining in the Pennines* (Longmans, 1965)

RHODES, John *Derbyshire Lead Mining in the Eighteenth Century* (Sheffield: University of Sheffield Institute of Education, 1973)

RIDEN, Philip J. *The Butterley Company 1790–1830: A Derbyshire Ironworks in the Industrial Revolution* (Chesterfield: Private Publication, 1973)

RIEUWERTS, James H. *Derbyshire's Old Lead Mines and Miners* (Buxton: Moorland Press, 1972)

RIEUWERTS, James H. *Lathkill Dale: Its Mines and Miners* (Rugeley: Moorland, 1973)

RIEUWERTS, James H. *History and Gazetteer of the Lead Mine Soughs of Derbyshire* (Private Publication, 1987)

RIEUWERTS, James H. *See* FORD, Trevor D. & RIEUWERTS, James H.

ROCHE, V.S. *See* BROWN, Ivor J., ROCHE, V.S. & FORD, Trevor D.

SLACK, Ronald *Pauper's Venture: Children's Fortune. Lead Mines of Brassington* (Cromford: Scarthin Books, 1986)

SOMERVILLE, R. *History of the Duchy of Lancaster* 2 Volumes (Duchy of Lancaster, 1953)

STRAHAN, A. *See* CARRUTHERS, R.G. & STRAHAN, A.

WAITE, Peter *See* BURT, Roger, WAITE, Peter, ATKINSON, Michael & BURNLEY, Raymond

WATSON, W. *The Strata of Derbyshire* (Buxton: Moorland, 1973. Reprint of 1811 Edition)

WILLIES, Lynn *See* PARKER, H.M. & WILLIES, Lynn

Theses

BLANCHARD, I.S.W. *Economic Change in Derbyshire in the Late Middle Ages 1272–1540* (University of London PhD Thesis, 1967)

BUTCHER, N.J.D. *Some Aspects of Structure and Fluorite Mineralisation in the Southern Pennines* (University of Leicester PhD Thesis, 1976)

HOPKINSON, G.G. *The Development of Lead Mining and of Coal and Iron Industries in North Derbyshire and South Yorkshire* (University of Sheffield PhD Thesis, 1958)

NICHOLS, H. *Local Maps of Derbyshire to 1770: An Inventory and Introduction* (University of Leicester MA Thesis, 1973)

OAKMAN, C. *Sough Hydrology of the Wirksworth–Matlock–Youlgreave Area of Derbyshire* (University of Leicester MPhil Thesis, 1979)

OTTERY, F.S. *The Development of Wirksworth 1800–1965* (University of Nottingham MA Thesis, 1965)

RIEUWERTS, James H. *A Technological History of the Drainage of Derbyshire Lead Mines* (University of Leicester PhD Thesis, 1981)

WILLIES, Lynn *Technical and Organisational Development of the Derbyshire Lead Mining Industry in the Eighteenth and Nineteenth Centuries* (University of Leicester PhD Thesis, 1980)

Articles

AMNER, Ronald "Recovery of the Second Steam Pumping Engine from Putwell Hill Mine, Monsal Dale" *Bulletin of the Peak District Mines Historical Society*, Vol.5 No.6 (October 1974), pp.335–340

AMNER, Ronald "Conservation and Restoration Practices used at Goodluck Mine" *Bulletin of the Peak District Mines Historical Society*, Vol.6 No.1 (May 1975), pp.40–46

AMNER, Ronald & NAYLOR, Peter J. "Goodluck Mine, Via Gellia" *Bulletin of the Peak District Mines Historical Society*, Vol.5 No.4 (October 1973), pp.217–240

ANKERS, A. "Discoveries at Ashley Hay Lead Mines near Wirksworth, Derbyshire" *Bulletin of the Peak District Mines Historical Society*, Vol.1 No.4 (April 1961), p.24

ANON "A Lead Mining Revival" *The Derbyshire Countryside*, Vol.18 No.8 (1951), p.163

ANON "Some Terms Used by the Lead Miners of Derbyshire, Part I" *Bulletin of the Peak District Mines Historical Society*, Vol.1 No.3 (October 1960), pp.19–22

ANON "The Derbyshire Lead Mining Customs" *Sheffield Clarion Ramblers Booklet of Membership*, (1960–61), pp.101–106

ANON "Lead Boom" [First Published 1923] *Bulletin of the Peak District Mines Historical Society*, Vol.1 No.6 (May 1962), pp.15–17

ANON "Peakland Mining" [First Published 1923] *Bulletin of the Peak District Mines Historical Society*, Vol.1 No.6 (May 1962), pp.43–44

ANON "Derbyshire Mining Find" *British Caver*, Vol.34 (1964), pp.52–53

ANON "Fluorspar Flotation at Glebe Mines" *Mining Magazine*, (October 1965), pp.276–283

ANON "Hoo Valley Mine (North)" *Manifold Caver*, (1984), pp.30–31

ATKINSON, Michael *See* BURT, Roger & ATKINSON, Michael

AUSTIN, M.R. "Religion and Society in Derbyshire During the Industrial Revolution" *Journal of the Derbyshire Archaeological and Natural History Society*, Vol.XCIII (1973), pp.75–89

BAND, Stuart "Lead Mining in Ashover: A Preliminary Survey. Part 1" *Bulletin of the Peak District Mines Historical Society*, Vol.6 No.2 (October 1975), pp.113–115

BAND, Stuart "Lead Mining in Ashover: A Preliminary Survey. Part 2" *Bulletin of the Peak District Mines Historical Society*, Vol.6 No.3 (April 1976), pp.129–134

BAND, Stuart "The Steam Engines of Gregory Mine, Ashover" *Bulletin of the Peak District Mines Historical Society*, Vol.8 No.5 (Summer 1983), pp.269–295

BAND, Stuart R. "John Allen, Miner, on Board H.M.S. Investigator 1801–1804" *Bulletin of the Peak District Mines Historical Society*, Vol.10 No.1 (Summer 1987), pp.67–68

BARRETT, F.A. "William Duesbury's Interest in Derbyshire Lead Mines" *Journal of the Derbyshire Archaeological and Natural History Society*, Vol.75 (1955), pp.156–158

BAYLISS, J.M., INESON, P.R. & RORISON, I.H. "The Extent of Belland Ground Adjacent to Tideslow and Maiden Rakes, Little Hucklow" *Bulletin of the Peak District Mines Historical Society*, Vol.7 No.3 (March 1979), pp.153–157

BECK, John S. "The Caves, Mines and Soughs of the Wardlow Basin and Cressbrook Dale" *Bulletin of the Peak District Mines Historical Society*, Vol.7 No.2 (October 1978), pp.106–115

BECK, John S. & WORLEY, Noel E. "Nickergrove Mine, Eyam, Derbyshire" *Bulletin of the Peak District Mines Historical Society*, Vol.6 No.5 (May 1977), pp.175–179

BECK, J.S. *See* WORLEY, Noel E. & BECK, J.S.

BEET, A.E. "J.W. Puttrell" *Bulletin of the Peak District Mines Historical Society*, Vol.1 No.2 (May 1960), pp.7–8

BIRD, Richard H. "Notes on the Derbyshire Map Surveyed and Produced By Peter Perez Burdett, 1762–1767" *Bulletin of the Peak District Mines Historical Society*, Vol.4 No.1 (March 1969), pp.75–82

BIRD, Richard H. "Notes on the Western Elton Mining Field" *Bulletin of the Peak District Mines Historical Society*, Vol.4 No.4 (October 1970), pp.306–311

BIRD, Richard H. "The Mineral Fields of Derbyshire and Cornwall: A Brief Comparison" *Bulletin of the Peak District Mines Historical Society*, Vol.4 No.4 (October 1970), pp.312–323

BIRD, Richard H. "Recollections of a Mill Close Lead Miner" *Bulletin of the Peak District Mines Historical Society*, Vol.5 No.1 (April 1972), pp.50–53

BIRD, Richard H. "Putwell Hill Lead Mine, Monsal Dale" *Bulletin of the Peak District Mines Historical Society*, Vol.5 No.1 (April 1972), pp.54–60

BIRKETT, N. *See* WARRINER, David J. & BIRKETT, N.

BLANCHARD, I.S.W. "Derbyshire Lead Production, 1195–1505" *Journal of the Derbyshire Archaeological and Natural History Society*, Vol.XCI (1971), pp.119–140

BLANCHARD, I.S.W. "Derbyshire Lead Production 1195–1505" *Derbyshire Archaeological Journal*, Vol.XCI (1974), pp.119–140

BRANIGAN, K., HOUSLEY, John & HOUSLEY, Catherine "Two Roman Lead Pigs from Carsington" *Journal of the Derbyshire Archaeological and Natural History Society*, Vol.CVI (1986), pp.5–17

BRASSINGTON, M. "Lead–Glazed Roman Pottery Found near Derby" *Bulletin of the Peak District Mines Historical Society*, Vol.4 No.1 (March 1969), pp.35–36

BROOK, E.S. "Mill Close Mine" *Bulletin of the Peak District Mines Historical Society*, Vol.1 No.1 (December 1959), pp.6–9

BROOKE–TAYLOR, W. Michael "The Ballard of the Great Barmote Court" *Bulletin of the Peak District Mines Historical Society*, Vol.7 No.1 (May 1978), p.50

BROOKE–TAYLOR, W. Michael "Memoranda Concerning the Broadmeadow and Wheels Rake Mines, Alport" *Bulletin of the Peak District Mines Historical Society*, Vol.7 No.6 (October 1980), pp.345–352

BROWN, Ivor J. "A General Survey of Present–Day Mining in Derbyshire" *Bulletin of the Peak District Mines Historical Society*, Vol.2 No.4 (1964), pp.204–205

BROWN, Ivor J. "Mine Fatalities in the Derbyshire Metalliferous Mining Area, 1874–1939 inclusive" *Bulletin of the Peak District Mines Historical Society*, Vol.4 No.1 (March 1969), pp.59–66

BROWN, Ivor J. "Magpie Mine and the Garlick Family 1881–1930" *Bulletin of the Peak District Mines Historical Society*, Vol.4 No.4 (October 1970), pp.324–336

BROWN, Ivor J. "Magpie Mine and the Bacon Family, 1930–1951" *Bulletin of the Peak District Mines Historical Society*, Vol.5 No.1 (April 1972), pp.10–13

BRYDEN, David J. "Roman Lead Mining in Derbyshire" *Bulletin of the Peak District Mines Historical Society*, Vol.2 No.5 (May 1965), pp.291–296

BULL, Christopher "The Warl Gate Extension in Goodluck Mine, Via Gellia, Cromford, Derbyshire" *Bulletin of the Peak District Mines Historical Society*, Vol.7 No.3 (March 1979), pp.175–176

BULL, Christopher "The Clay Vein Extension in Goodluck Mine, Via Gellia, Cromford, Derbyshire" *Bulletin of the Peak District Mines Historical Society*, Vol.7 No.4 (October 1979), pp.206–207

BURT, Roger & ATKINSON, Michael "The Mineral Statistics and Derbyshire Mining" *Bulletin of the Peak District Mines Historical Society*, Vol.6 No.3 (April 1976), pp.164–167

BUTCHER, N.J.D. "Some Recent Surface and Underground Observations at Magpie Mine" *Bulletin of the Peak District Mines Historical Society*, Vol.4 No.6 (December 1971), pp.403–412

BUTCHER, N.J.D. "The Geology of Magpie Sough and Mine" *Bulletin of the Peak District Mines Historical Society*, Vol.6 No.2 (October 1975), pp.64–70

CHALLIS, Peter J. "William Bray's Sketch of a Tour into Derbyshire" *Bulletin of the Peak District Mines Historical Society*, Vol.6 No.6 (December 1977), pp.297–302

CHALLIS, Peter J. "C.C.T.V. Inspection of Yatestoop Mine Shaft" *Bulletin of the Peak District Mines Historical Society*, Vol.7 No.4 (October 1979), p.194

CHANDLER, B. "The S.P. Mine, Perryfoot, Derbyshire" *British Caver*, Vol.23 (1953), pp.73–75

CHANDLER, B. "The Perryfoot Lead Rake" *British Caver*, Vol.25 (1954) pp.54–58

CHATBURN, Henry E. "Recollections of a Descent of the Cart Gate of the Odin Mine, Castleton" *Bulletin of the Peak District Mines Historical Society*, Vol.1 No.4 (April 1961), pp.35–36

CHATBURN, Henry E. "The Surface Remains on Dirtlow Rake" *Bulletin of the Peak District Mines Historical Society*, Vol.1 No.7 (October 1962), pp.22–26

COCKERTON, R.W.P. "Notes on a Pig of Lead from Carsington" *Journal of the Derbyshire Archaeological and Natural History Society*, Vol.73 (1953), p.110

CRITCHLEY, Martin F. "A Survey of Little Milldam Mine, Great Hucklow" *Bulletin of the Peak District Mines Historical Society*, Vol.6 No.5 (May 1977), pp.191–199

DANIEL, Clarence "Epics of the Edgeside Vein: Unusual Stories of Lead Mining Old and New Around Great Hucklow and Eyam" *The Derbyshire Countryside*, Vol.23 No.4 (1958), pp.22–23

DANIEL, Clarence "A Guest at the Court of King Barmote" *The Derbyshire Countryside*, Vol.24 No.5 (1959), pp.22–23

DANIEL, Clarence "The Derbyshire Barmote Courts" *Bulletin of the Peak District Mines Historical Society*, Vol.4 No.1 (March 1969), pp.89–96

DANIEL, Clarence "A Miner's Porringer Found on Longstone Edge" *Bulletin of the Peak District Mines Historical Society*, Vol.4 No.2 (November 1969), pp.177–178

DANIEL, Clarence "Eyam Cottage Museum Project" *Bulletin of the Peak District Mines Historical Society*, Vol.5 No.2 (October 1972), pp.107–108

DANIEL, Martin "A Note on the Anglo–Saxon Lead Industry of the

Peak" *Bulletin of the Peak District Mines Historical Society*, Vol.7 No.6 (Autumn 1980), pp.339–341

DANIEL, Martin "The Origins of the Barmote Court System: A New Theory" *Bulletin of the Peak District Mines Historical Society*, Vol.8 No.3 (Summer 1982), pp.166–167

DANIEL, Martin "The Early Lead Industry and the Ancient Demesne of the Peak" *Bulletin of the Peak District Mines Historical Society*, Vol.8 No.3 (Summer 1982), pp.168–170

DARNBOROUGH, G. "A Wirksworth Mine Agent's Letter" *Bulletin of the Peak District Mines Historical Society*, Vol.7 No.6 (Autumn 1980), p.326

DIAS, Jill R. "Lead, Society and Politics in Derbyshire before the Civil War" *Midland History*, Vol.VI (1981), pp.39–57

DIXON, A.G. "A Few Notes on the Jingler Site, Wakebridge, Crich" *Bulletin of the Peak District Mines Historical Society*, Vol.8 No.3 (Summer 1982), pp.185–186

DOOL, Josephine "Two Roman Pigs of Lead Found Near Ashbourne" *Bulletin of the Peak District Mines Historical Society*, Vol.6 No.2 (October 1975), pp.111–112

DOOL, Josephine & HUGHES, Roy G. "Two Roman Pigs of Lead from Derbyshire" *Journal of the Derbyshire Archaeological and Natural History Society*, Vol.XCVI (1976), pp.15–16

EMBLIN, Robert "A Pennine Model for the Diagenetic Origin of Base-Metal Ore Deposits in Britain" *Bulletin of the Peak District Mines Historical Society*, Vol.7 No.1 (May 1978), pp.5–20

EVANS, S. "Descent into a Derbyshire Lead Mine" *British Caver*, Vol.31 (1959), pp.18–21

EVANS, S. "The Magpie Mine Tragedy" *British Caver*, Vol.31 (1959), p.24

FAREY, J "Extract from 'General View of the Agriculture and Minerals of Derbyshire', Volume I, (1811) List of Lead Mines" *Bulletin of the Peak District Mines Historical Society*, Vol.1 No.7 (October 1962), pp.38–47

FISHER, F.N. "Sir Cornelius Vermuyden and the Dovegang Lead Mines" *Journal of the Derbyshire Archaeological and Natural History Society*, Vol.72 (1952), pp.74–118

FLETCHER, George & WILLIES, Lynn "Brightside Mine, Hassop" *Bulletin of the Peak District Mines Historical Society*, Vol.6 No.1 (May

1975), pp.33–39

FLINDALL, Roger B. "Lead Mining in Cromford Liberty, 1698–1714" *Bulletin of the Peak District Mines Historical Society*, Vol.5 No.5 (April 1974), pp.317–323

FLINDALL, Roger B. "A Survey of a Mine in Tearsall Rough, Wensley" *Bulletin of the Peak District Mines Historical Society*, Vol.5 No.6 (October 1974), pp. 373–380

FLINDALL, Roger B. "Merry Tom Vein, Middleton–by–Wirksworth: A Supplementary Note" *Bulletin of the Peak District Mines Historical Society*, Vol.6 No.6 (December 1977), pp.292–293

FLINDALL, Roger B. "An Historical Account of Middlepeak Mine and the Northern Part of Ratchwood Title, Wirksworth" *Bulletin of the Peak District Mines Historical Society*, Vol.8 No.4 (December 1982), pp.201–239

FLINDALL, Roger B. & HAYES, Andrew J. "The Adit Workings on the North Side of Via Gellia" *Bulletin of the Peak District Mines Historical Society*, Vol.4 No.6 (December 1971), pp.429–450

FLINDALL, Roger B. & HAYES, Andrew J. "A Survey of Good Luck Mine and Adjacent Levels in Via Gellia" *Bulletin of the Peak District Mines Historical Society*, Vol.5 No.1 (April 1972), pp.61–80

FLINDALL, Roger B. & HAYES, Andrew J. "Wapping Mine and Cumberland Cavern, Matlock Bath" *Bulletin of the Peak District Mines Historical Society*, Vol.5 No.2 (October 1972), pp.114–127

FLINDALL, Roger B. & HAYES, Andrew J. "The Mines East of Hoptonwood Quarries, Via Gellia" *Bulletin of the Peak District Mines Historical Society*, Vol.5 No.3 (May 1973), pp.137–148

FLINDALL, Roger B. & HAYES, Andrew J. "The Mines near Upperwood, Matlock Bath Part 1: The Tear Breeches–Hopping–Fluor Spar–Speedwell Complex" *Bulletin of the Peak District Mines Historical Society*, Vol.5 No.4 (October 1973), pp.182–199

FLINDALL, Roger B. & HAYES, Andrew J. "Notes on Some Early Techniques Used in Derbyshire Lead Mining" *Bulletin of the Peak District Mines Historical Society*, Vol.6 No.2 (October 1975), pp.93–95

FLINDALL, Roger & WOOD, K. "The Dig in the Level of Groaning Tor, Via Gellia" *Bulletin of the Peak District Mines Historical Society*, Vol.8 No.1 (Summer 1981), p.64

FLINDALL, Roger B., HAYES, Andrew J. & RIEUWERTS, James H. "Mines in the Slingtor Wood Area, Cromford" *Bulletin of the Peak District Mines Historical Society*, Vol.6 No.6 (December 1977), pp.263–279

FLINDALL, Roger B., SWAIN, J. & HAYES, Andrew J. "A Survey of the Masson Cave–cum–Mine Complex, Matlock" *Bulletin of the Peak District Mines Historical Society*, Vol.8 No.2 (Autumn 1981), pp.103–108

FLINDALL, Roger B. *See* WARRINER, David J., WILLIES, Lynn & FLINDALL, Roger B.

FLINDALL, Roger B. *See* WILLIES, Lynn, RIEUWERTS, James H. & FLINDALL, Roger B.

FORD, Trevor D. "The Speedwell Cavern, Castleton, Derbyshire" *Transactions of the Cave Research Group*, Vol.4 No.2 (1956), pp.97–124

FORD, Trevor D. "The Speedwell Mine in the Eighteenth Century" *The Derbyshire Countryside*, Vol.25 No.3 (1960), pp.20–21;55

FORD, Trevor D. "Agricola and the History of the Derbyshire Mines" *Bulletin of the Peak District Mines Historical Society*, Vol.1 No.4 (April 1961), pp.30–34

FORD, Trevor D. "Recent Studies of Mineral Distribution in Derbyshire and their Significance" *Bulletin of the Peak District Mines Historical Society*, Vol.1 No.5 (October 1961), pp.3–9

FORD, Trevor D. "Long Cliff Mine, Castleton, Derbyshire" *Bulletin of the Peak District Mines Historical Society*, Vol.1 No.7 (October 1962), pp.1–4

FORD, Trevor D. "White Watson: Pioneer Derbyshire Geologist" *Bulletin of the Peak District Mines Historical Society*, Vol.1 No.7 (October 1962), pp.27–37

FORD. Trevor D. "The Peak District in the Great Exhibition" *Bulletin of the Peak District Mines Historical Society*, Vol.2 No.2 (1963), pp.87–92

FORD, Trevor D. "Hurdlo Steel Pipe, Castleton" *Bulletin of the Peak District Mines Historical Society*, Vol.2 No.4 (1964), pp.230–234

FORD, Trevor D. "Biographical Notes: Faujas de St. Fond" *Bulletin of the Peak District Mines Historical Society*, Vol.2 No.5 (May 1965), pp.235–240

FORD, Trevor D. "A Visit to the Tri–State Lead Mining District, U.S.A." *Bulletin of the Peak District Mines Historical Society*, Vol.2 No.6 (December 1965), pp.335–338

FORD, Trevor D. "Biographical Notes of Authors on Derbyshire: Johann Jacob Ferber" *Bulletin of the Peak District Mines Historical Society*, Vol.3 No.1 (July 1966), pp.68–70

FORD Trevor D. "Biographical Notes on Derbyshire Authors: Karl Philipp Moritz 1756–1793" *Bulletin of the Peak District Mines Historical Society*, Vol.3 No.4 (December 1967), pp.243–246

FORD, Trevor D. "Biograpgical Notes on Derbyshire Authors: William Adam (1794?–1873) and the 'Gem of the Peak' " *Bulletin of the Peak District Mines Historical Society*, Vol.5 No.2 (October 1972), pp.81–89

FORD, Trevor D. "Biographical Notes on Derbyshire Authors: John Whitehurst, 1713–1788" *Bulletin of the Peak District Mines Historical Society*, Vol.5 No.6 (October 1974), pp.362–369

FORD, Trevor D. & SARJEANT, William, A.S. "The Peak District Mineral Index" *Bulletin of the Peak District Mines Historical Society*, Vol.2 No.3 (1964), pp.122–150

FORD, Trevor D. & SMITH, A. "Some Adits in the Via Gellia" *Bulletin of the Peak District Mines Historical Society*, Vol.4 No.5 (June 1971), pp.378–383

FORD, Trevor D. *See* RIEUWERTS, James H. & FORD, Trevor D.

FORD, Trevor D. *See* TUNE, R.N., HURT, L. & FORD, Trevor D.

FORD, Trevor D. *See* WORLEY, Noel E. & FORD, Trevor D.

FOSTER–SMITH, J.R. "A Personal Memoir of Mill Close Mine in 1939" *Bulletin of the Peak District Mines Historical Society*, Vol.10 No.1 (Summer 1987), pp.24–45

FULLER, G.Joan "Lead Mining in Derbyshire in the Mid–nineteenth Century" *East Midland Geographer*, Vol.3 Pt.7 No.23 (June 1965), pp.373–393

FULLER, G.Joan "Early Lead Smelting in the Peak District: Another Look at the Evidence" *East Midland Geographer*, Vol.5 No.3 (1970), pp.1–8

GARDINER, J. "Great Hucklow: A Lead Mining Village in the Nineteenth Century; Population and Occupations" *Derbyshire Miscellany*, Vol.X No.2 (1983), pp.37–44

GARLIC, S.C. (notes by) "Crich Lot and Cope" *Bulletin of the Peak District Mines Historical Society*, Vol.5 No.3 (May 1973), pp.174–181

GARLIC, S.L. "Extracts from the Chesterfield Gazette in 1828" *Bulletin of the Peak District Mines Historical Society*, Vol.4 No.5 (June 1971), pp.347,368,373,400

GARLIC, S.L. "Snippetts from the Derbyshire Times" *Bulletin of the Peak District Mines Historical Society*, Vol.6 No.3 (April 1976), p.161

GARLIC, S.L. "Letter to the Editor of the Chesterfield Gazette, June 14th. 1828" *Bulletin of the Peak District Mines Historical Society*, Vol.9 No.3 (Summer 1985), p.200

GILBERT, J.C. "Hillocks Mine, Monyash, Derbyshire" *Cave Science*, Vol.3 No.21 (1952), pp.223–226

GOLDBY, John "Thoughts on Derbyshire Caves and Mines" *Bulletin of the Peak District Mines Historical Society*, Vol.5 No.4 (October 1973), pp.215–216

GOULD, Robert "Capital Formation in the Wirksworth Lead Mining Industry, 1700–1800. Part 1" *Bulletin of the Peak District Mines Historical Society*, Vol.6 No.5 (May 1977), pp.233–240

GOULD, Robert "Capital Formation in the Wirksworth Lead Mining Industry, 1700–1800. Part 2" *Bulletin of the Peak District Mines Historical Society*, Vol.7 No.1 (May 1978), pp.21–27

GOULD, Robert "The Activities of the London Lead Companies in Wirksworth: A Brief Summary" *Bulletin of the Peak District Mines Historical Society*, Vol.7 No.1 (May 1978), pp.28–30

GOULD, Robert "A Visit to Blobber Mine, Wirksworth, in the 1920s" *Bulletin of the Peak District Mines Historical Society*, Vol.7 No.2 (October 1978), pp. 93–95

GREGORY, Nevil "Stafford's Dream" *Bulletin of the Peak District Mines Historical Society*, Vol.2 No.5 (May 1965), pp.297–302

GREGORY, Nevil "Notes and Impressions of Jingler (or Rolley) Mine, Wakebridge, Crich" *Bulletin of the Peak District Mines Historical Society*, Vol.3 No.1 (July 1966), pp.58–62

GREGORY, Nevil "A Manhole Cover for Snake Mine" *Bulletin of the Peak District Mines Historical Society*, Vol.4 No.1 (March 1969), pp.31–34

GREGORY, Nevil "Discovery of an Unusual Lime Kiln at Hassop" *Bulletin of the Peak District Mines Historical Society*, Vol.4 No.1 (March 1969), pp.83–87

GREGORY, Nevil "A Report on the Crich Mining Display" *Bulletin of the Peak District Mines Historical Society*, Vol.4 No.3 (May 1970), pp.240–243

GREGORY, Nevil & TUNE, R.N. "Ore Buddles at Snake Mine, Hopton and at Bonsall Leys" *Bulletin of the Peak District Mines Historical Society*, Vol.3 No.4 (December 1967), pp.253–255

GRIGOR–TAYLOR, W.R. "Notes on the Lathkill Gold Mine 1854–1856" *Bulletin of the Peak District Mines Historical Society*, Vol.5 No.1 (April 1972), pp.43–49

GUTHRIE, Joan "Lead Mining in Derbyshire" *Memoirs of the Northern Cavern and Mine Research Society*, No.1 (April 1964), pp.10–11

HALL, R. "Occupation and Population Structure in Part of the Derbyshire Peak District in the Mid–Nineteenth Century" *East Midland Geographer*, Vol.6 Pt.2 No.42 (December 1974), pp.66–78

HALL, R. "Economy and Society in the Derbyshire Peak District, 1861" *Journal of the Derbyshire Archaeological and Natural History Society*, Vol.XCVIII (1978), pp.72–82

HAYES, Andrew *See* FLINDALL, Roger B. & HAYES, Andrew A.

HAYES, Andrew *See* FLINDALL, Roger B., HAYES, Andrew & RIEUWERTS, James H.

HAYES, Andrew *See* FLINDALL, Roger B., SWAIN, J. & HAYES, Andrew

HAYWARD, R.A. "The Watergrove Pumping Engine of 1838" *Bulletin of the Peak District Mines Historical Society*, Vol.5 No.4 (October 1973), pp.200–214

HEALD, Derek "The Exploration of Wills Founder Mine, Winster" *Bulletin of the Peak District Mines Historical Society*, Vol.7 No.2 (October 1978), pp.51–66

HENSTOCK, Adrian "The Ashbourne Inquisition of 1288: A Reply" *Bulletin of the Peak District Mines Historical Society*, Vol.7 No.2 (October 1978), pp.96–98

HODGKINS, D.J. "The Origins and Independent Years of the Cromford and High Peak Railway" *Journal of Transport History*, Vol.VI No.1 (May 1863), pp.39–55

HOLMES, James F. "Lead Mining in Derbyshire" *Mining Magazine*, Vol.107 No.3 (September 1962), pp.137–148

HOPKINSON, G.G. "Lead Mining in Eighteenth Century Ashover" *Journal of the Derbyshire Archaeological and Natural History Society*, Vol.72 (1952), pp.1–21

HOPKINSON, G.G. "Five Generations of Derbyshire Lead Mining and Smelting" *Journal of the Derbyshire Archaeological and Natural History Society*, Vol.78 (1958), pp.9–28

HOPKINSON, G.G. "Lead Mining in the Eyam District in the Eighteenth Century" *Journal of the Derbyshire Archaeological and Natural History Society*, Vol.LXXX (1960), pp.80–97

HOSKINS, W.G. "Derbyshire Mines and Mills" *The Listener*, 18th May 1978, pp.631–632

HOUSLEY, Catherine *See* BRANIGAN, K., HOUSLEY, John & HOUSLEY, Catherine

HOUSLEY, John *See* BRANIGAN, K.,HOUSLEY, John & HOUSLEY, Catherine

HOUSTON, William J. "Fluorspar Production in Derbyshire and Yorkshire" *Quarry Managers Journal*, (April 1964), pp.149–161

HOUSTON, William J. "Calcite (and Galena) Mining at Arbor Low" *Mine and Quarry Engineering*, Vol.30 (July 1964), pp.302–306

HUGHES, Roy G. *See* DOOL, Josephine & HUGHES, Roy G.

HURT, L. "A Report on Nestus Mine and Other Shafts on the Heights of Abraham, Matlock Bath, Derbyshire" *Bulletin of the Peak District Mines Historical Society*, Vol.3 No.6 (October 1968), pp.369–380

HURT, L. "A Survey of Ball Eye Mines, Bonsall" *Bulletin of the Peak District Mines Historical Society*, Vol.4 No.4 (October 1970), pp.289–305

HURT, L. "Mawstone Mine, Youlgreave" *Bulletin of the Peak District Mines Historical Society*, Vol.8 No.3 (Summer 1982), pp.175–180

HURT, L *See* TUNE, R.N., HURT, L. & FORD, Trevor D.

INESON, P.R. *See* BAYLISS, J.M., INESON, P.R. & RORISON, I.H.

INESON, P.R. *See* WALTERS, S.G. & INESON, P.R.

IXER, R. *See* LUNN, P.E., ROGERS, P.J. & IXER, R.

JEFFERSON, D.P. "The Development of Middleton Dale, Derbyshire" *Bulletin of the Peak District Mines Historical Society*, Vol.1 No.4 (April 1961), pp.37–43

JONES, J. "Mineralogy of Bage Mine" *Bulletin of the Peak District Mines Historical Society*, Vol.8 No.4 (December 1982), pp.260–261

KAY, Robert "Songs of the Derbyshire Lead Miners" *Bulletin of the Peak District Mines Historical Society*, Vol.6 No.1 (May 1975), pp.6–11

KIRKHAM, Nellie "Woughs, Soughs and Main Rakes" *The Derbyshire Countryside*, Vol.15 No.57 (1945), pp.104–108

KIRKHAM, Nellie "Water: the Cheapest Commodity" *The Derbyshire Countryside*, Vol.16 No.8 (1947), pp.137–138

KIRKHAM, Nellie "Old Drowned Workings in Derbyshire" *Journal of the Derbyshire Archaeological and Natural History Society*, Vol.70 (1950), pp.1–20

KIRKHAM, Nellie "Lead Mine Soughs of Eyam, Stony Middleton and Calver, Derbyshire. Part 1" *British Caver*, Vol.22 (1951), pp.56–67

KIRKHAM, Nellie "The Soughs of Dovegang Mine" *Mine and Quarry Engineering*, Vol.17 (March 1951), pp.91–94

KIRKHAM, Nellie "Hillcar Sough" *Mine and Quarry Engineering*, Vol.18 (March 1952), pp.91–94

KIRKHAM, Nellie "Lead Mine Soughs of Eyam, Stony Middleton and Calver, Derbyshire. Part 2" *British Caver*, Vol.23 (1952), pp.64–67

KIRKHAM, Nellie "Lead Mine Soughs of Eyam, Stony Middleton and Calver, Derbyshire. Part 3" *British Caver*, Vol.24 (1953), pp.82–100

KIRKHAM, Nellie "A Coronation Procession of Lead Miners in 1821 for the Coronation of George V" *The Derbyshire Countryside*, Vol.19 No.6 (1953), p.135

KIRKHAM, Nellie "Gregory Mine and Cockwell Sough" *Mine and Quarry Engineering*, Vol.19 (January 1953), pp.21–25

KIRKHAM, Nellie "The Tumultuous Course of Dovegang" *Journal of the Derbyshire Archaeological and Natural History Society*, Vol.73 (1953), pp.1–35

KIRKHAM, Nellie "Lead Mine Soughs of Eyam, Stony Middleton and Calver, Derbyshire. Part 4" *British Caver*, Vol.25 (1954), pp.66–80

KIRKHAM, Nellie "Underground Water and Some Derbyshire Lead Mine Soughs" *Transactions of the Cave Research Group*, Vol.3 No.1 (1954)

KIRKHAM, Nellie "A Royal Mine in Nether Haddon" *Journal of the Derbyshire Archaeological and Natural History Society*, Vol.75 (1955), pp.20–35

KIRKHAM, Nellie "Lead Mine Soughs of Eyam, Stony Middleton and Calver, Derbyshire. Part 5" *British Caver*, Vol.27 (1956), pp.10–28

KIRKHAM, Nellie "The Tumultuous Course of Dovegang" *British Caver*, Vol.27 (1956), pp.73–105

DERBYSHIRE

KIRKHAM, Nellie "Lead Mine Shafts and Hillocks" *Derbyshire Miscellany*, Vol.1 No.3 (1956), pp.29–31

KIRKHAM, Nellie "An Account of Lead Mining in Derbyshire. Part 1" *The Plumbing Trade Journal*, Vol.36 No.6 (1956–7), pp.41–42

KIRKHAM, Nellie "An Account of Lead Mining in Derbyshire. Part 2" *The Plumbing Trade Journal*, Vol.36 No.7 (1956–7), pp.49–50

KIRKHAM, Nellie "An Account of Lead Mining in Derbyshire. Part 3" *The Plumbing Trade Journal*, Vol.36 No.8 (1956–7), pp.43–44

KIRKHAM, Nellie "On Lead Mines and Soughs" *Derbyshire Miscellany*, Vol.1 No.6 (1957), pp.71–72

KIRKHAM, Nellie "Ridgeway Level, Whatstandwell" *Derbyshire Miscellany*, Vol.1 No.6 (1957), pp.72–75

KIRKHAM, Nellie "Glebe Mine, Eyam" *Derbyshire Miscellany*, Vol.1 No.7 (1957), pp.92–97

KIRKHAM, Nellie "The Drainage of the Alport Lead Mines, Derbyshire" *Transactions of the Newcomen Society*, Vol.33 (1960–61), pp.67–93

KIRKHAM, Nellie "Winster Sough" *Bulletin of the Peak District Mines Historical Society*, Vol.1 No.5 (October 1961), pp.10–29

KIRKHAM, Nellie "Lead Miners and Royalists" *Derbyshire Miscellany*, Vol.2 No.5 (1961), pp.292–301

KIRKHAM, Nellie "The Magpie Mine and Sough, Sheldon, Derbyshire" *Sorby Record*, Vol.1 (1961), pp.31–39

KIRKHAM, Nellie "Tearsal and Dalefield Soughs, Wensley" *Bulletin of the Peak District Mines Historical Society*, Vol.1 No.6 (May 1962), pp.3–14

KIRKHAM, Nellie "Yatestoop Sough" *Bulletin of the Peak District Mines Historical Society*, Vol.1 No.7 (October 1962), pp.5–21

KIRKHAM, Nellie "Magpie Mine and its Tragedy" *Derbyshire Miscellany*, Vol.II (1962), pp.359–362

KIRKHAM, Nellie "Great Hucklow Mines" *Bulletin of the Peak District Mines Historical Society*, Vol.2 No.1 (1963), pp.31–47

KIRKHAM, Nellie "Old Mill Close Lead Mine, Derbyshire" *Bulletin of the Peak District Mines Historical Society*, Vol.2 No.2 (1963), pp.70–83

KIRKHAM, Nellie "Wheels Rake, Alport-by-Youlgreave" *Bulletin of the Peak District Mines Historical Society*, Vol.2 No.3 (1964), pp.153–174

KIRKHAM, Nellie "Whale Sough and Hubberdale Mine" *Bulletin of the Peak District Mines Historical Society*, Vol.2 No.4 (1964), pp.206–229

KIRKHAM, Nellie "The Ventilation of the Hillcar Sough" *Transactions of the Newcomen Society*, Vol.37 (1964–65), pp.133–139

KIRKHAM, Nellie "Eyam Edge Mines and Soughs" *Bulletin of the Peak District Mines Historical Society*, Vol.2 No.5 (May 1965), pp.241–254

KIRKHAM, Nellie "Eyam Edge Mines and Soughs: Part II" *Bulletin of the Peak District Mines Historical Society*, Vol.2 No.6 (December 1965), pp.315–334

KIRKHAM, Nellie "Steam Engines in Derbyshire Lead Mines" *Transactions of the Newcomen Society*, Vol.38 (1965–66), pp.69–89

KIRKHAM, Nellie "Eyam Edge Mines and Soughs: Part III" *Bulletin of the Peak District Mines Historical Society*, Vol.3 No.1 (July 1966), pp.43–57

KIRKHAM, Nellie "Eyam Edge Mines and Soughs: Part IV" *Bulletin of the Peak District Mines Historical Society*, Vol.3 No.2 (December 1966), pp.103–118

KIRKHAM, Nellie "Longstone Edge Area Mines and Soughs. Part 1" *Cave Science*, Vol.V No.39 (1966), pp.354–368

KIRKHAM, Nellie "Longstone Edge Area Mines and Soughs. Part 2" *Cave Science*, Vol.V No.40 (1966), pp.440–469

KIRKHAM, Nellie "Ball Eye Mine and Sough, Cromford" *Bulletin of the Peak District Mines Historical Society*, Vol.3 No.3 (May 1967), pp.165–174

KIRKHAM, Nellie "Oakenedge, Streaks, and Watergrove Soughs" *Bulletin of the Peak District Mines Historical Society*, Vol.3 No.4 (December 1967), pp.197–218

KIRKHAM, Nellie "The Derbyshire Lead Miners' Dish" *Derbyshire Miscellany*, Vol.IV No.2 (1967), pp.110–115

KIRKHAM, Nellie "Watergrove Mine: A Supplementary Note" *Bulletin of the Peak District Mines Historical Society*, Vol.3 No.5 (May 1968), pp.285–286

KIRKHAM, Nellie "Soughs in Middleton Dale, Part I" *Bulletin of the Peak District Mines Historical Society*, Vol.3 No.6 (October 1968), pp.329–338

KIRKHAM, Nellie "A Sough to Mill Close Grove and Windmill Sough" *Derbyshire Miscellany*, Vol.IV Part 4 (1968), pp.220–232

KIRKHAM, Nellie "Early Lead Smelting in Derbyshire" *Transactions of the Newcomen Society*, Vol.41 (1968–69), pp.119–139

KIRKHAM, Nellie "Lead Smelting Boles in Derbyshire" *Derbyshire Miscellany*, Vol.V Part 4 (1970), pp.191–196

KIRKHAM, Nellie "The Leeke Family in the Civil War" *Derbyshire Miscellany*, Vol.VII Part 1 (1974), pp.1–9

KIRKHAM, Nellie "Royalist Conspiracies and Derbyshire" *Derbyshire Miscellany*, Vol.VII Part 2 (1974), pp.55–73

KIRKHAM, Nellie "Maypit and Redsoil Mines: Comment on Lynn Willies' Article" *Bulletin of the Peak District Mines Historical Society*, Vol.6 No.1 (May 1975), pp.49–50

KITCHEN, G. & PENNEY, D. "New Pumps for Old" *Bulletin of the Peak District Mines Historical Society*, Vol.5 No.3 (May 1973), pp.129–136

LAWSON, John "Index to the Mining Records in the Bagshaw Collection in the John Rylands Library, Manchester. Part I: Documents 8/3/–90" *Bulletin of the Peak District Mines Historical Society*, Vol.3 No.5 (May 1968), pp.305–312

LAWSON, John "Index to the Mining Records in the Bagshaw Collection in the John Rylands Library, Manchester. Part 2: Documents 12/1/59–61" *Bulletin of the Peak District Mines Historical Society*, Vol.3 No.6 (October 1968), pp.353–356

LAWSON, John "Index to the Mining Records in the Bagshawe Collection in the John Rylands Library, Manchester." *Bulletin of the Peak District Mines Historical Society*, Vol.4 No.1 (March 1969), pp.41–48

LEA, H. "Nicking of a Derbyshire Lead Mine" *The Derbyshire Countryside*, Vol.16 No.61 (1946), p.167

LORD, P.J. & THOMPSON, S.J. "The Mines of Long Rake, Bradwell. Part 1" *Journal of the Sheffield University Spelaeological Society*, Vol.1 No.3 (1968)

LORD, P.J. & THOMPSON, S.J. "The Mines of Long Rake, Bradwell. Part 2" *Journal of the Sheffield University Spelaeological Society*, Vol.1 No.4 (1969), pp.166–170

LUDDITT, R. *See* PEARCE, Adrian J., LUDDITT, R., STRAW, M., TAYLOR, W., WATSON, J. & WATSON, R.

LUNN, P.E. "The Preservation of Mining Remains in the Peak District: Report of Meeting" *Bulletin of the Peak District Mines Historical Society*, Vol.4 No.5 (June 1973), pp.339–347

LUNN, P.E., ROGERS, P.J. & IXER, R. "Notes on Bravoite in Derbyshire" *Bulletin of the Peak District Mines Historical Society*, Vol.5 No.6 (October 1974), pp.332–334

MARTEL, M.E. "The Caves of Derbyshire: Bagshawe Cave and Mine" *British Caver*, Vol.14 (1946), p.50

MATKIN, R.B. "An Account of a Visit by John Rennie to Peak Cavern" *Bulletin of the Peak District Mines Historical Society*, Vol.7 No.6 (October 1980), pp.333–334

MATTHEWS, J. "The Magpie Sough and Mine" *Bulletin of the Peak District Mines Historical Society*, Vol.1 No.3 (October 1960), pp.13–14

MICHELL, F.B. "The Dressing of Complex Lead–Zinc Ores (Mill Close and Halkyn)" *Mine and Quarry Engineering*, Vol.12 (November 1946), pp.135–144

MILLWOOD, John "A Letter about Mill Close Mine in 1918" *Bulletin of the Peak District Mines Historical Society*, Vol.4 No.5 (June 1971), pp.375–377

MOSTAGHEL, Mohammad A. "Evolution of the South Pennine Orefield" *Bulletin of the Peak District Mines Historical Society*, Vol.8 No.6 (October 1983), pp.337–351

MOSTAGHEL, Mohammad A. "Evolution of the South Pennine Orefield. Part 2 Mineral Associations" *Bulletin of the Peak District Mines Historical Society*, Vol.9 No.2 (Winter 1984), pp.101–107

MOTT, R.A. "Lead Smelting in Derbyshire" *Bulletin of the Historical Metallurgy Group*, No.8 (January 1967), pp.6–11

MURPHY, S. "'Hand-Built' for the Job. An Example of Early Metallurgical Craftsmanship" *Bulletin of the Peak District Mines Historical Society*, Vol.4 No.4 (October 1970), pp.281–288

NASH, D.A. "Seven Rakes Mine at Matlock" *British Caver*, Vol.31 (1959), pp.16–18

NASH, Douglas A. "The Liberties of Grindlow and Foolow Report on the P.D.M.H.S. Excursion of August 7th., 1977" *Bulletin of the Peak District Mines Historical Society*, Vol6. No.6 (December 1977), pp.280–291

NASH, Douglas A. "Anecdotes on Mill Close Mine" *Bulletin of the Peak District Mines Historical Society*, Vol.7 No.2 (October 1978), pp.67–68

B.H.B.M.—G

NASH, Douglas A. "Hubberdale Mine and Associated Veins, 1836–1848" *Bulletin of the Peak District Mines Historical Society*, Vol.7 No.2 (October 1978), pp.87–92

NASH, Douglas A. "Miss Nellie Kirkham (Mrs. J.H.D. Myatt)" *Bulletin of the Peak District Mines Historical Society*, Vol.7 No.4 (October 1979), pp.195–198

NASH, Douglas A. *See* WORLEY, Noel E. & NASH, Douglas A.

NAYLOR, Peter J. "Analysis of Membership of the Society" *Bulletin of the Peak District Mines Historical Society*, Vol.5 No.5 (April 1974), p.316

NAYLOR, Peter J. "James Croston's On Foot Through the Peak" *Bulletin of the Peak District Mines Historical Society*, Vol.6 No.1 (May 1975), pp.12–14

NAYLOR, Peter J. "The Engines at Mill Close Mine 1920–1939" *Bulletin of the Peak District Mines Historical Society*, Vol.7 No.3 (March 1979), pp.165–168

NAYLOR, Peter J. "The Mawstone Mine Tragedy of 1932" *Bulletin of the Peak District Mines Historical Society*, Vol.8 No.3 (Summer 1982), pp.171–174

NAYLOR, Peter J. "Index to Mines, Soughs and Veins in Volume 8" *Bulletin of the Peak District Mines Historical Society*, Vol.8 No.6 (Autumn 1983), pp.383–394

NAYLOR, Peter J. "The Pumps at Mill Close Mine" *Bulletin of the Peak District Mines Historical Society*, Vol.9 No.2 (Winter 1984), pp.123–126

NAYLOR, Peter J. "Two Old Miners" *Bulletin of the Peak District Mines Historical Society*, Vol.9 No.2 (Winter 1984), pp.127–128

NAYLOR, Peter J. "Hopping Mine, Upperwood, Matlock Bath" *Bulletin of the Peak District Mines Historical Society*, Vol.10 No.1 (Summer 1987), pp.1–3

NAYLOR, Peter J. "John Burton of Bonsall, Derbyshire and Iowa, U.S.A. 1795–1854" *Bulletin of the Peak District Mines Historical Society*, Vol.10 No.1 (Summer 1987), pp.4–12

NAYLOR, Peter J. *See* AMNER, Ronald & NAYLOR, Peter J.

NEWTON, S.C. "The Gentry of Derbyshire in the Seventeenth Century" *Journal of the Derbyshire Archaeological and Natural History Society*, Vol.LXXXVI (1966), pp.1–30

NIXON, F. "The Early Steam Engines in Derbyshire" *Transactions of the Newcomen Society*, Vol.31 (1957–9), pp.1–28

NIXON, F. "Eighteenth Century Steam Engines in Derbyshire Lead Mines" *Derbyshire Miscellany*, Vol.1 No.9 (1958), p.128

OAKLEY, Margaret "A Recent Exploration of Hillcarr Sough" *Bulletin of the Peak District Mines Historical Society*, Vol.2 No.2 (1963), pp.100–104

OAKMAN, Colin D. "Derbyshire Sough Hydrogeology and the Artificial Drainage of the Stanton Syncline, near Derbyshire" *Transactions of the British Cave Research Association*, Vol.6 No.4 (December 1979), pp.169–194

OAKMAN, Colin D. "The Artificial Drainage of the Wirksworth/Cromford Area" *Bulletin of the Peak District Mines Historical Society*, Vol.7 No.5 (Spring 1980), pp.231–240

O'NEAL, R.A.H. "T'Owd Mon. A Study of the Old Lead Miner, based on the Literary Evidence" *The Derbyshire Countryside*, Vol.22 No.4 (1957), pp.18–21

OTTERY, F.S. "Lead Mining in the Wirksworth District During the Late Eighteenth and Early Nineteenth Centuries" *Bulletin of the Peak District Mines Historical Society*, Vol.4 No.2 (November 1969), pp.137–144

PARKER, Harry "The Capping of Knotlow Engine Shaft" *Bulletin of the Peak District Mines Historical Society*, Vol.3 No.6 (October 1968), pp.313–314

PARKER, Harry "Exploring Underground History the Easy Way: Using Modern Methods to Find an Ancient Engine" *Bulletin of the Peak District Mines Historical Society*, Vol.7 No.4 (October 1979), pp.192–193

PEARCE, Adrian J. "An Ecological Survey of Mines in Cucklet Delph, Stoney Middleton" *Bulletin of the Peak District Mines Historical Society*, Vol.5 No.5 (April 1974), pp.243–257

PEARCE, Adrian J. "To Remove or not to Remove" *Bulletin of the Peak District Mines Historical Society*, Vol.6 No.6 (December 1977), pp.295–296

PEARCE, Adrian J. "The Extravaganza or Introductory Weekend" *Bulletin of the Peak District Mines Historical Society*, Vol.7 No.2 (October 1978), pp.99–105

PEARCE, Adrian J. "The Peak District Mines Historical Society" *Industrial Archaeology*, Vol.14 No.2 (1979), pp.174–176

PEARCE, Adrian J. "Snake Mine: Some Recent Findings" *Bulletin of the Peak District Mines Historical Society*, Vol.7 No.6 (October 1980), pp.335–338

PEARCE, Adrian J., LUDDITT, R.; STRAW, M.; TAYLOR, W.; WATSON, J. & WATSON, R. "Mouldridge Mine, Pikehall, Derbyshire" *Bulletin of the Peak District Mines Historical Society*, Vol.9 No.2 (Winter 1984), pp.108–122

PEARMAN, Harry "Some Archival Sources of Information on Mines" *Bulletin of the Peak District Mines Historical Society*, Vol.4 No.3 (May 1970), pp.252–254

PENNEY, D. "Peakshole Sough, Castleton" *Bulletin of the Peak District Mines Historical Society*, Vol.9 No.3 (Summer 1985), pp.171–185

PENNEY, D. *See* KITCHEN, G. & PENNEY, D.

PENNY, S.R. *See* RADLEY, Jeffrey & PENNY, S.R.

PICKIN, John "A Sharpening Stone from a Level on Hassop Common" *Bulletin of the Peak District Mines Historical Society*, Vol.5 No.6 (October 1974), pp.360–361

PICKIN, John "The Mines of Hassop Common" *Bulletin of the Peak District Mines Historical Society*, Vol.6 No.2 (October 1975), pp.96–99

PICKIN, John "Smallpenny Sough, Lathkill Dale" *Bulletin of the Peak District Mines Historical Society*, Vol.6 No.2 (October 1975), pp.100–101

PICKIN, John "Watts Shaft Engine House, Old Mill Close Mine" *Bulletin of the Peak District Mines Historical Society*, Vol.8 No.4 (December 1982), pp.240–242

PICKIN, John "A Trial Excavation on High Tor Rake, Matlock" *Bulletin of the Peak District Mines Historical Society*, Vol.9 No.3 (Summer 1985), pp.197–199

PILL, A.L. "Origins of Some Derbyshire Cave and Lead Mine Names" *Cave Science*, Vol.2 No.16 (1951), pp.362–364

PILL, A.L. "Some Derbyshire Lead Mine Names" *The Derbyshire Countryside*, Vol.18 No.5 (1951), p.102

PILL, A.L. "Two Thousand Years of Lead Smelting. Part 1" *The Derbyshire Countryside*, Vol.18 No.7 (1952), pp.141–143

PILL, A.L. "Two Thousand Years of Lead Smelting. Part 2" *The Derbyshire Countryside*, Vol.18 No.8 (1952), pp.161–163

PRICE, D. "Mandale Mine Engine House, Lathkill Dale" *Bulletin of the Peak District Mines Historical Society*, Vol.1 No.3 (October 1960), p.16

P.S.M. "A Lead Mine in Derbyshire (Riber Mine, Matlock)" *East Midland Geographer*, No.10 (1958), pp.47–48

PUTTRELL, J.W. "A Visit to the Great Barmote Court" *Bulletin of the Peak District Mines Historical Society*, Vol.1 No.3 (October 1960), pp.7–9

QUIRK, David "Mineralization and Stress History in North Derbyshire" *Bulletin of the Peak District Mines Historical Society*, Vol.9 No.6 (Winter 1986), pp.333–386

QUIRK, David G. "Ringing Rake, Old Jant Mine and Gentlewoman's Pipes and the Genesis of the Masson Deposits, Matlock Bath, Derbyshire" *Bulletin of the Peak District Mines Historical Society*, Vol.10 No.1 (Summer 1987), pp.46–66

RADLEY, Jeffrey "Peak District Roads Prior to the Turnpike Era" *Journal of the Derbyshire Archaeological and Natural History Society*, Vol.LXXXIII (1963), pp.39–50

RADLEY, Jeffrey "The Transport of Lead: A Contribution to the Geography of Lead Mining" *Bulletin of the Peak District Mines Historical Society*, Vol.2 No.1 (1963), pp.1–8

RADLEY, J. & PENNY, S.R. "The Turnpike Roads of the Peak District" *Journal of the Derbyshire Archaeological and Natural History Society*, Vol.XCII (1972), pp.93–109

RHODES, J.N. "Derbyshire Influences on Lead Mining in North Wales in the 17th and 18th Centuries" *Bulletin of the Peak District Mines Historical Society*, Vol.3 No.6 (October 1968), pp.339–352

RIDEN, Philip "Joseph Butler, Coal and Iron Master 1763–1837" *Derbyshire Archaeological Journal*, Vol.CIV (1984)

RIEUWERTS, James H. "Lathkill Dale Mine" *Bulletin of the Peak District Mines Historical Society*, Vol.1 No.1 (December 1959), pp.12–14

RIEUWERTS, James H. "Preserving the Peak District Mines" *The Derbyshire Countryside*, Vol.25 No.2 (1960), pp.16–17

RIEUWERTS, James H. "The Merlin Mine" *Bulletin of the Peak District Mines Historical Society*, Vol.1 No.2 (May 1960), pp.3–6

RIEUWERTS, James H. "The Mines of Calver, Coombs Dale and Longstone Edge, May 1960" *Bulletin of the Peak District Mines Historical Society*, Vol.1 No.3 (October 1960), pp.3–5

RIEUWERTS, James H. "The Lead Mines and Soughs of Eyam Edge, August 1960" *Bulletin of the Peak District Mines Historical Society*, Vol.1 No.3 (October 1960), pp.10–12

RIEUWERTS, James H. "The Matlock Thermal Springs: Some further Investigations" *Bulletin of the Peak District Mines Historical Society*, Vol.1 No.4 (April 1961), pp.28–29

RIEUWERTS, James H. "Lathkilldale: Its Mines and Miners" *Bulletin of the Peak District Mines Historical Society*, Vol.2 No.1 (1963), pp.9–30

RIEUWERTS, James H. "Notes on the High Rake Lead Mine, Windmill" *Bulletin of the Peak District Mines Historical Society*, Vol.2 No.4 (1964), pp.175–178

RIEUWERTS, James H. "A List of the Soughs of the Derbyshire Lead Mines" *Bulletin of the Peak District Mines Historical Society*, Vol.3 No.1 (July 1966), pp.1–42

RIEUWERTS, James H. "Lathkill Dale: Its Mines and Miners (Supplementary Notes)" *Bulletin of the Peak District Mines Historical Society*, Vol.3 No.1 (July 1966), pp.71–74

RIEUWERTS, James H. "The Kirby Lead Mining Manuscript Collection" *Bulletin of the Peak District Mines Historical Society*, Vol.3 No.6 (October 1968), pp.357–362

RIEUWERTS, James H. "On Being Elected to the Grand Jury of the Barmote Court" *Bulletin of the Peak District Mines Historical Society*, Vol.3 No.6 (October 1968), pp.385–388

RIEUWERTS, James H. "Charles Henry Millington, 1878–1968: An Appreciation" *Bulletin of the Peak District Mines Historical Society*, Vol.4 No.1 (March 1969), pp.53

RIEUWERTS, James H. "The Soughs of Derbyshire Lead Mines: Supple-mentary List" *Bulletin of the Peak District Mines Historical Society*, Vol.4 No.2 (November 1969), pp.119–136

RIEUWERTS, James H. "The Inquisition or Quo Warrento of 1288" *Bulletin of the Peak District Mines Historical Society*, Vol.7 No.1 (May 1978), pp.41–49

RIEUWERTS, James H. "The Earliest Lead Mine Soughs in Derbyshire"

Bulletin of the Peak District Mines Historical Society, Vol.7 No.5 (Spring 1980), pp.241–314

RIEUWERTS, James H. "The Drainage of the Alport Mining Field" *Bulletin of the Peak District Mines Historical Society*, Vol.8 No.1 (June 1981), pp.1–28

RIEUWERTS, James H. "The Development of Mining and Drainage in the Wensley, Winster and Elton Areas" *Bulletin of the Peak District Mines Historical Society*, Vol.8 No.2 (Autumn 1981), pp.109–150

RIEUWERTS, James H. "Cromford Sough and the Early Use of Gunpowder" *Bulletin of the Peak District Mines Historical Society*, Vol.8 No.5 (Summer 1983), pp.315–329

RIEUWERTS, James H. "Derbyshire Lead Mining and Early Geological Concepts" *Bulletin of the Peak District Mines Historical Society*, Vol.9 No.2 (Winter 1984), pp.51–100

RIEUWERTS, James H. & FORD, Trevor D. "Odin Mine, Castleton, Derbyshire" *Bulletin of the Peak District Mines Historical Society*, Vol.6 No.4 (September 1976), pp.1–54

RIEUWERTS, James H. & FORD, Trevor D. "The Mining History of the Speedwell Mine or Oakden Level, Castleton, Derbyshire" *Bulletin of the Peak District Mines Historical Society*, Vol.9 No.3 (Summer 1985), pp.129–170

RIEUWERTS, James H. *See* FLINDALL, Roger B., HAYES, Andrew J. & RIEUWERTS, James H.

RIEUWERTS, James H. *See* TOFT, D. & RIEUWERTS, James H.

RIEUWERTS, James H. *See* WILLIES, Lynn, RIEUWERTS, James H. & FLINDALL, Roger B.

RILEY, Leslie J. "Gank Hole Mine, Lathkill Dale" *Bulletin of the Peak District Mines Historical Society*, Vol.6 No.6 (December 1977), pp.293–294

RILEY, Leslie J. & WILLIES, Lynn "The Recovery of the Pumps from Wills Founder Shaft in Winster" *Bulletin of the Peak District Mines Historical Society*, Vol.7 No.4 (October 1979), pp.199–205

RILEY, Leslie J. *See* WORLEY, Noel E., WORTHINGTON, Terence & RILEY, Leslie J.

RILEY, Peter "Peak District Mine Names: A Preliminary Survey" *Bulletin of the Peak District Mines Historical Society*, Vol.6 No.5 (May 1977), pp.241–248

ROBEY, John A. "The Mines North–West of Monyash, Derbyshire. Part I. The Chapel Dale Mine and Level" *Bulletin of the Peak District Mines Historical Society*, Vol.1 No.5 (October 1961), pp.30–36

ROBEY, John A. "The Mines North West of Monyash, Derbyshire, Part II, Ancient Mining in the Area" *Bulletin of the Peak District Mines Historical Society*, Vol.1 No.6 (May 1962), pp.29–35

ROBEY. John A. "The Mines North–West of Monyash. Part III, The Whalf and Crimbo Soughs" *Bulletin of the Peak District Mines Historical Society*, Vol.2 No.1 (1963), pp.51–58

ROBEY, John A. "Discovery of a Cavern on Crosslow Rake, Foolow, Derbyshire" *Bulletin of the Peak District Mines Historical Society*, Vol.2 No.3 (1964), pp.151–152

ROBEY, John A. "The Secular Variation of Magnetic North" *Bulletin of the Peak District Mines Historical Society*, Vol.2 No.6 (December 1965), pp.311–313

ROBEY, John A. "Field Grove Mine, Sheldon, Derbyshire" *Bulletin of the Peak District Mines Historical Society*, Vol.3 No.2 (December 1966), pp.93–102

ROBEY, John A. "Field Meeting to Millers Dale: 21st May 1967" *Bulletin of the Peak District Mines Historical Society*, Vol.3 No.4 (December 1967), pp.247–248

ROBEY, John A. "Early Mining Techniques in the Peak District" *Bulletin of the Peak District Mines Historical Society*, Vol.4 No.1 (March 1969), pp.49–52

ROBEY, John A. "Copper Smelting in Derbyshire" *Bulletin of the Peak District Mines Historical Society*, Vol.4 No.5 (June 1971), pp.348–356

ROBEY, John A. "Supplementary Notes on the Lead Mines in the Monyash–Flagg area of Derbyshire" *Bulletin of the Peak District Mines Historical Society*, Vol.5 No.3 (May 1973), pp.149–155

ROCHE, V.S. "The Magpie Mine Engine House, Sheldon, Derbyshire, 1864" *Bulletin of the Peak District Mines Historical Society*, Vol.3 No.6 (October 1968), pp.381–384

ROGERS, P.J. *See* LUNN, P.E., ROGERS, P.J. & IXER, R.

RORISON, I.H. *See* BAYLISS, J.M., INESON, P.R. & RORISON, I.H.

SARJEANT, William A.S. "The Water Grove Chimney: an attempt that failed" *Bulletin of the Peak District Mines Historical Society*, Vol.1 No.4 (April 1961), pp.13–15

SARJEANT, William A.S. "Comments on an Extract from a Paper by Thos.Short, M.D. 1733" *Bulletin of the Peak District Mines Historical Society*, Vol.1 No.4 (April 1961), p.27

SARJEANT, William A.S. "Further Notes on Croil Glossary, Part III" *Bulletin of the Peak District Mines Historical Society*, Vol.1 No.5 (October 1961), p.49

SARJEANT, William A.S. "The Formation of the Peak District Mines Historical Society" *Bulletin of the Peak District Mines Historical Society*, Vol.3 No.3 (May 1967), pp.185–190

SARJEANT, William A.S. "Folksongs of the Peak District Miners: a Letter" *Bulletin of the Peak District Mines Historical Society*, Vol.5 No.5 (April 1974), p.315

SARJEANT, William A.S. *See* FORD, Trevor D. & SARJEANT, William A.S.

S.C.R. "Blue John Mine, Derbyshire" *British Caver*, Vol.18 (1948), p.51

S.G.R. "Lead Mining in Derbyshire" *East Midland Geographer*, No.2 (1954),pp.42–43

SHAW, Richard P. "A Survey of the Geology of Putwell Hill Mine, Monsall Dale" *Bulletin of the Peak District Mines Historical Society*, Vol.7 No.6 (Autumn 1980), pp.342–344

SHAW, Richard P. "Pilkington's Cavern, Castleton" *Bulletin of the Peak District Mines Historical Society*, Vol.8 No.5 (Summer 1983), pp.296–300

SHORT, Thos. "The Warm Springs of Matlock: an Extract of a paper (1873)" *Bulletin of the Peak District Mines Historical Society*, Vol.1 No.4 (April 1961), pp.25–27

SLACK, Ronald "The Slack Family: Brassington Lead Miners" *Bulletin of the Peak District Mines Historical Society*, Vol.8 No.5 (Summer 1983), pp.301–314

SLACK, Ronald "Brassington Mining" *Bulletin of the Peak District Mines Historical Society*, Vol.9 No.3 (Summer 1985), pp.186–199

SLACK, Ronald "Land Tenure in a Lead Mining Village. Brassington 1834" *Derbyshire Miscellany*, Vol.XI No.1 (1986), pp.14–19

SLACK, R. "Great Rake Mine in the 1920s: Recalled by Joe Gould" *Bulletin of the Peak District Mines Historical Society*, Vol.10 No.1 (Summer 1987), pp.13–16

SMITH, A. *See* FORD, Trevor D. & SMITH, A.

SMITH, Michael E. "Water Grove Mine" *Bulletin of the Peak District Mines Historical Society*, Vol.1 No.1 (December 1959), p.10

SMITH, Michael E. "The Watergrove Mine" *Bulletin of the Peak District Mines Historical Society*, Vol.1 No.2 (May 1960), p.2

SMITH, Michael E. "The Small Penny Sough" *Bulletin of the Peak District Mines Historical Society*, Vol.1 No.3 (October 1960), pp.17–18

SMITH, Michael E. "The Drainage of the Victory and Burnt Heath Mines" *Bulletin of the Peak District Mines Historical Society*, Vol.1 No.4 (April 1961), pp.16–23

SMITH, Michael E. "The Odin Mine, Castleton, Derbyshire" *Bulletin of the Peak District Mines Historical Society*, Vol.1 No.6 (May 1962), pp.18–23

SMITH, Michael E. "Water Icicle Close Mine, Monyash" *Bulletin of the Peak District Mines Historical Society*, Vol.3 No.5 (May 1968), pp.281–284

SMITH, Michael E. "Bamforth Hole, Stony Middleton" *Bulletin of the Peak District Mines Historical Society*, Vol.4 No.5 (June 1971), pp.370–374

SMITH, Michael E. & TUNE, R.N. "A Report on a Preliminary Meeting of the Proposed Derbyshire Natural History Trust" *Bulletin of the Peak District Mines Historical Society*, Vol.1 No.4 (April 1961), p.44

SPALDING, David A.E. "Biographical Notes of Authors on Derbyshire, Gideon Algernon Mantell (1790–1852)" *Bulletin of the Peak District Mines Historical Society*, Vol.3 No.2 (December 1966), pp.85–92

STOKES, A.H. "Lead and Lead Mining in Derbyshire" *Peak District Mines Historical Society*, Special Publication No.2 (1973)

STRAW, M. *See* PEARCE, Adrian J., LUDDITT, R., STRAW, M., TAYLOR, W., WATSON, J. & WATSON, R.

SWAIN, J. *See* FLINDALL, Roger B., SWAIN, J. & HAYES, Andrew J.

TAYLOR, L.F. "The Mill Close Mine" *The Derbyshire Countryside*, Vol.23 No.6 (1958), pp.28–29

TAYLOR, W. *See* PEARCE, Adrian J., LUDDITT, R., STRAW, M., TAYLOR, W., WATSON, J. & WATSON, R.

THOMAS, Michael "The Rioting Crowd in Derbyshire in the Eighteenth Century" *Journal of the Derbyshire Archaeological and Natural History Society*, Vol.XCV (1975), pp.37–47

THOMPSON, S.J. "Lead Ore Production in the High Peak, 1832–1848: Part 1 Winster Liberty" *Memoirs of the Northern Cavern and Mine Research Society*, Vol.2 No.2 (May 1972), pp.74–79

THOMPSON, S.J. "Lead Ore Production in the High Peak, 1832–1848: Part 2 Chelmorton, Flagg, Monyash, Taddington & Upper Haddon Liberties" *Memoirs of the Northern Cavern and Mine Research Society*, Vol.2 No.3 (September 1973), pp.133–138

THOMPSON, S.J. *See* LORD, P.J. & THOMPSON, S.J.

THOMPSON, Steve "The Recovery of a Steam Engine from Putwell Hill Mine, Monsal Dale:" *Bulletin of the Peak District Mines Historical Society*, Vol.4 No.6 (December 1971), pp.413–416

THORNHILL, Robert "Washing Ore in Longstone" *Derbyshire Miscellany*, Vol.1 No.6 (1957), pp.76–77

THORNHILL, Robert "The Seedlow Lead Mine, 1764–1771" *Bulletin of the Peak District Mines Historical Society*, Vol.1 No.6 (May 1962), pp.24–28

THORNHILL, Robert "Lead Mining Near Calver" *Derbyshire Miscellany*, Vol.III No.6 (1965), pp.588–596

THORNHILL, Robert "Candles and Powder for Lead Mines" *Derbyshire Miscellany*, Vol.III No.8 (1966), pp.657–96

THORNHILL, Robert "Some Accounts of an 18th Century Lead Mining Agent in Great Longstone 1766–1827" *Bulletin of the Peak District Mines Historical Society*, Vol.3 No.4 (December 1967), pp.219–232

THORNHILL, Robert "Notes on Some Derbyshire Toll Houses and Turnpike Roads" *Derbyshire Miscellany*, Vol.IV Part 4 (1968), pp.185–216

THORNHILL, Robert "The Lead Miner of Longstone Church" *Bulletin of the Peak District Mines Historical Society*, Vol.4 No.1 (March 1969), pp.37–40

THORNTON, D.R. "Recent Developments at the Mandale Mine, Lathkill Dale" *Bulletin of the Peak District Mines Historical Society*, Vol 1. No.3 (October 1960), p.6

TOFT, D. & RIEUWERTS. James H. "Some Notes on a Thermal Spring Encountered in the Wragg Mine, Matlock Bath" *Bulletin of the Peak District Mines Historical Soceity*, Vol.1 No.3 (October 1960), p.15

TUNE. R.N. "Field Meeting to Snake Mine and Wester Hollow: 25th June 1967. Leader" *Bulletin of the Peak District Mines Historical Society*, Vol.3 No.4 (December 1967), pp.249–254

TUNE, R.N. "A Survey of Mandale Mine, Lathkilldale" *Bulletin of the Peak District Mines Historical Society*, Vol.4 No.1 (March 1969), pp.67–74

TUNE, R.N., HURT, L. & FORD, Trevor D. "Snake Mine, Hoptonwood, Derbyshire" *Bulletin of the Peak District Mines Historical Society*, Vol.3 No.5 (May 1968), pp.291–298

TUNE, R.N. *See* GREGORY, Neville & TUNE, R.N.

TUNE, R.N. *See* SMITH, Michael & TUNE, R.N.

VARVILL, W.W. "Secondary Enrichment by Natural Flotation (Mill Close and British Lead Mines). Part 1" *Mine and Quarry Engineering*, Vol.28 (February 1962), pp.64–73

VARVILL, W.W. "Secondary Enrichment by Natural Flotation. Part 2" *Mine and Quarry Engineering*, Vol.28 (March 1962), pp.112–118

VARVILL, W.W. "Secondary Enrichment by Natural Flotation. Part 3" *Mine and Quarry Engineering*, Vol.28 (April 1962), pp.156–161

VARVILL, W.W. "Secondary Enrichment by Natural Flotation. Part 4" *Mine and Quarry Engineering*, Vol.28 (May 1962), pp.208–214;219

WALTERS, S.G. "Clear–the–Way or Black Hillock Mine, Tideslow Moor" *Bulletin of the Peak District Mines Historical Society*, Vol.7 No.6 (Autumn 1980), pp.327–333

WALTERS, S.G. & INESON, P.R. "Mineralisation within the Igneous Rocks of the South Pennine Orefield" *Bulletin of the Peak District Mines Historical Society*, Vol.7 No.6 (Autumn 1980),pp.315–325

WALTERS, S.G. & INESON, P.R. "The Geology of the Hillicar Wood Adit, Via Gellia" *Bulletin of the Peak District Mines Historical Society*, Vol.7 No.6 (Autumn 1980), pp.353–356

WARD, G.H.B. "Holmesfield's Medieval Bole Hills" *Sheffield Clarion Ramblers' Booklet*, (1953–4), pp.74–83

WARREN, K. "The Derbyshire Iron Industry Since 1780" *East Midland Geographer*, No.16 (December 1961), pp.17–33

WARRINER, David J. "Exploration of Fritchley Sough and Old End Mine, Crich" *Bulletin of the Peak District Mines Historical Society*, Vol.8 No.1 (June 1981), pp.49–53

WARRINER, David J. "Examination and Survey of Bage Mine" *Bulletin of the Peak District Mines Historical Society*, Vol.8 No.4 (December 1982), pp.243–259

WARRINER, David J. & BIRKETT, N. "Ratchwood Founder Shaft, Wirksworth" *Bulletin of the Peak District Mines Historical Society*, Vol.8 No.3 (Summer 1982), pp.151–158

WARRINER, David J., WILLIES, Lynn & FLINDALL, Roger B. "Ringing Rake and Masson Soughs and the Mines on the East Side of Masson Hill, Matlock" *Bulletin of the Peak District Mines Historical Society*, Vol.8 No.2 (Autumn 1981), pp.65–102

WARWICK, G.T. "An Early Descent of Eldon Hole and an Account of the Entrance to Speedwell Mine" *British Caver*, Vol.XVII (1947), pp.48–50

WATSON, J. *See* PEARCE, Adrian J., LUDDITT, R., STRAW, M., TAYLOR, W., WATSON, J. & WATSON, R.

WATSON, R. *See* PEARCE, Adrian J., LUDDITT, R., STRAW, M., TAYLOR, W., WATSON, J. & WATSON, R.

WIGLEY, D.M. "John Wigley of Wigwell" *Derbyshire Miscellany*, Vol.V Part 4 (1970), pp.229–238

WILES, A.E. "The North Side of Ashford Lordship 1750–1850. A General Survey" *Bulletin of the Peak District Mines Historical Society*, Vol.2 No.2 (1963), pp.93–99

WILLIAMS, Christopher J. "Lead Mining Documents in the Derbyshire Record Office" *Bulletin of the Peak District Mines Historical Society*, Vol.3 No.6 (October 1968), pp.323–328

WILLIAMS, Christopher J. & WILLIES, Lynn "Stone Edge Cupola" *Bulletin of the Peak District Mines Historical Society*, Vol.3 No.6 (October 1968), pp.315–322

WILLIES, Lynn "Winster and 18th Century Lead Mining" *Bulletin of the Peak District Mines Historical Society*, Vol.3 No.5 (May 1968), pp.271–279

WILLIES, Lynn "Lead Smelting in Derbyshire 1737–1900" *Bulletin of the Historical Metallurgy Group*, Vol.3 No.2 (1969)

WILLIES, Lynn "Cupola Lead Smelting Sites in Derbyshire, 1737–1900" *Bulletin of the Peak District Mines Historical Society*, Vol.4 No.1 (March 1969), pp.97–115

WILLIES, Lynn "Regional Geochemical Reconnaissance of the Derbyshire Area (Review)" *Bulletin of the Peak District Mines Historical Society*, Vol.4 No.4 (October 1970), pp.337–338

WILLIES, Lynn "The Introduction of the Cupola to Derbyshire" *Bulletin of the Peak District Mines Historical Society*, Vol.4 No.5 (June

1971), pp.384–394

WILLIES, Lynn "Biographical Notes: Richard Watson, 1737–1816" *Bulletin of the Peak District Mines Historical Society*, Vol.4 No.5 (June 1971), pp.395–399

WILLIES, Lynn "Gabriel Jars (1732–1769) and the Derbyshire Lead Industry" *Bulletin of the Peak District Mines Historical Society*, Vol.5 No.1 (April 1972), pp.31–39

WILLIES, Lynn "Lead Smelting Sites at Beeley Moor, Barbrook and Stonedge: Report of Field Meeting" *Bulletin of the Peak District Mines Historical Society*, Vol.5 No.1 (April 1972), pp.40–42

WILLIES, Lynn "The Barker Family and the Eighteenth Century Lead Business" *Journal of the Derbyshire Archaeological and Natural History Society*, Vol.XCIII (1973), pp.55–74

WILLIES, Lynn "The Lords' Cupola, Middleton Dale" *Bulletin of the Peak District Mines Historical Society*, Vol.5 No.5 (April 1974), pp.288–302

WILLIES, Lynn "Lead Poisoning in the Derbyshire Lead Industry" *Bulletin of the Peak District Mines Historical Society*, Vol.5 No.5 (April 1974), pp.302–311

WILLIES, Lynn "The Reopening of Magpie Sough" *Bulletin of the Peak District Mines Historical Society*, Vol.5 No.6 (October 1974), pp.324–331

WILLIES, Lynn "A Survey of Maypit and Redsoil Mines, Sheldon" *Bulletin of the Peak District Mines Historical Society*, Vol.5 No.6 (October 1974), pp.349–359

WILLIES, Lynn "Report on Shaft Capping on Masson Hill, Matlock, June 1974" *Bulletin of the Peak District Mines Historical Society*, Vol.5 No.6 (October 1974), pp.370–372

WILLIES, Lynn "Maypit and Redsoil Mines. A Reply to Nellie Kirkham" *Bulletin of the Peak District Mines Historical Society*, Vol.6 No.1 (May 1975), pp.50–51

WILLIES, Lynn "The Washing of Lead Ore in Derbyshire during the Nineteenth Century" *Bulletin of the Peak District Mines Historical Society*, Vol.6 No.2 (October 1975), pp.53–59

WILLIES, Lynn "Two Wooden Lead Ore Measuring Dishes" *Bulletin of the Peak District Mines Historical Society*, Vol.6 No.2 (October 1975), pp.83–84

WILLIES, Lynn "Stanley Rowlands' Recollection of Magpie Mine in 1924" *Bulletin of the Peak District Mines Historical Society*, Vol.6 No.2 (October 1975), pp.102–106

WILLIES, Lynn "John Taylor in Derbyshire, 1839–1851. Part 1" *Bulletin of the Peak District Mines Historical Society*, Vol.6 No.3 (April 1976), pp.146–160

WILLIES, Lynn "The Recovery of the Wills Founder Water Pressure Engine" *Bulletin of the Peak District Mines Historical Society*, Vol.6 No.5 (May 1977), pp.180–190

WILLIES, Lynn "John Taylor in Derbyshire, 1839–1851. Part 2" *Bulletin of the Peak District Mines Historical Society*, Vol.6 No.5 (May 1977), pp.218–232

WILLIES, Lynn "Review: The Wolley Collection" *Bulletin of the Peak District Mines Historical Society*, Vol.7 No.1 (May 1978), p.4

WILLIES, Lynn "Technical Development in Derbyshire Lead Mining 1700–1880" *Bulletin of the Peak District Mines Historical Society*, Vol.7 No.3 (March 1979), pp.117–151

WILLIES, Lynn "Magpie Mine" *Industrial Archaeology*, Vol.14 No.3 (1979), pp.245–253

WILLIES, Lynn "Peak District Mining Museum: 2,000 Years of Derbyshire Lead Mining" *Industrial Archaeology*, Vol.14 No.4 (1979), pp.344–357

WILLIES, Lynn "John Fairburn: Stationer and Mining Entrepreneur" *Bulletin of the Peak District Mines Historical Society*, Vol.8 No.3 (Summer 1982), pp.159–165

WILLIES, Lynn "The Barker Family and Wyatt Lead Mining Businesses, 1730–1875" *Bulletin of the Peak District Mines Historical Society*, Vol.8 No.6 (Winter 1983), pp.331–368

WILLIES, Lynn "Prosperity and Decline in Derbyshire Lead Mining" *Bulletin of the Peak District Mines Historical Society*, Vol.9 No.5 (Summer 1986), pp.251–282

WILLIES, Lynn, RIEUWERTS, James H. & FLINDALL, Roger B. "Wind, Water and Steam Power on Derbyshire Lead Mines: A List" *Bulletin of the Peak District Mines Historical Society*, Vol.6 No.6 (December 1977), pp.303–320

WILLIES, Lynn *See* FLETCHER, George & WILLIES, Lynn

WILLIES, Lynn *See* RILEY, Leslie J. & WILLIES, Lynn

WILLIES, Lynn *See* WARRINER, David J., WILLIES, Lynn & FLINDALL, Roger B.

WILLIES, Lynn *See* WILLIAMS, Christopher J. & WILLIES, Lynn

WOOD, J. "The Lathkill Miner" *Bulletin of the Peak District Mines Historical Society*, Vol.6 No.5 (May 1977), p.200

WOOD, K. *See* FLINDALL, Roger B. & WOOD, K.

WOODHOUSE, H. "Recollections of Mill Close Mine, South Darley, Nr. Matlock, Derbyshire" *Bulletin of the Peak District Mines Historical Society*, Vol.9 No.4 (Winter 1985), pp.228–232

WOODWARD, M. "The Matlock Thermal Springs. Further Investigations II" *Bulletin of the Peak District Mines Historical Society*, Vol.1 No.5 (October 1961), pp.46–48

WORKMAN, G.H. "Excursion to Matlock Bath" *Bulletin of the Peak District Mines Historical Society*, Vol.1 No.2 (May 1960), pp.14–19

WORLEY, Noel E. "Geology of the Blende Vein, Magpie Sough" *Bulletin of the Peak District Mines Historical Society*, Vol.6 No.1 (May 1975), pp.28–32

WORLEY, Noel E. "The Geology of the Wills Founder Shaft, Winster" *Bulletin of the Peak District Mines Historical Society*, Vol.6 No.6 (December 1977), pp.257–262

WORLEY,Noel E. & BECK, J.S. "Moorfurlong Mine, Bradwell, Derbyshire and its Ecological Significance" *Transactions of the British Cave Research Association*, Vol.3 No.1 (April 1976), pp.49–53

WORLEY, Noel E. & FORD, Trevor D. "Mandale Forfield Shaft and Sough" *Bulletin of the Peak District Mines Historical Society*, Vol.6 No.3 (April 1976), pp.141–143

WORLEY, Noel E. & NASH, Douglas A. "The Winster Earth Tremors" *Bulletin of the Peak District Mines Historical Society*, Vol.7 No.3 (March 1979), pp.158–164

WORLEY, Noel E., WORTHINGTON, Terrence & RILEY, Leslie J. "The Geology and Exploration of the Hubberdale Mines, Taddington" *Bulletin of the Peak District Mines Historical Society*, Vol.7 No.1 (May 1978), pp.31–39

WORLEY, Noel E. *See* BECK, John S. & WORLEY, Noel E.

WORTHINGTON, Terrence *See* WORLEY, Noel E., WORTHINGTON, Terrence & RILEY, Leslie J.

CHESHIRE, SHROPSHIRE AND STAFFORDSHIRE

Books

ALLBUT, Martin *See* BROOK, Fred & ALLBUT, Martin

BROOK, Fred & ALBUTT, Martin *The Shropshire Lead Mines* (Hartington: Moorland, 1973)

BROWN, Ivor J. *The Mines of Shropshire* (Buxton: Moorland Press, 1976)

CARLON, Christopher *The Alderley Edge Mines* (Altringham: John Sherrett & Sons, 1979)

CARLON, C.J. *The Gallantry Bank Copper Mine, Bickerton, Cheshire* (Sheffield: Northern Mine Research Society, British Mining No.16, 1981)

DEWEY, H. & EASTWOOD, T. *Special Reports on the Mineral Resources of G.B. Vol.30: Copper Ores of the Midlands, Wales, the Lake District and the Isle of Man* (Sheffield: Mining Facsimiles, 1986. Reprint of the Geological Survey 1925 Edition)

DEWEY, H. *See* SMITH, B. & DEWEY, H.

EARP, J.R. & HAINS, B.A. *British Regional Geology. The Welsh Border Land* (Institute of Geological Sciences, H.M.S.O., 1981)

EASTWOOD, T. *See* DEWEY, H. & EASTWOOD, T.

FRANCE, R.S.(Ed.) *The Thievely Lead Mines 1629–1635* (Lancashire and Cheshire Record Society, 1951)

HAINS, B.A. *See* EARP, J.R. & HAINS, B.A.

HARRIS, John R. "Copper and Brass" in *The Victoria County History of Staffordshire* Vol.II (1967)

KIRKHAM, Nellie *Ecton Mines* (Clapham: Dalesman, 1949)

ROBEY, John A. *The Copper and Lead Mines of Ecton Hill, Staffordshire* (Cheddleton: Moorland & Peak District Mines Historical Society, 1972)

SMITH, B. & DEWEY, H. *Special Reports on the Mineral Resources of G.B. Vol.23. Lead and Zinc Ores in the Pre-Carboniferous Rocks of West Shropshire and North Wales* (Sheffield: Mining Facsimiles, 1986. Reprint of Geological Survey 1922 Edition.)

B.H.B.M.—H

Theses

BROWN, I.J. *Mineral Working and Land Reclamation in the Coalbrookdale Coalfield* (University of Leicester PhD Thesis, 1975)

LE GUILLOU, M. *Developments in the South Staffordshire Iron and Steel Industry 1850–1913, in the Light of Home and Foreign Competition* (University of Keele PhD Thesis, 1972–3)

NEWMAN, O.S. *Lead Mining in South West Shropshire 1780–1900* (University of Keele MA Thesis, 1983)

Articles

ADAMS, D.R. "Survey of the South Shropshire Lead Mining Area" *Shropshire Mining Club*, Account No.2 (1962)

ADAMS, D.R. "Survey of the South Shropshire Lead Mining Area, Part I: The Western Region" *Bulletin of the Peak District Mines Historical Society*, Vol.2 No.2 (1963), pp.105–110

ADAMS, D.R. "Survey of the South Shropshire Lead Mining Area, Part II: The Eastern Region" *Bulletin of the Peak District Mines Historical Society*, Vol.2 No.3 (1964), pp.111–121

ADAMS, D.R. "Survey of South Shropshire Mining Area: First Supplement" *Shropshire Mining Club*, Account No.4 (1968)

ADAMS, D.R. "Survey of Llanymynech Ogof Roman Copper Mine" *Shropshire Mining Club*, Account No.8 (1970)

ADAMS, D.R. "Mines and Caves in the Area between Llanymynech and the Dee" *Shropshire Mining Club*, Account No.9 (1972)

ADAMS, D.R. "A Short History of the Shropshire Mining Club" *Shropshire Mining Club Journal*, (1972–3), pp.29–35

ADAMS, D.R, & HAZELEY, J. "Survey of the Church Aston–Lilleshall Mining Area" *Shropshire Mining Club*, Account No.7 (1970)

ALLBUTT, Martin & BROOK, Frederick "Snailbeach Lead Mine" *Ports-mouth Polytechnic Industrial Archaeology Journal*, Vol.2

ALLBUTT, Martin & BROOK, Frederick "The Snailbeach Mining Company, 1767 to 1911" *Memoirs of the Northern Cavern and Mine Research Society*, (October 1969), pp.68–77

ALLBUTT, Martin & BROOK, Frederick "The South Shropshire Lead Mines" *Industrial Archaeology*, Vol.10 No.1 (1973), pp.40–63

ANON "Dale Mine, North Staffordshire" [First Published 1862] *Bulletin of the Peak District Mines Historical Society*, Vol.1 No.6 (May 1962), pp.37–38

ANON "To the Employees of the Shropshire Mines Ltd. December 1919. A Statement of Company Policy" *Shropshire Mining Club Journal*, (1978), pp.66–69

ANON "An Attempt to Save the Snailbeach Mining Area from Land Reclamation" *Shropshire Mining Club Journal*, (1978), pp.33–37

ASHWELL, Alan "Extract from Shrewsbury Chronical: February 1st, 1839" *Bulletin of the Peak District Mines Historical Society*, Vol.2 No.6 (December 1965), p.314

BICK, David E. "The Lead Mines of S.W. Shropshire" *Plymouth Mineral and Mining Club Journal*, Vol.4 No.3 (January 1974), pp.14–15

BROOK, Frank "Arthur Waters, Mining Agent" *Shropshire Mining Club Journal*, (1971–2), pp.37–42

BROOK, Frank "The Lawrences, Mining Entrepreneurs" *Shropshire Mining Club Journal*, (1972–3), pp.14–16

BROOK, Frank "Shropshire's Lead Mining Klondyke" *Shropshire Mining Club Journal*, (1973–4), pp.38–41

BROOK, Frank "The Snailbeach Lead Mine: A Company History" *Shropshire Mining Club Journal*, (1975–6), pp.33–41

BROOK, Frederick *See* ALLBUTT, Martin & BROOK, Frederick

BROWN, Ivor J. "Old Mining Ballads: A Collection of Old Ballads Commemorating Industrial Tragedies in the Coalbrookdale Coalfield" *Shropshire Mining Club*, Yearbook (1965–6), pp.45–47

BROWN, Ivor J. "The Mineral Wealth of Coalbrookdale: Part I" *Bulletin of the Peak District Mines Historical Society*, Vol.2 No.5 (May 1965), pp.255–290

BROWN, Ivor J. "The Mineral Wealth of Coalbrookdale: Part II" *Bulletin of the Peak District Mines Historical Society*, Vol.2 No.6 (December 1965), pp.339–366

BROWN, Ivor J. "Supplementary Notes on the Mineral Wealth of Coalbrookdale" *Bulletin of the Peak District Mines Historical Society*, Vol.3 No.2 (December 1966), pp.125–132

BROWN, Ivor J. "Mine Accidents in the South Shropshire Metalliferous Mining Area 1875–Present" *Shropshire Mining Club Journal*, (1971–2), pp.43–45

BROWN, Ivor J. "Salvaging Operations at Rock Mine, Ketley, Shropshire" *Shropshire Mining Club Journal*, (1972–3), pp.11–13

BROWN, Ivor J. "The Pontesford Mine Engine House, Near Shrewsbury" *Shropshire Mining Club Journal*, (1975–6), pp.22–24

BROWN, Ivor J. "Mineral Working in the Coalbrookdale Coalfield" *Shropshire Mining Club*, Yearbook (1978), pp.1–22

BROWN, Ivor J. (Ed.) "An Attempt to Save the Snailbeach Mining Area from Land Reclamation" *Bulletin of the Peak District Mines Historical Society*, Vol.7 No.4 (October 1979), pp.208–211

BROWN, Ivor J. "The Tunnels of the Coalbrookdale Coalfield Area" *Shropshire Mining Club Journal*, (1979), pp.37–44

BROWN, Ivor J. "Mines and Mineral Workings in the Coalbrookdale Coalfield" *Shropshire Caving and Mining Club*, Account No.11 (1979)

BROWN, Ivor J. "Notes on the Lead Smelt Houses of the South Shropshire Mining Field" *Shropshire Mining Club Journal*, (1980), pp.11–13

BROWN, Ivor J. & DAVIS, T.J. "Plans and Sections of the Metalliferous Mines of South West Shropshire" *Shropshire Mining Club*, Account No.10 (1972)

CARLON, Christopher J. "The Eardiston Copper Mine, Shropshire" *Bulletin of the Peak District Mines Historical Society*, Vol.8 No.1 (June 1981), pp.29–42

CHANDLER, B. "The Alderley Edge Copper Mines" *British Caver*, Vol.24 (1953), pp.37–41

CHAPMAN, G.J. *See* PEDRICK, P.D. & CHAPMAN, G.J.

CRITCHLEY, Martin F. "A Geological Outline of the Ecton Copper Mines, Staffordshire" *Bulletin of the Peak District Mines Historical Society*, Vol.7 No.4 (October 1979), pp.177–191

CRITCHLEY, Martin F. & WILSON, P.J. "A Survey of the Shafts at Bincliffe, Oversetts and Highfields Mine, Wetton, Staffordshire" *Bulletin of the Peak District Mines Historical Society*, Vol.6 No.2 (October 1975), pp.73–82

DAVIS, R.V. "A Brief Account of the Geology, History and Mechanisation of the Snailbeach Mine, Shropshire" *Memoirs of the Northern Cavern and Mine Research Society*, (January 1969), pp.52–62

DAVIS, Stuart "Mixon Mine: level in South Shaft" *Bulletin of the Peak District Mines Historical Society*, Vol.5 No.3 (May 1973), pp.159–160

DAVIS, T.J. "The Smaller Engine Houses in South Shropshire" *Shropshire Mining Club Journal*, (1975–6), pp.15–20

DAVIS, T.J. & JONES, V. "The Snailbeach Mining Company 1897" *Shropshire Mining Club Journal*, (1979), pp.35–36

DAVIS, T.J. *See* BROWN, Ivor J. & DAVIS, T.J.

DINES, H.G. "The West Shropshire Mining Region" *Bulletin of the Geological Survey of Great Britain*, No.14 (1958), pp.1–43

EFFORD, W. "Description of Famous Copper–Mine Belonging to His Grace the Duke of Devonshire at Ecton–Hill in the County of Stafford" *Bulletin of the Peak District Mines Historical Society*, Vol.1 No.5 (October 1961), pp.37–40

HAZELEY, J. *See* ADAMS, D.R. & HAZELEY, J.

HEATHCOTE, J.A. "A Survey of the Metal Mines of South West Shropshire" *Shropshire Cave and Mining Club*, Account No.12 (1979)

HEATHCOTE, J.A. "Huglith Mine, Shropshire" *Shropshire Mining Club Journal*, (1980), pp.21–29

JONES, T. "Impression of an East Shropshire Mine 1885–1953" *Shropshire Mining Club Journal*, (1973–4), pp.17–21

KIRKHAM, Nellie "Ecton Mines" *Journal of the Derbyshire Archaeological and Natural History Society*, Vol.67 (1947), pp.55–82

KIRKHAM, Nellie "Dale Lead Mine, Ecton" *Peakland Archaeological Newsletter*, No.4 (1948)

LAWSON, John "Statistics of the Mineral Production of the Pennines: Part 3 Staffordshire and Cheshire" *Memoirs of the Northern Cavern and Mine Research Society*, Vol.2 No.3 (September 1973), pp.119–122

LOCK, K. "Sale of Pennerley and Tankerville Mines 1902" *Shropshire Mining Club Journal*, (1972–3), pp.17–21

MIDDLETON, Terry "Caves and Mines of Hawkstone Park, Salop" *Cave Science*, Vol.14 No.3 (December 1987), pp.125–130

MORTON, John & ROBEY, John A. "Jacob Momma and the Ecton Copper Mines" *Bulletin of the Peak District Mines Historical Society*, Vol.9 No.3 (Summer 1985), pp.195–196

OSBORNE, G.V. "Rorrington Lead Mine, Shropshire" *British Caver*, Vol.39 (1964), pp.19–20

PEDRICK, P.D. & CHAPMAN, G.J. "A Preliminary Survey of the Bincliff Lead Mines, Wetton, Staffordshire" *Bulletin of the Peak District Mines Historical Society*, Vol.5 No.5 (April 1974), pp.258–270

PORTER, Lindsey "Ecton Hill: A Study of the Surface Features" *Bulletin of the Peak District Mines Historical Society*, Vol.4 No.2 (November 1969), pp.156–170

PORTER, Lindsey "Ecton Hill. Part II: Underground" *Bulletin of the Peak District Mines Historical Society*, Vol.4 No.3 (May 1970), pp.195–216

PORTER, Lindsey "Richard Niness, Mineral Agent of Warslow in Staffordshire" *Bulletin of the Peak District Mines Historical Society*, Vol.4 No.5 (June 1971), pp.362–369

PORTER, Lindsey & ROBEY, John A. "The Royledge and New York Copper Mines, Upper Elkstones, near Leek, Staffordshire" *Bulletin of the Peak District Mines Historical Society*, Vol.5 No.1 (April 1972), pp.1–9

PORTER, Lindsey & ROBEY, John A. "The Metalliferous Mines of the Weaver Hills, Staffordshire" *Bulletin of the Peak District Mines Historical Society*, Vol.5 No.1 (April 1972), pp.14–30

PORTER, Lindsey & ROBEY, John A. "The Dale Mine, Manifold Valley, North Staffordshire. Part 1" *Bulletin of the Peak District Mines Historical Society*, Vol.5 No.2 (October 1972), pp.93–106

PORTER, Lindsey & ROBEY, John A. "The Dale Mine, Manifold Valley, North Staffordshire. Part II" *Bulletin of the Peak District Mines Historical Society*, Vol.5 No.3 (May 1973), pp.161–173

PORTER, Lindsey & ROBEY, John A. "A History of the Bincliff Lead Mines, Wetton" *Bulletin of the Peak District Mines Historical Society*, Vol.5 No.5 (April 1974), pp.271–278

PORTER, Lindsey & ROBEY, John A. "The Dale Mine, Manifold Valley, North Staffordshire. Part III" *Bulletin of the Peak District Mines Historical Society*, Vol.5 No.5 (April 1974), pp.279–287

PORTER, Lindsey *See* ROBEY, John A. & PORTER, Lindsey

PRESERVATION SECRETARY "Preservation Work at the Ecton Mines, Staffordshire" *Bulletin of the Peak District Mines Historical Society*, Vol.1 No.3 (October 1960), p.2

PRICE, G.L.A. "Mineral Working in the Clee Hills" *Shropshire Mining Club Journal*, (1974–5), pp.18–29

PRICE, G.L.A. "The Boat Level Sough" *Shropshire Mining Club Journal*, (1978), pp.27–31

RIEUWERTS, James H. "Ecton Mines and Some Problems of Preservation" *Bulletin of the Peak District Mines Historical Society*, Vol.1 No.2 (May 1960), pp.20–21

ROBEY, John A. "The Ecton Copper Mines in the Seventeenth Century" *Bulletin of the Peak District Mines Historical Society*, Vol.4 No.2 (November 1969), pp.145–155

ROBEY, John A. "Two Lead Smelting Mills in North Staffordshire" *Bulletin of the Peak District Mines Historical Society*, Vol.4 No.3 (May 1970), pp.217–221

ROBEY, John A "The Burgoyne Mine at Ecton in the Seventeenth Century" *Bulletin of the Peak District Mines Historical Society*, Vol.6 No.2 (October 1975), pp.71–72

ROBEY, John A. & PORTER, Lindsey "The Copper and Lead Mines of the Mixon Area, Staffordshire" *Bulletin of the Peak District Mines Historical Society*, Vol.4 No.4 (October 1970), pp.256–280

ROBEY, John A. & PORTER, Lindsey "The Metalliferous Mines of the Weaver Hills, Staffordshire" *Bulletin of the Peak District Mines Historical Society*, Vol.4 No.6 (December 1971), pp.417–428

ROBEY, John A. *See* MORTON, John & ROBEY, John A.

ROBEY, John A. *See* PORTER, Lindsey & ROBEY, John A.

SARJEANT, William A.S. "Pyromorphite from the Mines of West Shropshire" *Bulletin of the Peak District Mines Historical Society*, Vol.3 No.3 (May 1967), pp.175–178

TRINDER, Barry "The Lead Smelters of the Ironbridge Gorge" *Shropshire Mining Club Journal*, (1979), pp.31–33

WARRINGTON, G. "Non–Ferrous Mining in North Shropshire and Cheshire" *Shropshire Mining Club Journal*, (1979), pp.9–20

WARRINGTON, G. "The Copper Mine at Alderly Edge" *Journal of the Chester Archaeology Society*, Vol.64 (1981), pp.47–73

WILSON, P.J. *See* CRITCHLEY, Martin F. & WILSON, P.J.

CORNWALL, DEVON AND SOMERSET

Books

ANON *Harvey's Hayle Foundry Catalogue* (Truro: Bradford Barton, Not Dated. Reprint of 1884 Edition.)

ANON *Williams' Perran Foundry Catalogue* (Truro: Bradford Barton, Not Dated. Reprint Edition.)

ANON *Tin and Copper Mines of Horrabridge (Horrabridge and District Part 2)* (Horrabridge: Private Publication, 1980)

ATKINSON, Michael, BURT, Roger & WAITE, Peter *Dartmoor Mines: The Mines of the Granite Mass* (Exeter: Department of Economic History, University of Exeter, 1978)

ATKINSON, Michael, BURT, Roger & WAITE, Peter *Dartmoor Mines: The Mines of the Granite Mass* (Exeter: Department of Economic History, University of Exeter, 1983. Reprint of 1978 Edition.)

ATKINSON, R.L. *Tin and Tin Mining* (Princes Risborough: Shire Books, 1985)

ATTHILL, R. *Old Mendip* (Newton Abbot: David & Charles, 1971)

BARTLETT, Steve "400 Mining Men of Liskeard" (Nantwich: Private Publication, 1987)

BARTON, Denys B. *The Redruth and Chasewater Railway 1824–1915* (Truro: Bradford Barton, 1960)

BARTON, Denys B. *A History of Copper Mining in Cornwall and Devon* (Truro: Truro Bookshop, 1961)

BARTON, Denys B. *A Guide to the Mines of West Cornwall* (Truro: Bradford Barton, 1963)

BARTON, Denys B. *A Historical Survey of the Mines and Mineral Railways of East Cornwall and West Devon* (Truro: Bradford Barton, 1964)

BARTON, Denys B. *The Cornish Beam Engine: A Survey of its History and Development in the Mines of Cornwall and Devon from before 1800 to the Present Day, with Something of its use Elsewhere in Britain and Abroad* (Truro: Bradford Barton, 1965)

BARTON, Denys B. *A Guide to the Mines of West Cornwall* (Truro: Bradford Barton, 1965. Second Edition)

BARTON, Denys B. *The Cornish Beam Engine: A Survey of its History and Development in the Mines of Cornwall and Devon fron before 1800 to the Present Day, with Something of its use Elsewhere in Britain and Abroad* (Truro: Bradford Barton, 1966. Second Edition)

BARTON, Denys B. *The Redruth and Chasewater Railway 1824–1915: A History of the Cornish Mineral Railway and Port which Served the Great Gwennap Copper Mines* (Truro: Bradford Barton, 1966. Revised Edition.)

BARTON, Denys B. (Ed.) *Historic Cornish Mining Scenes Underground* (Truro: Truro Bookshop, 1967)

BARTON, Denys B. *A History of Tin Mining and Smelting in Cornwall* (Truro: Bradford Barton, 1967)

BARTON, Denys B. *Essays in Cornish Mining History* Volume 1 (Truro: Bradford Barton, 1968)

BARTON, Denys B. *A History of Copper Mining in Cornwall and Devon* (Truro: Bradford Barton, 1968. Second Edition)

BARTON, Denys B. *Essays in Cornish Mining History* Volume 2 (Truro: Bradford Barton, 1971)

BARTON, Denys B. *A Historical Survey of the Mines and Mineral Railways of East Cornwall and West Devon* (Truro: Bradford Barton, 1971. Reprint of 1964 Edition.)

BARTON, Denys B. *A History of Copper Mining in Cornwall and Devon* (Truro: Bradford Barton, 1978. Third Edition)

BARTON, Denys B. *The Redruth and Chasewater Railway 1824–1915: A History of the Cornish Mineral Railway and Port which Served the Great Gwennap Copper Mines* (Truro: Bradford Barton, 1978. Reprint of 1966 Edition.)

BARTON, Denys B. *Historic Cornish Mining Scenes Underground* (Truro: Bradford Barton, 1980. Second Edition)

BARTON, R.M. *Introduction to the Geology of Cornwall* (Truro: Bradford Barton, 1964)

BOOKER, Frank *The Industrial Archaeology of the Tamar Valley* (Newton Abbot: David & Charles, 1967)

BOOKER, Frank *The Industrial Archaeology of the Tamar Valley* (Newton Abbot: David & Charles, 1971. Second Edition)

BROOKE, Justin *Stannary Tales: The Shady Side of Mining* (Twelveheads: Twelveheads Press, 1980)

BUCKLEY, J.A. *A History of South Crofty Mine* (Redruth: Dyllansow Truran, 1981)

BURNLEY, Raymond *See* BURT, Roger, WAITE, Peter & BURNLEY, Raymond

BURROW, J.C. & THOMAS, W. *'Mongst Mines and Miners: Being Underground Scenes by Flashlight Illustrating and Explaining the Methods of Working in the Cornish Mines About 1895* (Truro: Bradford Barton, 1965. Reprint of 1893 Edition.)

BURT, Roger (Ed.) *Cornish Mining: Essays on the Organisation of Cornish Mines and the Cornish Mining Economy* (Newton Abbot: David & Charles, 1969)

BURT, Roger (Ed.) *Industry and Society in the South West* (Exeter: University of Exeter, 1970)

BURT, Roger (Ed.) *Cornwall's Mines and Miners: Nineteenth Century Studies by George Henwood* (Truro: Bradford Barton, 1972)

BURT, Roger *John Taylor, Mining Entrepreneur and Engineer 1779–1863* (Buxton: Moorland, 1977)

BURT, Roger, WAITE, Peter & BURNLEY, Raymond *Devon and Somerset Mines* (Exeter: University of Exeter, 1984)

BURT, Roger, WAITE, Peter & BURNLEY, Raymond *Cornish Mines* (Exeter: University of Exeter, 1987)

BURT, Roger *See* ATKINSON, Michael, BURT, Roger & WAITE, Peter

CAUNTER, F.Lyde *Under the Surface* (St.Austell: H.E.Warne, 1957)

CAWTHORNE, Robert (Ed.) *All that Remains: A Survey of the Mines in the Kithill and Callington Areas, a Century After the Heyday of the Mining Industry in Devon and Cornwall* (Plymouth: Plymouth Caving Group, Not Dated)

CHESHER, Veronica *Industrial Housing in the Tin and Copper Mining Areas of Cornwall* (Cornwall: Trevithick Society, 1981)

CLARKE, A.G. *See* STANTON, W.I. & CLARKE, A.G.

COLLINS, John H. *A Handbook to the Mineralogy of Cornwall and Devon* (Truro: Bradford Barton, 1969. Reprint of 1892 Edition.)

COLLINS, John H. *Principles of Metal Mining* (Sheffield: Mining Facsimiles, 1985. Reprint of 1875 Edition.)

CORNISH CHAMBER OF MINES *Mining in Cornwall Today* (Truro: Cornish Chamber of Mines, 1974)

CORNISH MINING DEVELOPMENT ASSOCIATION *Mineral Areas in Cornwall Worthy of Investigation* (Cornwall: Cornish Mining Development Association, Third Issue, 1950)

CORNISH MINING DEVELOPMENT ASSOCIATION *Mineral Areas in Cornwall Worthy of Investigation* (Cornwall: Cornish Mining Development Association, Fifth Edition, 1960)

CROWLEY, T.E. *The Beam Engine: A Massive Chapter in the History of Steam* (Oxford: Senecio, 1982)

DAY, Joan *Bristol Brass: The History of the Industry* (Newton Abbot, David & Charles, 1973)

DEWEY, H. *British Regional Geology. South West England* (Geological Survey and Museum, H.M.S.O., 1948. Second Edition)

DEWEY, H. *Special Reports on the Mineral Resources of G.B. Vol.15: Arsenic and Antimony Ores* (Sheffield: Mining Facsimiles, 1986. Reprint of Geological Survey 1920 Edition.)

DEWEY, H. *Special Reports on the Mineral Resources of G.B. Vol.21: Lead, Silver–Lead and Zinc Ores of Cornwall, Devon and Somerset* (Sheffield: Mining Facsimiles, 1986. Reprint of Geological Survey 1921 Edition.)

DEWEY, H. *Special Reports on the Mineral Resources of G.B. Vol.27: Copper Ores of Cornwall and Devon* (Sheffield: Mining Facsimiles, 1986. Reprint of Geological Survey 1923 Edition.)

DICKASON, Graham B. *Cornish Immigrants to South Africa: The Cousin Jacks' Contribution to the Development of Mining and Commerce, 1820–1920* (Cape Town: A.A. Balkema, 1978)

DINES, Henry G. *The Metalliferous Mining Region of South West England* 2 Volumes (H.M.S.O., 1956)

DINES, Henry G. *The Metalliferous Mining Region of South West England* 2 Volumes (H.M.S.O., 1969. Second Edition)

DISUSED MINE SHAFT WORKING PARTY *Report of the Disused Mine Shaft Working Party* (Local Authorities Association Joint Minerals and Reclamation Group, 1984)

DOUCH, H.L. *East Wheal Rose: The History of Cornwall's Greatest Lead Mine* (Truro: Bradford Barton, 1964)

DOUCH, H.L. *East Wheal Rose: The History of Cornwall's Greatest Lead Mine* (Truro: Bradford Barton, 1979. Second Printing)

EARL, Bryan *Cornish Mining: The Techniques of Metal Mining in the West of England, Past and Present* (Truro: Bradford Barton, 1968)

EARL, Bryan *Cornish Explosives* (Cornwall: Trevithick Society, 1978)

EDMONDS, E.A., McKEOWN, M.C. & WILLIAMS, M. *British Regional Geology. South West England* (Institute of Geological Sciences, H.M.S.O. 1969. Third Edition.)

EDMONDS, E.A., McKEOWN, M.C. & WILLIAMS, M. *British Regional Geology. South West England* (Institute of Geological Sciences, H.M.S.O., 1975. Fourth Edition)

EDMONDS, E.A., McKEOWN, M.C. & WILLIAMS, M. *British Regional Geology. South West England* (British Geological Survey, H.M.S.O., 1985. Reprint of 1975 Edition)

FAIRCLOUGH, Tony & SHEPHERD, Eric *Mineral Railways of the West Country* (Truro: Bradford Barton, 1975)

GOUGH, John W. *The Mines of Mendip* (Newton Abbot: David & Charles, 1967. Second Edition)

GREEVES, T.A.P. *Tin Mines and Miners of Dartmoor: A Photographic Record* (Exeter: Devon Books, 1986)

HADFIELD, Charles *The Canals of South West England* (Newton Abbot: David & Charles, 1967)

HAMILTON, John & LAWRENCE, J.F. *Men and Mining in the Quantocks* (Bracknell: Town & Country Press, 1970)

HARRIS, Helen *The Industrial Archaeology of Dartmoor* (Newton Abbot: David and Charles, 1968)

HARRIS, Helen *The Industrial Archaeology of Dartmoor* (Newton Abbot: David & Charles, 1986. Second Edition)

HARRIS, John *Songs from the Earth: Selected Poems of John Harris, Cornish Miner 1820-84* (Padstow: Lodenek Press, 1977)

HARRIS, Thomas R. *Methodism and the Cornish Miner* (Cornwall: Cornish Methodist Historical Association, 1960)

HARRIS, Thomas R. *Arthur Woolf: the Cornish Engineer, 1766-1837* (Truro: Bradford Barton, 1966)

HARRIS, Thomas R. *Dolcoath: Queen of Cornish Mines* (Cornwall: Trevithick Society, 1974)

HATCHER, John *English Tin Production and Trade Before 1550* (Oxford: Clarendon Press, 1973)

HEFFER, Phillip *East Pool and Agar: A Cornish Mining Legend* (Redruth: Dyllansow Truran, 1985)

HEMMERY, Eric *Walking the Dartmoor Waterways: A Guide to Retracing the Leats and Canals of the Dartmoor Country* (Newton Abbot: David & Charles, 1986)

HENWOOD, George (Edited by Roger Burt) *Cornwall's Mines and Miners* (Truro: Bradford Barton, 1972)

JAMES, C.C. *A History of the Parish of Gwennap in Cornwall* (Wyman & Sons, 1963)

JENKIN, A.K.Hamilton *The Cornish Miner: An Account of His Life Above and Underground from Early Times* (Allen & Unwin, 1948. Second Edition)

JENKIN, A.K.Hamilton *The Cornish Miner: An Account of His Life Above and Underground from Early Times* (Allen & Unwin, 1962. Third Edition)

JENKIN, A.K.Hamilton *Mines and Miners of Cornwall: I. Around St. Ives* (Truro: Truro Bookshop, 1961)

JENKIN, A.K.Hamilton *Mines and Miners of Cornwall: II. St. Agnes-Perranporth* (Truro: Truro Bookshop, 1962)

JENKIN, A.K.Hamilton *Mines and Miners of Cornwall: III. Around Redruth* (Truro: Truro Bookshop, 1962)

JENKIN, A.K.Hamilton *Mines and Miners of Cornwall: IV. Penzance-Mount's Bay* (Truro: Truro Bookshop, 1962)

JENKIN, A.K.Hamilton *The Story of Cornwall* (Truro: Bradford Barton, 1962)

JENKIN, A.K.Hamilton *Mines and Miners of Cornwall: V. Hayle, Gwinear and Gwithian* (Truro: Truro Bookshop, 1963)

JENKIN, A.K.Hamilton *Mines and Miners of Cornwall: VI. Around Gwennap* (Truro: Truro Bookshop, 1963)

JENKIN, A.K.Hamilton *Mines and Miners of Cornwall: VII. Perranporth-Newquay* (Truro: Truro Bookshop, 1963)

JENKIN, A.K.Hamilton *Mines and Miners of Cornwall: VIII. Truro to the Clay District* (Truro: Truro Bookshop, 1964)

JENKIN, A.K.Hamilton *Mines and Miners of Cornwall: IX. Padstow, St. Columb and Bodmin* (Truro: Truro Bookshop, 1964)

JENKIN, A.K.Hamilton *Mines and Miners of Cornwall: X. Camborne-Illogan* (Truro: Truro Bookshop, 1965)

JENKIN, A.K.Hamilton *Mines and Miners of Cornwall: XI. Marazion, St. Hilary and Breage* (Truro: Truro Bookshop, 1965)

JENKIN, A.K.Hamilton *Mines and Miners of Cornwall: XII. Around Liskeard* (Truro: Truro Bookshop, 1966)

JENKIN, A.K. Hamilton *Mines and Miners of Cornwall: XIII. The Lizard–Falmouth–Mevagissey* (Truro: Truro Bookshop, 1967)

JENKIN, A.K.Hamilton *Mines and Miners of Cornwall: XIV. St. Austell to Saltash* (Truro: Truro Bookshop, 1967)

JENKIN, A.K.Hamilton *Mines and Miners of Cornwall: XV. Calstock, Callington and Launceston* (Cornwall: Federation of Old Cornwall Societies, 1969)

JENKIN, A.K.Hamilton *Mines and Miners of Cornwall: XVI. Wadebridge, Camelford and Bude* (Cornwall: Federation of Old Cornwall Societies, 1970)

JENKIN, A.K.Hamilton *Cornwall and Its People* (Newton Abbot: David & Charles, 1970)

JENKIN, A.K.Hamilton *The Cornish Miner: An Account of His Life Above and Underground from Early Times* (Newton Abbot: David & Charles, 1972. Reprint of 3rd Edition.)

JENKIN, A.K.Hamilton *Mines of Devon Volume 1: The Southern Area* (Newton Abbot: David & Charles, 1974)

JENKIN, A.K.Hamilton *Mines and Miners of Cornwall: I. Around St. Ives* (Bracknell: Forge Books, 1978. Reprint of 1961 Edition.)

JENKIN, A.K.Hamilton *Mines and Miners of Cornwall: II. St. Agnes–Perranporth* (Bracknell: Forge Books, 1978. Reprint of 1962 Edition.)

JENKIN, A.K.Hamilton *Wendron Tin* (Helston: Wendron Forge Ltd., 1978)

JENKIN, A.K.Hamilton *Mines and Miners of Cornwall: Index to Volumes 1–16* (St. Austell: Old Cornwall Publications, 1979)

JENKIN, A.K.Hamilton *Mines and Miners of Cornwall: III. Around Redruth* (Bracknell: Forge Books, 1979. Reprint of 1962 Edition.)

JENKIN, A.K.Hamilton *Mines and Miners of Cornwall: IV. Penzance–Mount's Bay* (Bracknell: Forge Books, 1979. Reprint of 1962 Edition.)

JENKIN, A.K.Hamilton *Mines and Miners of Cornwall: V. Hayle, Gwinear and Gwithian* (Bracknell: Forge Books, 1980. Reprint of 1963 Edition.)

JENKIN, A.K.Hamilton *Mines and Miners of Cornwall: VI. Around Gwennap* (Bracknell: Forge Books, 1981. Reprint of 1963 Edition.)

JENKIN, A.K.Hamilton *Mines of Devon Volume 2: North and East of Dartmoor* (Exeter: Devon Library Services, 1981)

KEAST, John *The King of Mid-Cornwall: The Life of Joseph Thomas Treffry 1782-1850* (Redruth: Dyllansow Truran,1982)

KNEEBONE, Derek A. *Fish, Tin and Copper* (Redruth: Dyllansow Truran, 1983)

LAWRENCE, J.F. *See* HAMILTON, John & LAWRENCE, J.F.

LAWS, Peter *Cornish Engines and Engine Houses* (National Trust, 1984)

LAWS, Peter *See* TODD, Arthur C. & LAWS, Peter

LEAN, Thomas *On the Steam Engines in Cornwall* (Truro: Bradford Barton, 1969. Reprint of 1839 Edition.)

LEIFCHILD, J.R. *Cornwall: Its Mines and Miners* (Frank Cass, 1968. Reprint of 1857 Edition)

LEWIS, George R. *The Stannaries: A Study of the Medieval Tin Miners of Cornwall and Devon* (Truro: Bradford Barton, 1965. Reprint of 1908 Edition.)

MADGE, Mervyn *The Tamerton Treacle Mines and Other Tales of Cornwall and the West Country* (Plymouth: Private Publication, 1984)

MAXWELL, I.S. *Historical Atlas of West Penwith* (Sheffield: University of Sheffield, 1976)

McKEOWN, M.C. *See* EDMONDS, E.A., McKEOWN, M. & WILLIAMS, M.

MESSENGER, Michael J. *Caradon and Looe: The Canal, Railways and Mines* (Twelveheads: Twelveheads Press, 1978)

MICHELL, F.Bice *Michell: A Family of Cornish Engineers 1740-1910* (Cornwall: Trevithick Society, 1984)

MORRISON, T.A. *Cornwall's Central Mines: The Northern District 1810-1895* (Penzance: Alison Hodge, 1980)

MORRISON, T.A. *Cornwall's Central Mines: The Southern District 1810-1895* (Penzance: Alison Hodge, 1983)

NOALL, Cyril *Levant: The Mine Beneath the Sea* (Truro: Bradford Barton, 1970)

NOALL, Cyril *Botallack* (Truro: Bradford Barton, 1972)

NOALL, Cyril *The St. Just Mining District* (Truro: Bradford Barton, 1973)

NOALL, Cyril *The St. Ives Mining District* Volume 1 (Redruth: Dyllansow Truran, 1982)

NOALL, Cyril *Geevor* (Pendeen: Geevor Tin Mines, 1983)

ORDISH, H.G. *Cornish Engine Houses: A Pictorial Survey* (Truro: Bradford Barton, 1967)

ORDISH, H.G. *Cornish Engine Houses: A Second Pictorial Survey* (Truro: Bradford Barton, 1968)

ORWIN, C.S. & SELLICK, Roger J. *The Reclamation of Exmoor Forest* (Newton Abbot: David & Charles, 1970. Second Edition)

PALMER, Marilyn *The Basset Mines: Their History and Industrial Archaeology* (Sheffield: Northern Mines Research Society, British Mining No.32, 1987)

PASCOE, W.H. *C.C.C.: The History of the Cornish Copper Company* (Redruth: Dyllansow Truran, 1982)

PAYNTER, William H. *Our Old Cornish Mines: East Cornwall* (Liskeard: Snell & Cowling, 1964)

PAYTON, Philip J. *The Cornish Miner in Australia* (Redruth: Dyllansow Truran, 1984)

PEARCE, F. *St.Agnes: Portrait of a Cornish Village* (Falmouth: Bantam, 1977)

PENHALE, Jack *The Mine Under the Sea* (Falmouth: J.H.Lake, 1962)

PENHALLURICK, Roger David *Tin in Antiquity: Its Mining and Trade Throughout the Ancient World, With Particular Reference to Cornwall* (Institute of Metals, 1986)

PENNINGTON, Robert R. *Stannary Law: A History of the Mining Law of Cornwall and Devon* (Newton Abbot: David & Charles, 1973)

PIPER, Lawrence P.S. *A Short History of the Camborne School of Mines* (Cornwall: Trevithick Society, 1975)

POPPLEWELL, Lawrence *The Railways, Canal and Mines of Looe and Liskeard* (Tarrant Hinton: Oakwood Press, 1977)

PRYCE, William *Mineralogia Cornubiensis* (Truro: Bradford Barton, 1972. Reprint of 1778 Edition.)

ROBINS, John *Follow the Leat with John Robins: A Series of Walks Along Some Dartmoor Leats* (Tavistock: Private Publication, 1982)

ROBINS, John *Supplement to Follow the Leat with John Robins* (Tavistock: Private Publication, 1983)

ROBINS, John *Follow the Leat with John Robins: A Series of Walks Along Dartmoor Leats and a Description of the Mines Some of Them Served* (Tavistock: Private Publication, 1984)

ROBINSON, Mandie *Cap'n 'Ancock: Ruler of Australia's Little Cornwall* (Melborne: Rigby, 1978)

ROGERS, K.H. *The Newcomen Engine in the West of England* (Bradford-on-Avon: Moonraker Press, 1976)

ROWE, John *Cornwall in the Age of the Industrial Revolution* (Liverpool: Liverpool University Press, 1953)

ROWE, John *The Hard-Rock Men: Cornish Immigrants and the North American Frontier* (Liverpool: Liverpool University Press, 1974)

SCHMITZ, Christopher J. *The Teign Valley Lead Mines* (Sheffield: Northern Cavern and Mine Research Society, Individual Survey Series No.6, 1973)

SCHMITZ, Christopher J. *The Teign Valley Lead Mines, 1806–1880* (Sheffield: Northern Mine Research Society, British Mining No.15, 1980)

SELLICK, Roger J. *The West Somerset Mineral Railway and the Story of the Brendon Hills Iron Mines* (Dawlish: David & Charles, 1962)

SELLICK, Roger J. *The West Somerset Mineral Railway and the Story of the Brendon Hills Iron Mines* (Newton Abbot: David & Charles, 1970. Second Edition.)

SELLICK, Roger J. *The Old Mineral Line: An Illustrated Survey of the West Somerset Mineral Railway from Watchet to the Brendon Hills as it was and is Today* (Dulverton: Exmoor Press, 1976)

SELLICK, Roger J. *See* ORWIN, C.S. & SELLICK, Roger J.

SHAMBROOK, H.R. *The Caradon and Phoenix Mining Area* (Sheffield: Northern Mine Research Society, British Mining No.20, 1982)

SHEPHERD, Eric *See* FAIRCLOUGH, Tony & SHEPHERD, Eric

SIVEWRIGHT, W.J. *Civil Engineering Heritage. Wales and Western England* (Thomas Telford Ltd, 1986)

SLADER, J.M. *Days of Renown: The Story of Mining on Exmoor and the Border Parishes* (Bracknell: West Country Publications, 1965)

SOMERSET ARCHAEOLOGICAL & NATURAL HISTORY SOCIETY *Parish Surveys in Somerset* (Luxborough, 1983)

SPARGO, Thomas *The Mines of Cornwall: I. The Land's End Peninsula* (Truro: Bradford Barton, 1959. Reprint of 1865 Edition.)

SPARGO, Thomas *The Mines of Cornwall: II. The Camborne Area* (Truro: Bradford Barton, 1960. Reprint of 1865 Edition.)

SPARGO, Thomas *The Mines of Cornwall: III. The Mount's Bay Area* (Truro: Bradford Barton, 1960. Reprint of 1865 Edition.)

SPARGO, Thomas *The Mines of Cornwall: IV. The Redruth Area* (Truro: Bradford Barton, 1961. Reprint of 1865 Edition.)

SPARGO, Thomas *The Mines of Cornwall: V. Mid-Cornwall* (Truro: Bradford Barton, 1961. Reprint of 1865 Edition.)

SPARGO, Thomas *The Mines of Cornwall: VI. East Cornwall* (Truro: Bradford Barton, 1961. Reprint of 1865 Edition.)

STANTON, W.I. & CLARKE, A.G. *Cornish Miners at Charterhouse-on-Mendip* (Stockwood: A.G.Clarke, 1984. Reprinted from the Proceedings of the University of Bristol Spelaeological Society)

STUCKEY, Douglas *Adventurer's Slopes: The Story of the Silver and Other Mines of Combe Martin in Devon* (Bracknell: West Country Handbooks, 1965)

TANGYE, Michael *Portreath: Some Chapters on its History* (Redruth: John Olson, 1968)

TANGYE, Michael *Tehidy and the Bassets* (Redruth: Dyllansow Truran, 1984)

THOMAS, Charles *Mining Fields of the West: Being a Practical Exposition of the Principal Mining Districts in Cornwall and Devon* (Truro: Bradford Barton, 1967. Reprint of 1871 Edition)

THOMAS, D.M. *Songs from the Earth: Selected Poems of John Harris Cornish Miner, 1820–1884* (Padstow: Lodenek Press, 1977)

THOMAS, W. *See* BURROW, J.C. & THOMAS, W.

TODD, Arthur C. *The Cornish Miner in America: The Contribution to the Mining History of the United States by Emigrant Cornish Miners: the Men Called Cousin Jack* (Truro: Bradford Barton, 1967)

TODD, Arthur C. *The Search for Silver: Cornish Miners in Mexico, 1824–1947* (Padstow: Lodenek Press, 1977)

TODD, Arthur C. & LAWS, Peter *The Industrial Archaeology of Cornwall* (Newton Abbot: David & Charles, 1972)

TRIVETT, Robert *An Industry of the Past* (Plymouth: Plymouth College of Art and Design, 1981)

TROUNSON, John H. *Historic Cornish Mining Scenes at Surface* (Truro: Bradford Barton, 1968)

TROUNSON, John H. *Mining in Cornwall 1850–1960* Volume 1 (Ashbourne: Moorland, 1980)

TROUNSON, John H. *Mining in Cornwall 1850–1960* Volume 2 (Ashbourne: Moorland, 1981)

TROUNSON, John H. *Mining in Cornwall 1850–1960* Volume 1 (Redruth: Dyllansow Truran, 1985. New Edition)

TROUNSON, John H. *Mining in Cornwall* Vol.2 (Redruth: Dyllansow Truran, 198?)

VALE, E. *The Harvey's of Hayle* (Truro: Bradford Barton, 1966)

VIVIAN, John *Tales of the Cornish Miners* (Truro: Tor Mark Press, 1981)

WAITE, Peter *See* ATKINSON, Michael, BURT, Roger & WAITE, Peter

WAITE, Peter *See* BURT, Roger, WAITE, Peter & BURNLEY, Raymond

WALMSLEY, Jessica *See* WALMSLEY, Mary & WALMSLEY, Jessica

WALLMSLEY, Mary & WALMSLEY, Jessica *The Old Men of the Moor* (Ilfracombe: Arthur H. Stockwell, 1982)

WATSON, Joseph Y. *Cornish Mining Notes, 1861* (Truro: Truro Bookshop, 1961. Reprint of 1861 Edition.)

WATSON, Joseph Y. *A Compendium of British Mining* (Truro: Truro Bookshop, 1962. Reprint of 1843 Edition)

WILLIAMS, H.V. *Cornwalls Old Mines* (Truro: Tor Mark Press, 1969)

WILLIAMS, M. *See* EDMONDS, E.A., McKEOWN, M.C. & WILLIAMS, M.

Theses

ALLEN, G.C. *The History of an Eighteenth Century Combination in the Copper Mining Industry* (University of Birmingham MComm Thesis, 1922)

AVERY, M. *Some Aspects of the Iron Age in South West England* (University of Oxford BLitt Thesis, 1971–2)

BRAYSHAY, W.M. *The Demography of Three West Cornwall Mining Communities 1851–1871: A Society in Decline* (University of Exeter PhD Thesis, 1977)

BURKE, G.M. *The Cornish Miner and the Cornish Mining Industry, 1870–1921* (University of London, Birkbeck, PhD Thesis, 1982)

DIXON, David G. *Mining and the Community in the Parishes of North Molton, South Molton, Molland and Twitchen, Devonshire* (University of Southampton MA Thesis, 1983)

GOODRIDGE, J.C. *The Historical Geography of the Copper Mining Industry in Devon and Cornwall from 1800 to 1900* (University of London PhD Thesis, 1967)

GREAVES, T.A.P. *The Devon Tin Industry,1450–1750: An Archaeological and Historical Survey* (University of Exeter PhD Thesis, 1981)

HALDANE, J.W. *A Study of Iron Working from Pre–Roman Sites in the South West of England* (University of London MPhil Thesis, 1969/70)

HATCHER, M.J.J.R. *The Assessionable Manors of the Duchy of Cornwall in the Later Middle Ages* (University of London PhD. Thesis, 1967)

McGUINNESS, T.W. *Changes in the Population of West Cornwall with the Rise and Decline of Mining* (University of London Thesis, 1938)

McGUINNESS, T.W. *Population Changes in Cornwall in Relation to Economic Resources* (University of London PhD Thesis, 1944)

O'HEA, J.D. *Economy and Society in the Upper Teign Valley 1801–1851, with Special Reference to Bridford* (University of Exeter MA Thesis, 1981)

PATRICK, A *The Evolution of Morwellham: A Tamar River Port* (Council for National Academic Awards MPhil Thesis, 1980)

PIPER, L.P.S. *The Development of Technical Education in Cornwall from the Early Nineteenth Century until 1902* (University of Leicester MEd Thesis, 1977)

POUNDS, N.J.G. *The Historical Geography of Cornwall* (University of London PhD Thesis, 1945)

REED, R.G. *Cornwall in the Neolithic and Bronze Age Period* (University of London PhD Thesis, 1970/71)

ROTTENBURY, F.John *Geology, Mineralogy and Mining History of the Metalliferous Mining Areas of Exmoor* (University of Leeds PhD Thesis, 1974)

ROWLANDS, M.J.J. *A Study of the Bronze Working Industries of the Middle Bronze Age in Southern Britain* (University of London Thesis, 1970/1)

RULE, John *The Labouring Miner in Cornwall c.1740–1870: A Study in Social History* (University of Warwick PhD Thesis, 1971)

TRETHOWAN, D.M. *The Rise and Decline of Porthleven Harbour, 1810–1960* (University of Exeter M.A. Thesis, 1972)

Articles

ALABASTER, C. "The Minerals of Mendip" *Somerset Mines Research Group Journal*, Vol.1 No.4 (July 1982), pp.1–52

AMHOF, Graham "Branch Channels of the Wheal Jewell Leat" *Dartmoor Magazine*, No.9 (Winter 1987), pp.14–15

ANDREW, C.K.Croft "The Cornish Miners (Militia Corps), 1796" *Devon and Cornwall Notes and Queries*, Vol.25 Pt.1 (January 1952), pp.18–19

ANDREW, C.K.Croft "Cornish Miner's Petition to Queen Victoria 1842" *Devon and Cornwall Notes and Queries*, Vol.26 Pt.2 (April 1954), pp.58–61

ANON "Tin and Copper" *Mining Magazine*, Vol.LXXIII No.1 (July 1945), pp.3–4

ANON "A Cornish Experimental Mine (Holman's)" *Mine and Quarry Engineering*, Vol.22 (December 1956), pp.513–515

ANON "Atlantic Plug (Levant)" *Mine and Quarry Engineering*, Vol.27 (February 1961), p.541

ANON "Reopening a Mine (Carnello)" *Mine and Quarry Engineering*, Vol.27 (February 1961), pp.62–63

ANON "Hydraulic Tin, Bissoe" *Mine and Quarry Engineering*, Vol.28 (January 1962), pp.2–9

ANON "Providence Mine, St.Just, Cornwall" *British Caver*, Vol.39 (1964), pp.59–62

ANON "Wheal Owles and Boscean United Mining Co.Ltd, St.Just, Penzance" *Memoirs of the Northern Cavern and Mine Research Society*, (August 1965), pp.39–40

ANON "Lamb Leer" *Mendip Nature Research Committee Journal*, Vol.2 (November 1965), pp.1–58

ANON "Lead Mining on Mendip" *British Caver*, Vol.49 (1968), pp.20–22

ANON "Avonmouth Zinc Smelting" *Mining Magazine*, (August 1975), pp.79–87

ANON "Cornwall's Latest Tin Mine (Mount Wellington)" *Mine and Quarry*, Vol.4 No.9 (September 1975), pp.18–26

ANON "Winning and Concentrating at Mount Wellington" *Mine and Quarry*, Vol.4 No.10 (October 1975), pp.48–53

ANON "Copper Ore Statistics: Public Ticketings, Cornwall 1814–1856; Public Ticketings, Swansea 1819–1856" *British Mining*, No.8 (1978), pp.40–42

ANON "Caradon Copper Mines" *Tamar Journal*, No.1 (1978), pp.23–26

ANON "West Devon Mine Re–Opens after 100 years" *Mine and Quarry*, Vol.8 No.5 (May 1979), p.49

ANON "Wheal Jane Tin Mine Moving Towards Production Again" *Mining Magazine*, (July 1980), pp.5–7

ANON "New Mineral Processing Equipment Improves Tin Plant Performance in Cornwall" *Mining Magazine*, (July 1981), pp.28–29

ANON "Developments in Mineral Processing in the Cornish Tin Industry" *Camborne School of Mines Journal*, (1984), pp.50–55

ANON "Carclaise Tin Mine" *Bulletin of the Association of Industrial Archaeology*, Vol.12 No.4 (1985), pp.4–5

ANON "What Future for Cornish Tin. Part 1" *Mine and Quarry*, Vol.16 No.1 (January/February 1987), pp.7–13

ANON "What Future for Cornish Tin. Part 2" *Mine and Quarry*, Vol.16 No.3 (March 1987), pp.19–21

ANON "Index to the Plymouth Caving Group Journal and Newsletters. Vol.1–100" *Plymouth Caving Club Journal and Newsletter*, No.101 (September 1987), pp.6–21

ASHWORTH, H.W.W. *See* PALMER, L.S. & ASHWORTH, H.W.W.

ATKINSON, Barry "The North Cliff Mines: Chapelporth to Hayle" *Plymouth Mineral and Mining Club Journal*, Vol.12 No.1 (May 1981), pp.4–5,14

ATKINSON, Barry "The Mines of Perranporth: A Recent Survey" *Plymouth Mineral and Mining Club Journal*, Vol.12 No.3 (February 1982), pp.3–4,8

ATKINSON, Barry "A Survey of the Lesser Known Mining Sites of Cornwall. List 1: The Liskeard Area" *Plymouth Mineral and Mining Club Journal*, Vol.13 No.3 (February 1983), pp.14–15

ATKINSON, Barry "A Survey of the Lesser Known Mining Sites of Cornwall. List 2: Calstock, Callington and Launceston" *Plymouth Mineral and Mining Club Journal*, Vol.14 No.1 (May 1983), p.17

ATKINSON, Barry "A Survey of the Lesser Known Mining Sites of Cornwall. List 3: St. Austell to Saltash" *Plymouth Mineral and Mining Club Journal*, Vol.14 No.2 (October 1983), p.13

ATKINSON, Barry "Portreath's Lost Mines" *Plymouth Mineral and Mining Club Journal*, Vol.14 No.3 (March 1984), pp.8–9

ATKINSON, Barry "A Survey of the Lesser Known Mining Sites of Cornwall. List 4: Around St. Ives" *Plymouth Mineral and Mining Club Journal*, Vol.14 No.3 (March 1984), p.16

ATKINSON, Barry "Industrial Archaeology: Portheras Cove to Letcha Cliff" *Plymouth Mineral and Mining Club Journal*, Vol.15 No.1 (August 1984), pp.3–5

ATKINSON, Barry "A Survey of the Lesser Known Mining Sites of Cornwall. List 5: St.Agnes to Perranporth" *Plymouth Mineral and Mining Club Journal*, Vol.15 No.1 (August 1984), p.9

ATKINSON, Barry "A Survey of the Lesser Known Mining Sites of Cornwall. List 6: Wendron to the Porkellis Area" *Plymouth Mineral and Mining Club Journal*, Vol.15 No.3 (May 1985), p.11

ATKINSON, Barry "A Survey of the Lesser Known Mining Sites of Cornwall. List 7: Newquay to Perranporth" *Plymouth Mineral and Mining Club Journal*, Vol.16 No.1 (August 1985), p.10

ATKINSON, Barry "South of Tavistock: The Mines of the Bere Alston Peninsula, the Tavy and the Walkham Valleys" *Plymouth Mineral and Mining Club Journal*, Vol.16 No.2 (February 1986), pp.3–6

ATKINSON, Barry "A Survey of the Lesser Known Mining Sites of Cornwall. List 8: The Lizard–Falmouth–Mevagissey" *Plymouth Mineral and Mining Club Journal*, Vol.16 No.2 (February 1986), p.12

ATKINSON, Barry "A Survey of the Lesser Known Mining Sites of Cornwall. List 9: Padstow–St.Columb and Bodmin" *Plymouth Mineral and Mining Club Journal*, Vol.16 No.3 (August 1986), p.11

ATKINSON, Barry "A Survey of the Lesser Known Mining Sites of Cornwall. List 10: Hayle, Gwinear–Gwithian" *Plymouth Mineral and Mining Club Journal*, Vol.17 No.1 (December 1986), p.7

ATKINSON, Barry "A Survey of the Lesser Known Mining Sites of Cornwall. List 11: Penzance to Mounts Bay" *Plymouth Mineral and Mining Club Journal*, Vol.17 No.2 (April 1987), p.5

ATKINSON, Barry "A Survey of the Lesser Known Mining Sites of Cornwall. List 12: Around Gwennap" *Plymouth Mineral and Mining Club Journal*, Vol.18 No.1 (February 1988), p.9

ATKINSON, Barry *See* McKENNA, Neil & ATKINSON, Barry

ATKINSON, C. "The Excelsior Tunnel" *Old Cornwall*, Vol.9 No.5 (Autumn 1981), pp.246–247

ATKINSON, Michael & BURT, Roger "Mining in the Duchy of Cornwall" in C.Gill(Ed), *The Duchy of Cornwall* (Newton Abbot; David & Charles, 1987)

ATKINSON, Michael & SCHMITZ, Christopher "Kelly Iron Mine, near Bovey Tracey" *Devon Historian*, No.11 (October 1975), pp.27–34

ATKINSON, Michael, WAITE, Peter & BURT, Roger "The Iron Mining Industry in Devon" *British Mining*, No.19 (1982), pp.27–33

BAINBRIDGE, B.C.L. "The Tin Streaming Industry in Cornwall: A Survey" *Cornish Archaeology*, No.7 (1968), pp.61–62

BAINSMITH, B.F. "The Fuggan Pit at Little Wheal Speed" *Old Cornwall*, Vol.5 (1951–1961), pp.463–464

BAKER, Owen A. "Notes on the Tamar Valley Arsenic Industry" *Plymouth Mineral and Mining Club Newsletter*, Vol.2 No.2 (August 1971), pp.12–13

BAKER, Owen A. "Old Gunnislake: Tribute to a Classic Locality" *Plymouth Mineral and Mining Club Newsletter*, Vol.2 No.3 (December 1971), pp.14–15

BAKER, Owen A. "Mining at Tamerton" *Plymouth Mineral and Mining Club Journal*, Vol.4 No.3 (January 1974), pp.16–18

BAKER, W.G. "Stannary Parliament" *Plymouth Mineral and Mining Club Journal*, Vol.7 No.2 (Autumn 1976), pp.3–5

BAYLES, Russell "Great Devon Consols" *Transactions of the Northern Cavern and Mine Research Society*, Vol.1 No.1 (June 1961), pp.4–6

BAYLES, Russell "The Cornish Beam Pumping Engine at the Dorothea Slate Quarry" *Memoirs of the Northern Cavern and Mine Research Society*, Vol.2 No.1 (April 1971) pp.19–20

BEAGRIE, Neil "The St.Mawes Ingot" *Cornish Archaeology*, No.22 (1983), pp.107–111

BEAUMONT, J. "The Discovery of Lamb Leer in 1681" *British Caver*, Vol.16 (1947), pp.59–60

BEER, K.E. "Mineralisation in the Teign Valley" *Transactions of the Devonshire Association*, Vol.110 (1978), pp.77–80

BICK, David E. "Cornish Engine Houses at Welsh Metal Mines" *Industrial Archaeology*, Vol.5 No.3 (1968), pp.262–265

BICK, David E. "North Devon and Exmoor" *Plymouth Mineral and Mining Club Journal*, Vol.3 No.2 (August 1972), pp.3–4

BIRD, Richard H. "The Mineral Fields of Derbyshire and Cornwall: A Brief Comparison" *Bulletin of the Peak District Mines Historical Society*, Vol.4 No.4 (October 1970), pp.312–323

BIZLEY, Alice C. "New Chiverton Mine in the Parish of Perranzabuloe" *Old Cornwall*, Vol.9 No.9 (Autumn 1983), pp.424–426

BLUNDEN, J.R. "The Redevelopment of the Cornish Tin Mining Industry" in Gregory, K.T. & Ravenhill, W.L.D., *Exeter Essays in Honour of Arthur Davies* (Exeter: University of Exeter, 1971) pp.169–184

BLUNDEN, J.R. "The Renaissance of the Cornish Tin Industry" *Geography*, Vol.55 (1970), pp.331–335

BOOKER, Frank "The Tamar Valley" *Industrial Archaeology*, Vol.4 No.1 (1967), pp.1–7

BOOKER, Frank "More about Drakewalls" *Tamar Journal*, No.5 (1983), pp.13–17

BRAYSHAY, Mark "The Duke of Bedford's Model Cottages in Tavistock, 1840–1870" *Transactions of the Devonshire Association*, Vol.114 (1982), pp.115–131

BREWER, David "An Investigation into the Holne Moor Leat and My Conclusions" *Dartmoor Magazine*, No.4 (Autumn 1986), pp.11–13

BREWER, David "More on the Holne Town Leat" *Dartmoor Magazine*, No.7 (Summer 1987), pp.24–25

BREWER, David "A Leat from the Avon" *Dartmoor Magazine* No.10 (Spring 1988), pp.7–10

BROOKE, Justin "New Light on Devon Great Consols" *Devon and Cornwall Notes and Queries*, Vol.30 Pt.7 (July 1966), pp.183–184

BROOKE, Justin "The Lighter Side of Mining" *Devon and Cornwall Notes and Queries*, Vol.31 Pt.1 (January 1968), pp.19–22

BROOKE, Justin "Historical Notes on Wheal Jane" *Memoirs of the Northern Cavern and Mine Research Society*, Vol.2 No.3 (September 1973), pp.161–162

BROOKE, Justin "Brixham Iron Mines" *Devon and Cornwall Notes and Queries*, Vol.33 Pt.5 (Autumn 1975), p.180

BROOKE, Justin "South Devon Iron Mines" *Plymouth Mineral and Mining Club Journal*, Vol.6 No.3 (January 1976), pp.7–8

BROOKE, Justin "Wheal Buller" *Journal of the Trevithick Society*, No.4 (1976), pp.65–72

BROOKE, Justin "The Gold Mines of Devon" *Plymouth Mineral and Mining Club Journal*, Vol.7 No.3 (January 1977), pp.5–7

BROOKE, Justin "Two Cornish Companies" *Devon and Cornwall Notes and Queries*, Vol.33 Pt.8 (Spring 1977), p.313

BROOKE, Justin "Miners' Songs" *Devon and Cornwall Notes and Queries*, Vol.33 Pt.8 (Spring 1977), p.313

BROOKE, Justin "The Gold Mines of Devon" *Plymouth Mineral and Mining Club Journal*, Vol.8 No.1 (Spring 1977), pp.3–5

BROOKE, Justin "The Gold Mines of Devon" *Plymouth Mineral and Mining Club Journal*, Vol.8 No.2 (Autumn 1977), pp.3–4

BROOKE, Justin "Who Discovered Devon Great Consols" *British Mining*, No.5 (1977), pp.21–22

BROOKE, Justin "Stannary Tales" *British Mining*, No.8 (1978), pp.16–21

BROOKE, Justin "Frank Mills" *Plymouth Mineral and Mining Club Journal*, Vol.11 No.1 (May 1980), pp.11–13,16

BROOKE, Justin "Elborough Mine" *Somerset Mines Research Group Journal*, Vol.1 No.1 (December 1980), pp.2–3

BROOKE, Justin "The Last Years of Devon Great Consols" *Journal of the Trevithick Society*, No.9 (1982), pp.69–72

BROOKE, Justin "Cornwall Sites of Interest Old and New, 1981" *British Mining*, No.19 (1982), pp.55–57

BROOKE, Justin "Devon United Mines" *Plymouth Mineral and Mining Club Journal*, Vol.15 No.3 (May 1985), p.12

BROOKE, Justin "Wheal Zion" *Tamar Journal*, No.8 (1986), pp.15–20

BROOKE, Justin "Wheal Vor and the Gundry Bankruptcies" *Journal of the Trevithick Society*, No.14 (1987), pp.67–82

BROOKS, A.W. "King Edward Mine, West Cornwall 1897–1921" *Camborne School of Mines Journal* (1986), pp.57–68

BROUGHTON, D.G. "Tin Working in the Eastern District of the Parish of Chagford, Devon" *Proceedings of the Geologists Association*, Vol.78 (1967), pp.447–462

BROUGHTON, D.G. "Dartmoor Tin Working: Its Effect upon Scenery and Land Use" *The Kingston Geographer*, Vol.1 No.1 (October 1968), pp.31–39

BROUGHTON, D.G. "The Birch Tor and Vitifer Tin Mining Complex" *Transactions of the Cornish Institute of Engineers*, Vol.XXIV (1968–69), pp.25–49

BROWN, Kenneth "The Incredible Ookiep Copper Mine: Its Riches, its Railways and its Cornish Engines" *Journal of the Trevithick Society*, No.11 (1984), pp.41–59

BROWN, L.G. "Fifty Years of Cornish Mining" *Transactions of the Cornish Institute of Engineers*, Vol.XVIII (1962–3), pp.17–28

BROWN, P.D.C. "A Roman Pewter Mould from St. Just in Penwith" *Cornish Archaeology*, No.9 (1970), pp.107–110

BUCKLEY, J.Allen "History of South Crofty Mine" Pts 1–8 *Wheals Magazine* Nos.2–9 (May 1979–May 1981)

BUCKLEY, J.Allen "Upheavals among Tudor Tinners" *Wheals Magazine*, No.11 (December 1981)

BUCKLEY, J.Allen "The Introduction of Blasting into Cornish Mines" *Wheals Magazine*, No.12 (December 1982)

BURGESS, R.L., HAWTIN, Frank & RICHARDS, C. "Mendip Survey (lead)" *Journal of the Bristol Industrial Archaeology Society*, Vol.4 (1971)

BURKE, Gillian "The Cornish Diaspara in the Nineteenth Century" in Marks, Sheila & Richardson, Peter, *International Labour Migration: Historical Perspective* (1984), pp.57–75

BURKE, Gillian "The Decline of the Independent Bal Maiden: The Impact of Change in the Cornish Mining Industry" in John, Angela V.(Ed.) *Unequal Opportunities: Women's Employment in England 1800–1918* (Oxford: Blackwell, 1986), pp.179–204

BURKE, Gillian & RICHARDSON, Peter "The Decline and Fall of the Cost Book System in the Cornish Tin Industry, 1895–1914" *Business History*, Vol.XXIII No.1 (1981), pp.4–18

BURKE, Gillian & RICHARDSON, Peter "The Adaptability of the Cornish Cost Book System: A Response" *Business History*, Vol.XXV No.2 (1983), pp.193–199

BURT, Roger & KUDO, Norikazu "The Adaptability of the Cornish Cost Book System" *Business History*, Vol.XXV No.1 (1983), pp.30–41

BURT, Roger & TIMBRELL, Martin "Diversification as a Response to Decline in the Mining Industry: Arsenic and South–Western Metal Production 1850–1914" *Journal of Interdisciplinary Economics*, Vol.2 (1987), pp.31–54

BURT, Roger & WILKIE, Ian "Manganese Mining in the South West of England" *Journal of the Trevithick Society*, No.11 (1984), pp.18–40

BURT, Roger *See* ATKINSON, Michael & BURT, Roger

BURT, Roger *See* ATKINSON, Michael, WAITE, Peter & BURT, Roger

BURT, R.O. "Mineral Recovery from the Old Red River Valley, Cornwall" *Transactions of the Cornish Institute of Engineers*, Vol.XXV (1969–70), pp.42–57

CLARKE, A.G. *See* STANTON, W.I. & CLARKE, A.G.

CLARKE, A.J. & RABJOHNS, E.W. "The History of Wheal Grenville" *Camborne School of Mines Journal*, (1975), pp.41–52

CLAUGHTON, Peter F. "The Metalliferous Mines of North Devon and Exmoor" *Plymouth Mineral and Mining Club Journal*, Vol.4 No.1 (Spring 1973) pp.4–9

CLAUGHTON, Peter F. "The Metalliferous Mines of North Devon and Exmoor: Additions and Corrections" *Plymouth Mineral and Mining Club Journal*, Vol.5 No.1 (Spring 1974), pp.9–10

CLAUGHTON, Peter F. "Fullabrook Mine" *Plymouth Mineral and Mining Club Journal*, Vol.6 No.1 (Spring 1975), pp.4–5

CLAUGHTON, Peter F. "Mining in the Parish of Georgeham, North Devon" *Plymouth Mineral and Mining Club Journal*, Vol.6 No.3 (January 1976), pp.15–16

CLAUGHTON, Peter F. "The Mining Industry at Combe Martin, North Devon" *Plymouth Mineral and Mining Club Journal*, Vol.7 No.2 (Autumn 1976), pp.13–15

CLAUGHTON, Peter F. "The Mining Industry at Combe Martin, North Devon. Part 2" *Plymouth Mineral and Mining Club Journal*, Vol.7 No.3 (January 1977), pp.11–14

CLAUGHTON, Peter F. "The Mining Industry at Combe Martin, North Devon. Part 3" *Plymouth Mineral and Mining Club Journal*, Vol.8 No.1 (Spring 1977), pp.16–18

CLAUGHTON, Peter F. "The Mining Industry at Combe Martin, North Devon. Part 4" *Plymouth Mineral and Mining Club Journal*, Vol.8 No.2 (Autumn 1977), pp.15–18

COCKS, J.V.Somers "The Stannary Bounds of Plympton and Tavistock" *Devon and Cornwall Notes and Queries*, Vol.32 Pt.3 (Winter 1971), pp.76–79

COCKS, J.V.Somers "The Stannary Bounds of Plympton and Tavistock, a Correction" *Devon and Cornwall Notes and Queries*, Vol.32 Pt.4 (Spring 1972), p.124

COOK, R.M.L., GREEVES, Thomas A.P. & KILVINGTON, C.C. "Eylesbarrow (1814–1852): A Study of a Dartmoor Tin Mine" *Transactions of the Devonshire Association*, Vol.106 (1974), pp.161–214

COOMBE, M.O. "The Industrial History of Hayle" *Industrial Archaeology*, Vol.10 No.1 (1973), pp.64–76

CORBYN, A. "The Method of Ore Extraction Employed at a Cornish Tin Mine" *Shropshire Mining Club*, Yearbook (1961–2), pp.36–37

COSTELLO, Lynette M. "The Bradford Pool Case" *Transactions of the Devonshire Association*, Vol.113 (1981), pp.59–77

COX, T. "A Mendip Mining Law" *British Caver*, Vol.49 (1968), pp.59–60

CROOK, Christopher "Observations on Surface Features at Middlehope, Kewstoke which Indicate Possible Mine Workings" *Somerset Mines Research Group Journal*, Vol.1 No.2 (July 1981), pp.21–22

CURTIS, B.A. (Compiler) "The Cornish Man Engine" *Old Cornwall*, Vol.7 (1967–1973), pp.502–506

DELTA "A Note on Early Cornish Mine Pumps" *Industrial Archaeology*, Vol.16 No.2 (1981), pp.110–115

DENHAM, P.V. "The Duke of Bedford's Tavistock Estate, 1820–1838" *Transactions of the Devonshire Association*, Vol.110 (1978), pp.19–51

DICKINSON, M.G. "Dartmoor Mining Leats 1786–1836" *Devon and Cornwall Notes and Queries*, Vol.33 Pt.4 (1975), pp.102–108

DICKINSON, M.G. "An Early Tinworks Deed: Some Implications" *Devon and Cornwall Notes and Queries*, Vol.33 Pt.6 (Spring 1976), pp.185–188

DICKINSON, M.G. "Mining Activity and Cornish Migration at Mary Tavy" *Devon and Cornwall Notes and Queries*, Vol.34 Pt.5 (Spring 1980), pp.184–188

DICKINSON, Michael "The Duke's Men, the Wheal Maria People and Others: The Story of the Devon Great Consols 'Ghost' Railway" *Tamar Journal*, No.7 (1985), pp.41–50

DICKINSON, Neil "Uranium and Radium in South West England" *Plymouth Mineral and Mining Club Journal*, Vol.11 No.2 (September 1980), pp.4–8

DOUCH, H.L. "An Early Mining Agreement" *Journal of the Royal Institution of Cornwall*, New Series, Vol.2 Pt.2 (1954), pp.107–111

EARL, Bryan "Arsenic Winning and Refining Methods in the West of England" *Journal of the Trevithick Society*, No.10 (1983), pp.9–29

EARL, Bryan "Melting Tin in the West of England: A Study of an Old Art. Part 1" *Journal of the Historical Metallurgy Society*, Vol.19 No.2 (1985) pp.153–161

EARL, Bryan "Melting Tin in the West of England. Part 2" *Journal of the Historical Metallurgy Society*, Vol.20 No.1 (1986), pp.17–32

EARL, Bryan "A New Look at West of England Industrial Archaeology" *Journal of the Trevithick Society*, No.13 (1986), pp.46–59

EDMONDS, Eric W.A. "Great Dowgas Mine, St.Stephen" *Journal of the Trevithick Society*, No.12 (1985), pp.78–84

EDWARDS, Charles S. "A Cornish Miner Emigrates to Australia: Leaves from a Diary of 1852 and some Reminiscences" *Journal of the Royal Institution of Cornwall*, New Series, Vol.2 Pt.1 (1953), pp.33–43

EVANS, Colin J. "Adapt and Survive: Patterns of Tin Usage" *Mining Magazine*, (June 1985), pp.557–561

EVANS, H.R. "A Cornish Family of Tin–Bounders" *Devon and Cornwall Notes and Queries*, Vol.28 Pt.7 (July 1960), pp.209–215

EVANS, H.R. "A Cornish Family of Tin–Bounders" *Devon and Cornwall Notes and Queries*, Vol.28 Pt.8 (October 1960), pp.229–233

EVANS, Jane "Man and Mining on and around Mendip: Notes on the Display in Woodspring Museum, Weston–super–Mare" *Somerset Mines Research Group Journal*, Vol.1 No.2 (July 1981), pp.23–28

EVERARD, C.E. "Mining and Shore–Line Evolution Near St.Austell, Cornwall" *Transactions of the Royal Geological Society of Cornwall*, Vol.XIX (1959–60), pp.199–219

FINBERG, H.P.R. "The Stannary of Tavistock" *Transactions of the Devonshire Association*, Vol.81 (1949), pp.155–184

FINBERG, H.P.R. "An Unrecorded Stannary Parliament" *Transactions of the Devonshire Association*, Vol.82 (1950), pp.295–310

FLEMING, Andrew "Prehistoric Tin Extraction on Dartmoor: A Cautionary Note" *Transactions of the Devonshire Association*, Vol.119 (1987), pp.117–122

FORBES, James "Tour into Cornwall to the Land's End" *Journal of the Royal Institution of Cornwall*, Vol.9 (1983), pp.146–206

FYFIELD–SHAYLER, Brian A. & NORTON, C.P. "Tolgus Tin: Sole Survivor of the Traditional Cornish Tin Streaming Industry" *Industrial Archaeology*, Vol.15 No.1 (1980), pp.34–66

GARNETT, R.H.T. "Divers Investigate the Levant Mine" *Mining Magazine*, Vol.104 No.2 (February 1961), pp.73–78

GARNETT, R.H.T. & OBIAL, R. "Undersea Sampling at Levant Mine" *Mining Magazine*, (December 1968), pp.448–453

GERRARD, Sandy "Retallack: A Late Medieval Tin Milling Complex in the Parish of Constantine, and its Cornish Context" *Cornish Archaeology*, No.24 (1985), pp.175–182

GERRARD, Sandy "Stream Working in Medieval Cornwall" *Journal of the Trevithick Society*, No.14 (1987), pp.7–31

GETTINS, G.L. "The Exmoor Mineral Railway" *Exmoor Review*, (1967), pp.36–37

GILL, Michael C. "An Account of the Accident at Wheal Agar" *British Mining*, No.3 (1976), pp.10–11

GILLET, T.E. "The Geology of South Crofty Mine" *Transactions of the Northern Cavern and Mine Research Society*, Vol.1 No.2 (April 1964), pp.23–27

GLANVILL, Peter "Wheal Friendship Mine, Devon" *Journal of the Cerberus Spelaeological Society*, Vol.15 No.4 (1985), pp.109–110

GLOSSON, Michael "Rules and Laws Governing Lead and Calamine Mining in Backwell, 1709" *Somerset Mines Research Group Journal*, Vol.1 No.3 (February 1982), pp.43–45

GOODRIDGE, J.C. "Devon Great Consols: A Study of Victorian Mining Enterprise" *Transactions of the Devonshire Association*, Vol.96 (1964), pp.228–268

GOODRIDGE, J. "A New Life for Tin Revival in Cornwall" *Geographical Magazine*, (August 1985), pp.424–429

GREEN, G.W. "The Central Mendip Lead–Zinc Orefield" *Bulletin of the Geological Survey of Great Britain*, No.14 (1958), pp.70–90

GREEVES, Thomas A.P. "A Mine in the Deancombe Valley" *Transactions of the Devonshire Association*, Vol.101 (1969), pp.197–201

GREEVES, Thomas A.P. "A Tinners' Mill in Walkhampton Parish" *Transactions of the Devonshire Association*, Vol.103 (1971), pp.197–199

GREEVES, Thomas A.P. "Wheal Prosper: A Little Known Dartmoor Tin Mine" *Plymouth Mineral and Mining Club Journal*, Vol.6 No.1 (Spring 1975), pp.6–7

GREEVES, Thomas A.P. "Merrivale Bridge Mine, Wheal Fortune and Staple Tor Sett, 1806–1887" *Plymouth Mineral and Mining Club Journal*, Vol.6 No.3 (January 1976), pp.3–5,11

GREEVES, Thomas A.P. "Wheal Cumpston Tin Mine, Holne, Devon" *Transactions of the Devonshire Association*, Vol.110 (1978), pp.161–171

GREEVES, Thomas A.P. "A History of Whiteworks Tin Mine" *Plymouth Mineral and Mining Club Journal*, Vol.11 No.2 (September 1980), pp.11–16

GREEVES, Thomas A.P. "An Outline Archaeological and Historical Survey of Tin Mining in Devon 1500–1900" in Wachtler, E. & Engewald, G. (Eds.),*International Symposium Zur Geschichte Des Bergbaus Und Huttenwesens, Vortrage Band I* (ICOHTEC, 1980), pp.73–89

GREEVES, Thomas A.P. "Steeperton Tor Mine, Dartmoor, Devon" *Transactions of the Devonshire Association*, Vol.117 (1985), pp.101–127

GREEVES, Thomas A.P. "The Great Courts or Parliaments of Devon Tinners 1474–1786" *Transactions of the Devonshire Association*, Vol.119 (1987), pp.145–167

GREEVES, Thomas A.P. See COOK, R.M.L., GREEVES, Thomas A.P. & KILVINGTON, C.C.

HAMILTON, J.R. "The Mines and Minerals of Exmoor" *Camborne School of Mines Journal*, (1950), pp.45–48

HANNAM, Mervyn "Mendip Mining" *British Caver*, Vol.29 (1958), pp.31–34;63–65

HARKER, Roger S. "The House of Water" *Transactions of the Northern Cavern and Mine Research Society*, Vol.1 No.1 (June 1961), pp.23–27

HARKER, Roger S. "The Flooding of Wheal Owles" *Memoirs of the Northern Cavern and Mine Research Society*, (August 1965), pp.35–39

HARPER, Peter "The Treacle Mines of Dunchideock" *Devon and Cornwall Notes and Queries*, Vol.31 Pt.3 (October 1968), pp.85–86

HARRIS, Helen B.M. "Manganese Mining in West Devon" *Tamar Journal*, No.9 (1987), pp.20–24

HARRIS, John R. & ROBERTS, R.O. "Eighteenth Century Monopoly: The Cornish Metal Company Agreements of 1785" *Business History*, Vol.V No.2 (1962), pp.69–82

HARRIS, T.R. "Arthur Woolf (1766–1837) Cornish Engineer and Inventor" *Transactions of the Cornish Institute of Engineers*, Vol.XIX (1963–4), pp.15–25

HARRIS, T.R. "A Short History of the Cornish Explosives Industries" *Transactions of the Cornish Institute of Engineers*, Vol.XXVI (1970–1), pp.2–15

HARRIS, T.R. "Some Lesser Known Cornish Engineers" *Journal of the Trevithick Society*, No.5 (1977), pp.25f

HARRIS, T.R. "The Cornish Copper Company 1754–1869: Copper Smelters, Merchants, Engineers and Ironfounders" *Journal of the Trevithick Society*, No.6 (1978), pp.7–19

HATCHER, John "A Diversified Economy: Later Medieval Cornwall" *Economic History Review*, Second Series Vol.XXII No.2 (1969), pp.208–227

HAWTIN, Frank "Industrial Archaeology at Charterhouse–on–Mendip" *Industrial Archaeology*, Vol.7 No.2 (1970), pp.171–175

HAWTIN, Frank *See* BURGESS, R.L., HAWTIN, Frank & RICHARDS, C.

HAYNES, R.G. "Suspected Early Iron–Smelting Site on Dartmoor" *Devon and Cornwall Notes and Queries*, Vol.32 Pt.7 (Spring 1973), p.215

HAYNES, R.G. "The Bottle Hill Mine Leat" *Devon and Cornwall Notes and Queries*, Vol.33 Pt.7 (Autumn 1976), pp.257–260

HAZARD, R. "Levant Mine" *Shropshire Mining Club*, Account No.3 (1963)

HAZARD, R. "The Devon Great Consols Mine" *Shropshire Mining Club*, Yearbook (1963–4), pp.48–50

HERBERT, Stanley "Life After Death for Cornish Tin" *Mine and Quarry*, Vol.10 No.3 (March 1981), pp.21–25

HICKS, Graham "The Bere Alston Silver Lead Mines" *Plymouth Mineral and Mining Club Journal*, Vol.4 No.3 (January 1974), pp.8–9

HICKS, Graham "Bere Alston Silver Lead Mines" *Tamar Journal*, No.1 (1978), pp.20–23

HIGGANS, John "Angarack Smelting House: Its History" *Journal of the Trevithick Society*, No.7 (1979–1980), pp.37–55

HOOPER, John "Mine Tunnels at Sharkham Point" *British Caver*, Vol.51 (1969), pp.1–4

HOUSTON, William J. "The Tolgus Tin Stamping Co.Ltd, Redruth, Cornwall" *Memoirs of the Northern Cavern and Mine Research Society*, (August 1965), pp.32–35

HUNTER, John " Visit to Wheal Jane Tin Mine" *British Mining*, No.3 (1976), pp.8–10

HUNTER, John "An Exercise in Mineral Exploration: Dartmoor, 1974" *British Mining*, No.5 (1977), pp.1–6

HUNTER, John "Hemerdon Ball: Rolling Again?" *British Mining*, No.8 (1978), pp43–48

JAMES, C.C. "Great Wheal Vor" *Transactions of the Royal Geological Society of Cornwall*, Vol.XVII Pt.4 (1944–5), pp.194–207

JAMES, C.C. "The Dating of the Earliest Copper Production in Cornwall, with a Note on the Makers of Bronze–Age Implements and Pottery" *Old Cornwall*, Vol.4 (1943–1950), pp.199–204

JAMES, C.C. "Cornwall and Mexico" *Old Cornwall*, Vol.4 (1943–1950), pp.349–352

JAMES, C.C. "Visitors to Botallack" *Old Cornwall*, Vol.5 (1951–1961), pp.61–64

JAMES, C.C. "The Cornish Copper Miners in Australia" *Old Cornwall*, Vol.5 (1951–1961), pp.139–142

JAMES, C.C. "Some Notes on Cornish Miners in Brazil" *Old Cornwall*, Vol.5 (1951–1961), pp.228–229

JAMES, C.C. "Early Tin Smelting in Cornwall" *Old Cornwall*, Vol.5 (1951–1961), pp.269–273

JENKINS, A.K.Hamilton "The Rise and Fall of Wheal Alfred" *Journal of the Royal Institution of Cornwall*, New Series, Vol.3 Pt.3 (1959), pp.124–137

JONES, J.L. "Forgotten Mines of Mendip" *Country Life*, 119 (16th February 1956), pp.260–261

JONES, M.H. "Extracts from a Brendon Hill Diary" *Exmoor Review*, No.3 (Summer 1961), pp.57–62

JONES, M.H. "Wartime Mining on Exmoor" *Exmoor Review*, (1979), pp.41–42

JONES, M.H. "The Incline at Brendon Hill" *Exmoor Review*, No.28 (1987), pp.35–45

KILVINGTON, C.C. *See* COOK, R.M.L., GREEVES, Thomas A.P. & KILVINGTON, C.C.

KUDO, Norikazu *See* BURT, Roger & KUDO, Norikazu

LAING, Lloyd R. "A Greek Tin Trade with Cornwall" *Cornish Archaeology*, No.7 (1968), pp.15–23

LAMMING, C.K.G. "Radioactivity in West Cornwall" *Mining Magazine*, Vol.LXXXVI No.5 (May 1952), pp.265–273

LAW, R.J. "A Glimpse of the Cornish Mineral Industry in 1873" *Journal of the Trevithick Society*, No.4 (1976), pp.57–61

LE MARCHANT, R. "The Reopening of George and Charlotte Mine" *Tamar Journal*, No.2 (1979–80), pp.46–49

LE MARCHANT, R. "Evidence of Pumping at George and Charlotte Mine" *Tamar Journal*, No.3 (1980–81), pp.24–26

LE MARCHANT, R. "The Dressing of Copper Ore" *Tamar Journal*, No.9 (1987), pp.4–7

LE MARCHANT, R. "Tin Streaming" *Tamar Journal*, No.10 (1988), pp.30–33

LEVY, J.F. "Decay of Timber at Tywarnhaile" *Mine and Quarry Engineering*, Vol.29 (March 1963), pp.119–124

LINEHAN, C.D. "A Forgotten Manor in Widecombe–in–the–Moor, with notes on its Geology, Archaeology and Mining by H.French" *Transactions of the Devonshire Association*, Vol.94 (1962), pp.463–492

LONG, E.C. "Anderton Tin Mine" *Tamar Journal*, No.6 (1984), pp.37–47

MARSHMAN, Ronald "South Crofty to Refurbish Shafts, Drive Decline" *Mining Magazine*, (March 1985), pp.248–249

McGUINNESS, T.W. "Occupational Change in Cornwall (Over a Period of Circa 100 Years)" *Royal Cornwall Polytechnic Society*, Vol.110 (1943), pp.78–107

McKENNA, Neil & ATKINSON, Barry "A Study of the Grylls and Bunny Adits, Botallack, St.Just" *Plymouth Mineral and Mining Club Journal*, Vol.15 No.3 (May 1985), pp.4–5

MESSENGER, Michael J. "Bulkamore Iron Mine and its Tramway" *Devon Historian*, No.14, (May 1977), pp.15–16

MESSENGER, Michael J. "Early Cornish Mineral Railways" *Journal of the Trevithick Society*, No.5 (1977), pp.70–75

MICHELL, F.B. "Mineral Pigments (Great Rock)" *Mine and Quarry Engineering*, Vol.10 (January 1945), pp.9–14

MICHELL, F.B. "The Dressing of Tin Ores (Geevor). Pt 1" *Mine and Quarry Engineering*, Vol.11 (January 1946), pp.15–19

MICHELL, F.B. "The Dressing of Tin Ores (Porkellis & East Pool). Pt 2" *Mine and Quarry Engineering*, Vol.11 (February 1946), pp.29–36

MICHELL, F.B. "Half a Century of Progress in Tin Dressing and Metallurgy" *Transactions of the Cornish Institute of Engineers*, Vol.XVIII (1962–3), pp.2–15

MICHELL, F.B. "The History of Mineral Processing in Cornwall" *Bulletin of the Historical Metallurgy Group*, Vol.4 No.1 (1970), pp.4–9

MICHELL, F.B. "The History of Mineral Processing in Cornwall" *Camborne School of Mines Journal*, (1972), pp.23–28

MICHELL, F.B. "Ore Dressing in Cornwall 1600–1900" *Journal of the Trevithick Society*, No.6 (1978), pp.25–52

MICHELL, F.B. "The Development of the Copper Mining Industry in Cornwall and the Industrial Revolution" *Camborne School of Mines Journal*, (1980), pp.55–59

MOORE, John McMahon "Exploration Prospects for Stockwork Tin-Tungsten Ores in South West England" *Mining Magazine*, (February 1977), pp.97–103

MORTON, John "The Cornish Copper Company, 1693 to 1697" *Journal of the Trevithick Society*, No.7 (1979–1980), pp.57–75

NEWELL, Edmund "Interpreting the Cornish Copper Standard" *Journal of the Trevithick Society*, No.13 (1986), pp.36–45

NEWMAN, Philip "Two Small Mines in the Newleycombe Valley" *Dartmoor Magazine*, No.8 (Autumn 1987), pp.8–10

NEWMAN, Philip "The Moorland Meavy: A Tinners' Landscape" *Transactions of the Devonshire Association*, Vol.119 (1987), pp.223–240

NICHOLAS, C. "Developments in Economic Geology in South West England: A Review of the 1970s" *Proceedings of the Ussher Society*, Vol.5 Pt.1 (1980), pp.4–6

NICHOLLS, Bryan "The Lady Elizabeth Mine, Ermington" *Plymouth Mineral and Mining Club Journal*, Vol.15 No.2 (December 1984), pp.3–6

NOALL, Cyril "The Tinners Riot of 1729" *Old Cornwall*, Vol.5 (1951–1961), pp.396–398, 418–421

NOALL, Cyril "The West Cornwall Railway" *Cornish Magazine*, Vol.1 No.7 (November 1958), pp.240–241;264

NOALL, Cyril "The Cornish Bal Maiden" *Cornish Magazine*, Vol.4 No.6 (October 1961), pp.176–180

NOALL, Cyril "Royal Visit to Cornwall. Part 1" *Cornish Magazine*, Vol.4 No.8 (December 1961), pp.239–243

NOALL, Cyril "Royal Visit to Cornwall. Part 2" *Cornish Magazine*, Vol.4 No.9 (January 1962), pp.272–276

NOALL, Cyril "Royal Visit to Cornwall. Part 3" *Cornish Magazine*, Vol.4 No.10 (February 1962), pp.298–302

NOALL, Cyril "Royal Visit to Botallack Mine" *Cornish Magazine*, Vol.6 No.3 (July 1963), pp.76–79

NOALL, Cyril "History of the Cornish Man Engine. Part 1" *Cornish Magazine*, Vol.7 No.3 (July 1964), pp.79–83

NOALL, Cyril "History of the Cornish Man Engine. Part 2" *Cornish Magazine*, Vol.7 No.4 (August 1964), pp.126–128

NORTON, C.P. *See* FYFIELD–SHAYLER, Brian A. & NORTON, C.P.

OBIAL, R. *See* GARNET, R.H.T. & OBIAL, R.

OXENFORD, P. "Virtuous Lady Copper Mine" *Plymouth Mineral and Mining Club Journal*, Vol.4 No.2 (October 1973), p.8

PADEL, Oliver "Cornish Mine Names" *Wheals Magazine*, No.13 (March 1983)

PADEL, Oliver "Early Place Names Indicating Tin Working" *Wheals Magazine*, No.15 (August 1983)

PALMER, L.S. & ASHWORTH, H.W.W. "Four Roman Pigs of Lead from the Mendips" *Proceedings of the Somerset Archaeological & Natural History Society*, Vols.101–102 (1956–1957), pp.52–87

PARSONS, Hamlyn "The Dartmoor Blowing House (Some Recent Investigations)" *Transactions of the Devonshire Association*, Vol.88 (1956), pp.189–196

PARSONS, Trevor "The Cornish Man Engine" *Plymouth Mineral and Mining Club Journal*, Vol.10 No.1 (June 1979), pp.17–18

PASCOE, W.Arthur "Notes on the Cornish Tin Industry" *Mining Magazine*, Vol.LXXIII No.2 (August 1945), pp.84–87

PASCOE, W. Arthur "Cornish Mining Adventure" *Old Cornwall*, Vol.5 (1951–1961), pp.108–118

PASCOE, W. Arthur "Cornish Saints and Tin Mining" *Old Cornwall*, Vol.6 (1961–1967), pp.234–235

PASCOE, W.H. "The Mines of Phillack Parish" *Plymouth Mineral and Mining Club Journal*, Vol.14 No.1 (May 1983), pp.3–5

PATRICK, Amber "The Growth and Decline of Morwellham" *Transactions of the Devonshire Association*, Vol.106 (1974), pp.95–117

PATRICK, Amber "Copper Production in the Tamar Valley in the Eighteenth Century" *Tamar Journal*, No.5 (1983), pp.35–42

PEARSON, Alan "William Pryce, M.D., 1735–1790" *Old Cornwall*, Vol.7 (1967–1973), pp.388–396

PEARSON, Alan "Cornish Miners in Coal Mines" *Old Cornwall*, Vol.9 No.5 (Autumn 1981), pp.222–225

PENNINGTON, Robert R. "The Cornish Metal Company, 1785–1792" *Journal of the Trevithick Society*, No.5 (1977), pp.76–88

PENNINGTON, Robert R. "The South Wheal Francis and West Wheal Basset Boundary Litigation" *Journal of the Trevithick Society*, No. 7 (1979–1980), pp.95–102

PIPER, L.P.S. "A Short History of Camborne School of Mines" *Journal of the Trevithick Society*, No.2 (1974), pp.9–44

POLKINGHORNE, J.P.R. "The Bridford Baryte Mine" *Transactions of the Royal Geological Society of Cornwall*, Vol.18 (1951), pp.240–254

POLKINGHORNE, J.P.R. "Bridford Baryta Mine, Devon" *Transactions of the Cornish Institute of Engineers*, Vol.IX (1953–54), pp.16–23

POOL, P.A.S. "William Borlase, the Scholar and the Man" *Journal of the Royal Institution of Cornwall*, New Series Vol.V Pt.2 (1966), pp.120–172

POUNDS, Norman J.G. "Ports and Shipping of the Fal" *Journal of the Royal Institution of Cornwall*, New Series Vol.1 Pt.1 (1946), pp.43–60

PREW, W.J. "On Metals in Devon: A Comparative Review of Origins and Principles" *Transactions of the Devonshire Association*, Vol.81 (1949), pp.333–340

PRICE, D.G. "Changing Perceptions of Prehistoric Tinning on Dartmoor" *Transactions of the Devonshire Association*, Vol.117 (1985), pp.129–138

RABJOHNS, E.W. *See* CLARKE, A.J. & RABJOHNS, E.W.

RAMSDEN, J.V. "Notes on the Mines of Devonshire" *Transactions of the Devonshire Association*, Vol.84 (1952), pp.81–104

REDGRAVE, Blaze "Wheal Betsy; A Dartmoor Lead Mine" *Dartmoor Magazine*, No.10 (Spring 1988), p.18

RENDALL, Michael "Wheal Coates, Polberrow and Dolcoath Adit" *Journal of the Cerberus Spelaeological Society*, Vol.15 No.3 (1985), pp.79–81

RICHARDS, C. *See* BURGESS, R.L., HAWTIN, Frank & RICHARDS, C.

RICHARDSON, Peter *See* BURKE, Gillian & RICHARDSON, Peter

RICHARDSON, P.H.G. "Hexworthy Tin Mine" *Plymouth Mineral and Mining Club Journal*, Vol.3 No.3 (December 1972), pp.3–4

RICHARDSON, P.H.G. "Hexworthy Tin Mine" *Plymouth Mineral and Mining Club Journal*, Vol.4 No.2 (Autumn 1973), pp.11–13

RICHARDSON, P.H.G. "Notes on the Old Burning House Near Ilsington" *Plymouth Mineral and Mining Club Journal*, Vol.7 No.3 (January 1977), pp.16–17

RICHARDSON, P.H.G. "Devon Great Consols After 1903" *Plymouth Mineral and Mining Club Journal*, Vol.10 No.1 (June 1979), pp.3–8

RICHARDSON, P.H.G. "Mining at Devon Great Consols after 1903" *Tamar Journal*, No.2 (1979–80), pp.33–42

RICHARDSON, P.H.G. "The Mary Tavy Mines: Some Recollections, 1932–1982" *Plymouth Mineral and Mining Club Journal*, Vol.14 No.2 (October 1983), pp.3–8

RICHARDSON, P.H.G. "South Devon United Mine, Peter Tavy" *Plymouth Mineral and Mining Club Journal*, Vol.15 No.2 (December 1984), pp.9–13

RICHARDSON, P.H.G. "Roborough Down Wolfram" *Plymouth Mineral and Mining Club Journal*, Vol.17 No.1 (December 1986), p.3

RICHARDSON, P.H.G. "Small Details: Snippets from the Devon Great Consols Workbooks for the early 1920s" *Plymouth Mineral and Mining Club Journal*, Vol.17 No.3 (Autumn 1987), pp.7–8

ROBERTS, Peter "Standon Hill and Wapsworthy" *Plymouth Mineral and Mining Club Journal*, Vol.12 No.2 (September 1981), p.12

ROBERTS, Peter "The Cruquis Engine" *Plymouth Mineral and Mining Club Journal*, Vol.16 No.1 (August 1985), p.10

ROBERTS, R.O. *See* HARRIS, John R. & ROBERTS, R.O.

ROBERTS, Steve "Kelly Mine: The First Year" *Plymouth Mineral and Mining Club Journal*, Vol.17 No.1 (December 1986), pp.9–12

ROBERTS, Steve "East Pool" *Plymouth Mineral and Mining Club Journal*, Vol.18 No.1 (February 1988), pp.3–4

ROBINS, J.A.C. "Bachelors Hall Tin Mine" *Plymouth Mineral and Mining Club Journal*, Vol.14 No.3 (March 1984), pp.3–7

ROBINS, J.A.C. "The Grimstone and Sortridge Leat" *Tamar Journal*, No.10 (1988), pp.24–29

ROBINS, John "A Fresh Concept of the Leats of Whiteworks Mine" *Dartmoor Magazine*, No.3 (Summer 1986), p.19

ROBINS, John "The Devonport and Vitifer Leats" *Dartmoor Magazine*, No.5 (Winter 1986), p.25

ROBINS, John "The Vitifer Leat" *Dartmoor Magazine*, No.7 (Summer 1987), p.26

RODERICK, G.W. *See* STEPHENS, M.D. & RODERICK, G.W.

ROTTENBURY, John "The Bampfylde Mine" *Exmoor Review*, (1969), pp.24–29

ROTTENBURY, John "The Mines of Combmartin" *Exmoor Review*, (1973), pp.47–50

ROWE, Geoff A. "The Three Wise Men" *Plymouth Mineral and Mining Club Journal*, Vol.6 No.1 (Spring 1975), p.3

ROWE, Geoff A. "Drakewall's Mine" *Tamar Journal*, No.3 (1980–81), pp.20–23

ROWE, Geoff A. "The Mines of Tamar–side. No.2 Old Gunnislake Mine" *Tamar Journal*, No.4 (1982), pp.30–33

ROWE, Geoff A. "The Mines of Tamar–side. No.3 South Hooe Mine" *Tamar Journal*, No.5 (1983), pp.7–8

ROWE, Geoff A. "The Mines of Tamar–side. No.4 Devon Great Consols" *Tamar Journal*, No.6 (1984), pp.37–47

ROWE, Geoff A. "New Great Consols" *Tamar Journal*, No.7 (1985), pp.26–30

ROWE, Geoff A. "The Mines of Tamar–side. No.6 Gawton Mine" *Tamar Journal*, No.8 (1984), pp.4–6

ROWE, John "The Rise of Foreign Competition to Cornish Tin–Mining" *Royal Cornwall Polytechnic Society Annual Report*, No.132 (1965), pp.22–39

ROWE, John "The Declining Years of Cornish Tin Mining" in Porter, J.H.(Ed.) *Education and Labour in the South West* (Exeter: University of Exeter, Papers in Economic History No.10, 1975)

ROWE, John "Humphry Davy and the Cornish Contribution to the Industrial Revolution" *Journal of the Trevithick Society*, No.6 (1978), pp.53–63

RUMBOLD, Richard "Radioactive Minerals in Cornwall and Devon" *Mining Magazine*, Vol.XCI No.1 (July 1954), pp.16–27

RUMING, G. "Religion in the Mining Communities in the Tamar Valley" *Tamar Journal*, No.7 (1985), pp.41–50

RUSSELL, Arthur "John Hawkins, F.G.S., F.R.H.S., F.R.S., 1761–1841: A Distinguished Cornishman and Early Mining Geologist" *Journal of the Royal Institution of Cornwall*, New Series, Vol.2 Pt.2 (1954), pp.98–106

RUSSELL, P.M.G. "Manganese Mining in Devon" *Devon and Cornwall Notes and Queries*, Vol.31 Pt.7 (Summer 1970), pp.205–213

SALTER, Christopher "Early Iron Working on Dartmoor" *Plymouth Mineral and Mining Club Journal*, Vol.9 No.2 (September 1978), pp.3–4

SALTER, Christopher "Seventeenth Century Tin–Mining Techniques" *Plymouth Mineral and Mining Club Journal*, Vol.10 No.2 (October 1979), pp.11–12

SALTER, Christopher "Seventeenth Century Tin–Mining Techniques. Part 2" *Plymouth Mineral and Mining Club Journal*, Vol.11 No.1 (May 1980), pp.7–8

SALTER, Christopher "Seventeenth Century Tin–Mining Techniques. Part 3" *Plymouth Mineral and Mining Club Journal*, Vol.12 No.1 (May 1981), pp.11–12,14

SCHMITZ, Christopher J. "The Early Growth of the Devon Barytes Industry, 1835–1875" *Transactions of the Devonshire Association*, Vol.106 (1974), pp.59–76

SCHMITZ, Christopher J. "An Account of Mendip Calamine Mining in the Early 1870s" *Proceedings of the Somerset Archaeological & Natural History Society*, Vol.120 (1976), pp.81–83

SCHMITZ, Christopher J. "The Development and Decline of the Devon Barytes Industry, 1875–1958" *Transactions of the Devonshire Association*, Vol.109 (1977), pp.117–133

SCHMITZ, Christopher J. "Capital Formation and Technological Change in South West England Metal Mining in the Nineteenth Century" in Minchinton, W.E.(Ed.) *Capital Formation in South West England* (Exeter: University of Exeter, Papers in Economic History No.9, 1978)

SCHMITZ, Christopher J. "Cornish Mine Labour and the Royal Commission of 1864" *Journal of the Trevithick Society*, No.10 (1983), pp.35–45

SCHMITZ, Christopher J. *See* ATKINSON, Michael & SCHMITZ, Christopher J.

SCHOFIELD, John "Early Blowing–Houses at Godolphin" *Cornish Archaeology*, No.7 (1968), p.107

SEVIER, W.E. "Progress at Geevor Tin Mine" *Mining Magazine*, Vol.73 No.4 (October 1945), pp.201–210

SHAMBROOK, H.R. "The Phoenix United Mines, Linkinhorne, East Cornwall" *British Mining*, No.5 (1977), pp.46–53

SHAMBROOK, H.R. "The Cornish Boiler" *British Mining*, No.19 (1982), pp.46–47

SHAMBROOK, H.R. "The Wherry Mine, Penzance" *British Mining*, No.19 (1982), pp.91–94

SHAMBROOK, H.R. "Mining, Methodism (Primitive and United), Bible Christian etc." *British Mining*, No.19 (1982), pp.95–96

SHAMBROOK, Roy "The Other Side of the Story" *Plymouth Mineral and Mining Club Journal*, Vol.7 No.2 (Autumn 1976), pp.6,19

SHAMBROOK, Roy "Some East Cornwall Mines" *Plymouth Mineral and Mining Club Journal*, Vol.7 No.3 (Spring 1977), pp.15,19

SHAMBROOK, Roy "The Devon Great Consolidated Copper Mining Company" *Journal of the Trevithick Society*, No.9 (1982), pp.62–68

SHAMBROOK, Roy "The Miners' Welfare" *Journal of the Trevithick Society*, No.12 (1985), pp.75–77

SHAW, Trevor "Iron Mine at Haytor Vale, Devon" *British Caver*, Vol.26 (1955), pp.83–84

SIMPSON, S. "Mendip Mines of Long Ago" *British Caver*, Vol.38 (Autumn 1963), pp.8–10

SLEEMAN, S.M. "The Great Tin Mining Era in West Cornwall" *Industrial Heritage*, Vol.2 (1971)

SPINK, Graeme "South Caradon: Victim of Man and Time" *Plymouth Mineral and Mining Club Journal*, Vol.4 No.3 (January 1974), pp.12–13

SPOONER, John "Tin: Trial of Errors" *Mining Magazine*, (June 1986), pp.475–477

STAAL, Cyril "Calenick Crucibles" *Royal Cornwall Polytechnic Society Annual Report*, Vol.124 (1957), pp.44–54

STANES, Robin G.F. "Iron Smelting Site at Hemyock" *Devon and Cornwall Notes and Queries*, Vol.34 Pt.1 (Spring 1978), pp.36–37

STANIER, Peter "Lost Mining Ports of the South Cornish Coast" *Industrial Archaeology Review*, Vol.III No.1 (1978), pp.1–16

STANIER, Peter "The Copper Trade of South West England in the Nineteenth Century" *Journal of Transport History*, Vol.V No.1 (Feruary 1979), pp.18–35

STANIER, Peter "Early Mining and Water Power in the Caradon Mining District of Eastern Cornwall" *Journal of the Trevithick Society*, No.14 (1987), pp.32–45

STANTON, W.I. & CLARKE, A.G. "Cornish Miners at Charterhouse-on-Mendip" *Proceedings of the University of Bristol Spelaeological Society*, Vol.17 No.1 (1984), pp.29–54

STENGELHOFFEN, John *See* STEPHENS, P. & STENGELHOFFEN, John

STEPHENS, M.D. & RODERICK, G.W. "Industry and Education in the Nineteenth Century: The Cornish Mine Worker. A Case Study" *Paedagogica Historica*, Vol.XI No.2 (1971), pp.516–540

STEPHENS, P. & STENGELHOFEN, John "Tin Stream Works at Tuckingmill" *Journal of the Trevithick Society*, No.1 (1973), pp.90–95

STEPHENS, W.B. "Elementary Education in the Cornish Mining Areas in the Mid Nineteenth Century" *Devon and Cornwall Notes and Queries*, Vol.31 Pt.5 (Autumn 1969), pp.135–140

STEWART, E.A. "Report on an Investigation of Mine Shafts on Sandford Hill, Mendips" *British Caver*, Vol.32 (1959), pp.51–55

STEWART, P.A.E. "Mendip: Emborough Adit" *British Caver*, Vol.27 (1956), pp.55–57

STILES, Robin "Some Documentary Evidence of Calamine Working at Shipham Manor, Somerset, in the Eighteenth Century" *Somerset Mines Research Group Journal*, Vol.2 No.1 (July 1983), pp.1–7

STOYEL, Alan "Brea Adit Works, Camborne" *Journal of the Trevithick Society*, No.4 (1976), pp.45–56

TANGYE, Michael "The Wesleyan Methodist Relief Fund for the Cornwall District, 1879" *Old Cornwall*, Vol.7 (1967–1973), pp.185–190

TAYLOR, Christopher "The Story of Devon Great Consols Mine 1844–1901" *Tamar Journal*, No.10 (1988), pp.34–43

TAYLOR, J., HARRISON, R.K. & TAYLOR, K. "Structure and Mineralisation at Roskrow United Mine, Ponsanooth, Cornwall" *Bulletin of the Geological Survey of Great Britain*, Vol.25 (1966), pp.33–40

TEW, D.H. "Man Engines in Cornwall" *Journal of the Trevithick Society*, No.8 (1981), pp.47–53

THOMAS, Charles "A Cornish Mine Captain: Josiah Thomas of Dolcoath 1833–1901" *Camborne School of Mines Journal*, (1986), pp.69–75

THOMAS, J.G. "Notes on Some Early Blowing and Smelting Sites in the Carn Brea–St. Agnes Area" *Journal of the Trevithick Society*, No.2 (1974), pp.71–83

TILLY, V.J. "The Proposed Revival of Cornish Mining" *Camborne School of Mines Journal*, (1949), pp.4–9

TIMBRELL, Martin *See* BURT, Roger & TIMBRELL, Martin

TODD, A.C. "Davies Gilbert: Patron, Politicial and Natural Philosopher" *Journal of the Royal Institution of Cornwall*, New Series Vol.IV Pt.4 (1964), pp.452–480

TOLL, R.W. "Water Power in West Devon" *Mining Magazine*, Vol.78 No.3 (March 1948), pp.137–141

TOLL, R.W. "Old Silver Lead Mines in West Devon" *Mining Magazine*, Vol.LXXVIII No.6 (March 1948), pp.335–342

TOLL, R.W. "The Tavistock–Morwelham Canal" *Mining Magazine*, Vol.79 No.3 (September 1948), pp.144–148

TOLL, R.W. "Radioactive Minerals in the Tavistock District" *Mining Magazine*, Vol.LXXXV No.3 (September 1951), pp.137–142

TOLL, R.W. "Arsenic in West Devon and East Cornwall" *Mining Magazine*, Vol.LXXXIX No.2 (August 1953), pp.83–88

TOLL, R.W. "Manganese in West Devon" *Mining Magazine*, Vol.XCIX No.1 (July 1958), pp.17–19

TRINICK, G.M.A. "The Tregurtha Downs Mines, Marazion 1700–1965" *Industrial Archaeology Review*, Vol.II No.2 (1978), pp.111–128

TRINICK, G.M.A. "The Tregurtha Downs Mines, Marazion, 1700–1965" *Journal of the Trevithick Society*, No.8 (1981), pp.7–25

TROUNSON, John H. "The Cornish Mineral Industry. Part 1" *Mining Magazine*, Vol.LXVI No.2 (February 1942), pp.47–52

TROUNSON, John H. "The Cornish Mineral Industry. Part 2" *Mining Magazine*, Vol.LXVI No.5 (May 1942), pp.195–205

TROUNSON, John H. "The Cornish Mineral Industry. Part 3. The St.Just and St.Ives Mining Districts" *Mining Magazine*, Vol.LXVII No.3 (September 1942), pp.119–130

TROUNSON, John H. "The Cornish Mineral Industry. Part 4 No.1. The Marazion, Wheal Vor, St.Erth, Gwinear and Crowan Districts" *Mining Magazine*, Vol.LXVIII No.1 (January 1943), pp.9–18

TROUNSON, John H. "The Cornish Mineral Industry. Part 4 No.2. The Marazion, Wheal Vor, St.Erth, Gwinear and Crowan Districts" *Mining Magazine*, Vol.LXVIII No.2 (February 1943), pp.78–85

TROUNSON, John H. "The Cornish Mineral Industry. Part 4 No.3. The Marazion, Wheal Vor, St.Erth, Gwinear and Crowan Districts" *Mining Magazine*, Vol.LXIX No.6 (December 1943), pp.329–342

TROUNSON, John H. "The Cornish Mineral Industry. Part 5. The Wendron District" *Mining Magazine*, Vol.LXXII No.2 (February 1945), pp.73–83

TROUNSON, John H. "Some Useful Prospects in Cornwall. Part 1" *Mining Magazine*, Vol.LXXXIV No.2 (February 1951), pp.73–84

TROUNSON, John H. "Some Useful Prospects in Cornwall Part 2" *Mining Magazine*, Vol.LXXXIV No.3 (March 1951), pp.139–149

TROUNSON, John H. "Some Useful Prospect in Cornwall Part 3" *Mining Magazine*, Vol.LXXXIV No.4 (April 1951), pp.209–216

TROUNSON, John H. "Cornish Engines and the Men Who Handled Them" *Journal of the Royal Institution of Cornwall*, New Series, Vol.5

Pt.3 (1967), pp.213–249

TROUNSON, John H. "Metal Mining in the West of England" *Bulletin of the Historical Metallurgy Group*, Vol.4 No.1 (1970), pp.2–3

TROUNSON, John H. "Engineering Marvels" *Journal of the Trevithick Society*, N0.7 (1979–1980), pp.7–33

TROUNSON, John H. "Cornish Stacks and Engine Houses" *Journal of the Trevithick Society*, No.9 (1982), pp.73–84

TROUNSON, John H. "The Cornish Mining Industry in the Eighteenth and Nineteenth Centuries" *Journal of the Trevithick Society*, No.11 (1984), pp.7–17

TROUNSON, John H. "The Boy Who Worked Up Mine" *Journal of the Trevithick Society*, No.12 (1985), pp.73–74

TUCKER, D.Gordon & TUCKER, Mary "The Story of Wheal Guskus in the Parish of Saint Hilary" *Journal of the Trevithick Society*, No.1 (1973), pp.49–62

TUCKER, Mary *See* TUCKER, D.Gordon & TUCKER, Mary

TYLECOTE, R.F. "The History of the Tin Industry in Cornwall: Some Suggested Lines of Research" *Cornish Archaeology*, No.5 (1966), pp.30–33

TYLECOTE, R.F. "Calenick: A Cornish Tin Smelter, 1702 to 1891" *Journal of the Historical Metallurgy Society*, Vol.14 No.1 (1980), pp.1–16

WAITE, Peter *See* ATKINSON, Michael, WAITE, Peter & BURT, Roger

WALTON, W.J. "The History of Underground Photography in Cornish Mines" *Camborne School of Mines Journal*, (1977), pp.30–37

WARNER, R.B. "The Carnanton Tin Ingot" *Cornish Archaeology*, No.6 (1967), pp.29–31

WEAVER, M.E. "Industrial Housing in West Cornwall" *Industrial Archaeology*, Vol.3 No.1 (1966)

WELLINGTON, John F. "Water Power in West Country Mining" *Tamar Journal*, No.7 (1985), pp.5–13

WELLS, A.P. "On Stream Analysis at Wheal Jane" *Mining Magazine*, (February 1983), pp.124–131

WHETTER, J.C.A. "Cornish Trade in the 17th Century: An Analysis of the Port Books" *Journal of the Royal Institution of Cornwall*, New Series Vol.IV Pt.4 (1964), pp.388–413

WHITEHEAD, J. "Geevor Tin Mine" *Camborne School of Mines Journal*, (1954), pp.31–44

WHITTICK, G.Clement "Roman Lead Ingots from the Mendips" *Proceedings of the Somerset Archaeological & Natural History Society*, Vol.125 (1981), pp.87–92

WHITTICK, G.Clement "The Earliest Roman Lead Mining on Mendip and in North Wales: A Reappraisal" *Britannia*, Vol.13 (1982), pp.113–123

WILKIE, Ian *See* BURT, Roger & WILKIE, Ian

WILLIAMS, Gerald "A History of Giew Mine" *Journal of the Trevithick Society*, No.11 (1984), pp.60–70

WILLIAMS, Gerald "Bal Du Mine or West Wheal Reeth" *Journal of the Trevithick Society*, No.13 (1986), pp.80–83

WOODROW, A. "Andrew Angwin M.Inst.M.M." *Journal of the Trevithick Society*, No.11 (1984), pp.71–75

YOUELL, R.F. "Eastern Exmoor" *Plymouth Mineral and Mining Club Journal*, Vol.5 No.1 (Spring 1974), pp.12–16

YOUNG, H.R. "Surface Water and Mining in the West Country" *Mining Magazine*, Vol.LXX No.6 (June 1944), pp.329–338

OTHER ENGLISH DISTRICTS

Books

BICK, David E. *Old Industries of Dean* (Newent: The Pound House, 1980)

CLEERE, Henry & CROSSLEY, David W. *The Iron Industry of the Weald* (Leicester: Leicester University Press, 1985)

COLLIDGE, W.H. *A Short History of Judkins of Heyford, Northamptonshire and Judkin Quarries at Nuneaton* (Nuneaton: Private Publication, 1966)

CROSSLEY, David W. *The Bewl Valley Ironworks, Kent c1300 to 1730* (Royal Archaeological Institute Monograph, 1975)

CROSSLEY, David W. *See* CLEERE, Henry & CROSSLEY, David W.

DREWETT, P.L. (Ed.) *Archaeology in Sussex to AD 1500* (Council for British Archaeology, Research Report No.29, 1978)

GALLOIS, R.W. *British Regional Geology. The Wealden District* (Institute of Geological Sciences, H.M.S.O., 1979)

HAINS, B.A. & HORTON, A. *British Regional Geology. Central England* (Institute of Geological Sciences, H.M.S.O., 1975)

HART, Cyril E. *The Industrial History of Dean* (Newton Abbot: David & Charles, 1971)

HART, Cyril E. *The Free Miners of the Royal Forest of Dean and Hundred of St.Briavels* (Gloucester: British Publishing Co., 1953)

HOLLINGWORTH, S.E. & TAYLOR, J.H. *The Mesozoic Ironstones of England: The Northampton Sand Ironstone: Stratigraphy, Structure and Reserves* (Memoirs of the Geological Survey, H.M.S.O., 1951)

HORTON, A. *See* HAINS, B.A. & HORTON, A.

MARFELL, A. *Forest Mines* (Coleford: Douglas McLean, 1980)

NICHOLLS, H.G. *The Forest of Dean and Iron Making in Olden Times* (Coleford: The Forest Bookshop, 1981. Reprint of 1866 Edition.)

RUTLAND RAILWAY MUSEUM *Ironstone Mining in the Cottesmore Area* (Rutland: Rutland Railway Museum, 1981)

STRAKER, Ernest *Wealden Iron* (Newton Abbot: David & Charles, 1969. Reprint of 1931 Edition)

TAYLOR, J.H. *The Mesozoic Ironstones of England. Petrology of the Northampton Sand Ironstone Formation* (Memoirs of the Geological Survey, H.M.S.O., 1949)

TAYLOR, J.H. *See* HOLLINGSWORTH, S.E. & TAYLOR, J.H.

WILSON, V. *The East Midlands Ironstone Fields* (Nottingham: Nottingham University, 1953)

Theses

CATTELL, C.S. *The Historical Geography of the Wealden Iron Industry* (University of London MA Thesis, 1972)

FISHER, C. *Free Miners and Colliers: Custom, the Crown and Trade Unionism in the Forest of Dean 1788-1886* (University of Warwick PhD Thesis, 1978)

HAMMERSLEY, G.F. *The History of the Iron Industry in the Forest of Dean Region 1562-1660* (University of London PhD Thesis, 1971/2)

Articles

ANON "Iron Ore at Corby" *Mine and Quarry Engineering*, Vol.18 (January 1952), pp.21–29

ANON "Ironstone Mining at Exton Park" *Mine and Quarry Engineering*, Vol.23 (September 1957), pp.400–405

ANON "Dragonby Mine (Frodingham). Part 1" *Mine and Quarry Engineering*, Vol.24 (January 1958), pp.2–8

ANON "Dragonby Mine. Part 2" *Mine and Quarry Engineering*, Vol.24 (February 1958), pp.46–51

ANON "Dragonby Mine. Part 3" *Mine and Quarry Engineering*, Vol.24 (March 1958), pp.104–110

ANON "Redbourn Ore Preparation Plant (Frodingham Ironstone)" *Mine and Quarry Engineering*, Vol.28 (September 1962), pp.396–403

ASHWORTH, G.J. "A Note on the Decline of the Wealden Iron Industry" *Surrey Archaeological Collections*, Vol.67 (1970), pp.61–65

B.H.B.M.—K

BIRD, M. "The Calcutta Pumping Engine, Swannington, Leicestershire" *Bulletin of the Peak District Mines Historical Society*, Vol.6 No.3 (April 1976), pp.161–163

BRIDGE, E.M. "New Land for Old in the East Midlands (Ironstone mining)" *East Midland Geographer*, Vol.4 Pt.3 No.27 (June 1967), pp.143–153

BRIDGEWATER, Norman P. "Iron Working Sites in and Around the Forest of Dean" *Bulletin of the Historical Metallurgy Group*, Vol.2 No.1 (1968), pp.27–32

BROWN, Ivor J. "Gazetteer of Ironstone Mines in the East Midlands: Lincolnshire Section" *Lincolnshire Industrial Archaeology Group*, Vol.6 Nos.2 & 3 (1971)

BROWN, Ivor J. "A Gazetteer of Ironstone Mines in the East Midlands" *Bulletin of the Peak District Mines Historical Society*, Vol.6 No.2 (October 1975), pp.107–110

CANNELL, Alfred E. & CANNELL, M. "Grime's Graves, Norfolk" *Memoirs of the Northern Cavern and Mine Research Society*, (January 1969), p.78

CANNELL, M. *See* CANNELL, Alfred & CANNELL, M.

CATTELL, C.S. "The 1574 Lists of Wealden Ironworks" *Sussex Archaeological Collections*, Vol.CXVII (1979)

CLEERE, H. "The Roman Iron Industry of the Weald and its Connection with Classis Britannica" *Archaeological Journal*, Vol.131 (1974), pp.179–188

COHEN, I "History of Iron Working in and Near the Forest of Dean" *Transactions of the Woolhope Naturalists Fell Club*, Vol.34 (1955), pp.161–177

DIXON, E. "Britain's Earliest Mines, Grimes Grave, Norfolk" *Memoirs of the Northern Cavern and Mine Research Society*, (December 1966), pp.49–50

DOVER, T.M. "The Development of Strip Mining in the Northampton Sand and Frodingham Ironstone Fields" *Mine and Quarry Engineering*, Vol.26 (January 1960), pp.14–20

ELKINGTON, David & VINER, David "A Roman Pig of Lead Found at Syde, Gloucester" *Transactions of the Bristol and Gloucestershire Archaeological Society*, Vol.103 (1985), pp.209–211

EVANS, D. "The Coastal Trade in Iron Ore for Sussex and Hampshire in the 18th Century" *Sussex Industrial History*, Vol.15 (1985-6)

GORTON, R. "The Hook Norton Ironstone Companies" *Cake and Cockhorse*, Vol.IX (1982)

HART, Cyril E. "A Resume of the History of the Forest of Dean's Ironworking Industries" *Bulletin of the Historical Metallurgy Group*, Vol.2 No.1 (1968), pp.7–15

HIGHLEY, David E. "The Economic Geology of the Weald" *Proceedings of the Geologists Association*, Vol.86 No.4 (1976), pp.559–569

JOHNSON, B.L.C. "New Light on the Iron Industry of the Forest of Dean" *Transactions of the Bristol and Gloucestershire Archaeological Society*, Vol.LXXII (1953), pp.129–143

KING, Robert J. & LUDHAM, B.A. "The Quest for a Lost Lead Mine in Leicestershire" *Bulletin of the Peak District Mines Historical Society*, Vol.4 No.1 (March 1969), pp.3–30

KING, Robert J. & LUDHAM, B.A. "Ticklow Lane, Shepshed; Leicestershire's Lost Lead Mine" *Bulletin of the Historical Metallurgy Group*, Vol.3 No.2 (1969),p.69

LAFFOLEY, Nicholas d'A. "A History of Mining on Sark and Herm, Channel Islands" *Bulletin of the Peak District Mines Historical Society*, Vol.9 No.4 (Winter 1985), pp.201–227

LUDHAM, B.A. *See* KING, Robert J. & LUDHAM, B.A.

McCORMICK, Alan G. & WILLIES, Lynn "A Great Pig of Lead found at Colwick, Nottinghamshire" *Bulletin of the Peak District Mines Historical Society*, Vol.6 No.3 (April1976), pp144–145

RAYBOULD, T.J. "The Development and Organisation of Lord Dudley's Mineral Estates 1774–1845" *Economic History Review*, Second Series Vol.XXI No.3 (1968), pp.529–544

SCOTT–GARRETT, C. "Roman Iron Mine in Lydney Park" *Transactions of the Bristol and Gloucestershire Archaeological Society*, Vol.78 (1959), pp.86–91

SHELTON, D.C. "Mining Frodingham Ironstone" *Transactions of the Cornish Institute of Mining, Mechanical and Metallurgical Engineers*, Vol.III (1947–48), pp.22–30

SISMEY, Ron. "A Century of Ironstone Mining in Northamptonshire 1880–1980" *Camborne School of Mines Journal*, (1986), pp.52–56

SWEETING, G.S. "The Mineral Resources of the Weald" *South East Naturalist and Antiquary*, Vol.55 (1951), pp.31–39

VINER, David *See* ELKINGTON, David & VINER, David

WILLIES, Lynn *See* McCORMICK, Alan G. & WILLIES, Lynn

WILSON, Vernon "The Geology of the East Midland Ironstone Fields. Part 1" *Mine and Quarry Engineering*, Vol.22 (August 1956), pp.322–328

WILSON, Vernon "The Geology of the East Midland Ironstone Fields. Part 2" *Mine and Quarry Engineering*, Vol.22 (September 1956), pp.372–375

THE ISLE OF MAN

Books

ATKINSON, Michael *See* BURT, Roger, WAITE, Peter, ATKINSON, Michael & BURNLEY, Raymond

BAWDEN,T.A. *See* GARRAD, Larch S. with BAWDEN, T.A., QUALTROUGH, J.K. & SCRATCHARD, W.S.

BURNLEY, Raymond *See* BURT, Roger, WAITE, Peter, ATKINSON, Michael & BURNLEY, Raymond

BURT, Roger, WAITE, Peter, ATKINSON, Michael & BURNLEY, Raymond *The Lancashire and Westmorland Mineral Statistics with the Isle of Man 1845–1913* (Exeter: Department of Economic History, University of Exeter, 1983)

CARRUTHERS, R.G. & STRAHAN, A. *Special Reports on the Mineral Resources of G.B. Vol.26: Lead and Zinc Ores of Durham, Yorkshire, Derbyshire and Notes on the Isle of Man* (Sheffield: Mining Facsimiles, 1986. Reprint of Geological Survey 1923 Edition)

CLARKE, Catherine, HORTON, Mark & STRATTON, Michael *A Survey of Mining Remains at Laxey, Isle of Man* (Ironbridge: Institute of Industrial Archaeology, Research Paper No.2, 1985)

DEWEY, H. & EASTWOOD, T. *Special Reports on the Mineral Resources of G.B. Vol.30: Copper Ores of the Midlands, Wales, the Lake District and the Isle of Man* (Sheffield: Mining Facsimiles, 1986. Reprint of the Geological Survey 1925 Edition)

EASTWOOD, T. *See* DEWEY, H. & EASTWOOD, T.

GARRAD, Larch S. with BAWDEN, T.A., QUALTROUGH, J.K. & SCRATCHARD, W.S. *The Industrial Archaeology of the Isle of Man* (Newton Abbot: David & Charles, 1972)

JESPERSEN, Anders *The Lady Isabella Waterwheel of the Great Laxey Mining Company, Isle of Man, 1854–1954* (Copenhagen: Private Publication, 1954)

QUALTROUGH, J.K. *See* GARRAD, Larch S. with BAWDEN, T.A., QUALTROUGH, J.K. & SCRATCHARD, W.S.

SCRATCHARD, W.S. *See* GARRAD, Larch S. with BAWDEN, T.A., QUALTROUGH, J.K. & SCRATCHARD, W.S.

THE ISLE OF MAN

STRAHAN, A. *See* CARRUTHERS, R.G. & STRAHAN, A.

WAITE, Peter *See* BURT, Roger, WAITE, Peter, ATKINSON, Michael & BURNLEY, Raymond

Theses

Articles

BICK, David E. "Comments on Unusual Water–Powered Engines on the Isle of Man" *Bulletin of the Peak District Mines Historical Society*, Vol.6 No.3 (April 1976), p.135

CHALLIS, Peter J. "The Snaefell Mine Accident, 1897" *British Mining*, No.23 (1983), pp.20–23

GARRAD, Larch S. "John Kelly's Ballawillan Carding Mill and the Ohio Mine, East Baldwin, Isle of Man" *Industrial Archaeology*, Vol.13 No.4 (1978) pp.331–334

GARRAD, Larch S. "Snaefell Mine, Lonan, Isle of Man, with Particular Reference to the Use of Water Power: Part I" *Industrial Archaeology*, Vol.16 No.2 (1981), pp.116–125

GARRAD, Larch S. "The Use of Water Power in the Cornaa Valley, Isle of Man: Part II: Corrany Bridge and Below" *Industrial Archaeology*, Vol.16 No.3 (1981), pp.218–222

GARRAD, Larch S. "Snaefell Mines, Lonan, Isle of Man: Part II: Surviving Remains other than those on the Main Washing Floors and about the Shaft" *Industrial Archaeology*, Vol.17 Nos.2–4 (Not Dated), pp.114–119

GILLINGS, Andy M. "Unusual Water–Powered Engines in the Isle of Man" *Bulletin of the Peak District Mines Historical Society*, Vol.6 No.2 (October 1975), pp.85–92

GILLINGS, Andy M. *See* KELLY, Bobby & GILLINGS, Andy M.

GILLINGS, Andy M. *See* WARRINER, David J. & GILLINGS, Andy M.

GRANT, R.F.M. "The Snaefell Mine" *Mining Magazine*, Vol.XCII No.2 (February 1955), pp.79–86

HOLLIS, David "The Great Laxey Winding Engine, Great Laxey Mine, Isle of Man" *Bulletin of the Peak District Mines Historical Society*, Vol.9 No.5 (Summer 1986), pp.306–312

HOLLIS, David B. "Further Comments About Great Laxey Winding Engine" *Bulletin of the Peak District Mines Historical Society*, Vol.10 No.1 (Summer 1987), pp.17–23

HOLLIS, David B. "Uranium in the Isle of Man" *British Mining*, No.34 (1987), pp.44–45

HOLLIS, David B. "The Forgotten Iron Mines of Kirk Maughold, Isle of Man" *British Mining*, No.34 (1987), pp.46–54

KELLY, Bobby & GILLINGS, A.M. "Recollections of a Laxey Miner" *Bulletin of the Peak District Mines Historical Society*, Vol.8 No.1 (June 1981), pp.43–48

KENYON, P. "The Great Laxey Mining Company, Isle of Man. Surviving Evidence April 1965" *Journal of Industrial Archaeology*, Vol.2 (1965), pp.154–157

LANDLESS, Jeremy "An Introduction to the Mines of the Isle of Man" *British Mining*, No.3 (1976), pp.24–41

PEARCE, Adrian J. & ROSE, G. "Mining Remains in the Isle of Man" *Bulletin of the Peak District Mines Historical Society*, Vol.7 No.4 (October 1979), pp.216–230

ROSE, G. *See* PEARCE, Adrian J. & ROSE, G.

SKELTON, R.H. "Manx Mines" *Mining Magazine*, Vol.XCII No.1 (January 1955), pp.9–18

VARLEY, H.D. "Lady Isabella Wheel, Isle of Man" *Industrial Archaeology*, Vol.7 No.3 (1970), pp.337–338

WARRINER, David J. & GILLINGS, Andy M "Exploration and Survey of the Great Laxey Mine, Isle of Man" *Bulletin of the Peak District Mines Historical Society*, Vol.8 No.6 (Autumn 1983), pp.373–382

WALES: GENERAL

Books

LEWIS, W.J. *Lead Mining in Wales* (Cardiff: University of Wales Press, 1967)

NORTH, Frederick John *Mining for Metals in Wales* (Cardiff: National Museum of Wales, 1962)

REES, D.Morgan *Mills, Mines and Furnaces: Industrial Archaeology in Wales* (H.M.S.O. National Museum of Wales, 1969)

REES, D.Morgan *The Metalliferous Mines of Wales* (Bulletin of the National Museum of Wales, 1972)

REES, D.Morgan *The Industrial Archaeology of Wales* (Newton Abbot: David & Charles, 1975)

SIVEWRIGHT, W.J. *Civil Engineering Heritage. Wales and Western England* (Thomas Telford Ltd, 1986)

SPARGO, Thomas *The Mines of Wales: Their Present Position and Prospects* (Talybont: Simon Hughes, 1975. Reprint Edition.)

THOMAS, Trevor Morgan *The Mineral Wealth of Wales and Its Exploitation* (Edinburgh: Oliver & Boyd, 1961)

Theses

JONES, L. *The Lead and Silver Industry in Wales 1558–1750* (University of Oxford BLitt Thesis, 1924)

Articles

ANON "Welsh Mining Laws" *British Caver*, Vol.31 (1959), pp.81–83

BICK, David E. "Forgotten Mines of Wales" *Country Quest*, Vol.10 No.7 (December 1969), pp.39–41

BICK, David E. "The Lost Silver Mines of Wales" *Country Quest*, Vol.19 No.9 (February 1979), pp.9–11

CONWAY, Alan "Welsh Goldminers in British Columbia" *National Library of Wales Journal*, Vol.10 (1957–8), pp.375–389

DELABOLE "Mines Down–Along" *British Caver*, Vol.19 (Spring 1949), pp.27–30

EGAN, David "Record Offices and Local History in Wales. Part 1" *The Local Historian*, Vol.13 No.6 (May 1979), pp.341–345

EGAN, David "Record Offices and Local History in Wales. Part 2" *The Local Historian*, Vol.13 No.7 (August 1979), pp.425–430

EGAN, David "Record Offices and Local History in Wales. Part 3" *The Local Historian*, Vol.13 No.8 (November 1979), pp.468–471

HARRIS, John R. "Michael Hughes of Sutton: the Influence of Welsh Copper on Lancashire Business, 1780–1815" *Transactions of the Historical Society of Lancashire and Cheshire*, Vol.CI (1949), pp.139–167

PHILLIPS, Seaton "Roman Lead Mines (Wales)" *British Caver*, Vol.29 (1958), pp.41–43

TUCKER, Mary "Source Material for Metal Mining History: The Druid Inn Papers at the National Library of Wales" *Bulletin of the Peak District Mines Historical Society*, Vol.6 No.5 (May 1977), pp.249–250

WILLIAMS, Moelwyn I. "Local History in Wales" *The Local Historian*, Vol.9 No.1 (February 1970), pp.16–22

NORTH WALES AND MERIONETH

Books

ANNELS, A.E. & BURNHAM, B.C.(Eds.) *The Dolaucothi Gold Mines* (University College Cardiff & University College Lampeter, 1983)

BEVAN–EVANS, M. *Gadlys and Flintshire Lead Mining in the 18th. Century* (Hawarden: Flintshire Record Office, 1963)

BICK, David E. *The Old Copper Mines of Snowdonia* (Newent: The Pound House, 1982)

BURNHAM, B.C. *See* ANNELS, A.E. & BURNHAM, B.C.

DEWEY, H. & EASTWOOD, T. *Special Report on the Mineral Resources of G.B. Vol.30: Copper Ores of the Midlands, Wales, the Lake District and the Isle of Man* (Sheffield: Mining Facsimiles, 1986. Reprint of Geological Survey 1925 Edition.)

DEWEY, H. *See* SMITH, B. & DEWEY, H.

DODD, Arthur Herbert *A History of Wrexham, Denbighshire* (Wrexham: Hughes & Son for Wrexham Borough Council, 1957)

DODD, Arthur Herbert *A History of Caernarvonshire 1284–1900* (Caernarvon: Caernarvonshire Historical Society, 1968)

DODD, Arthur Herbert *The Industrial Revolution in North Wales* (Cardiff: University of Wales Press, 1971)

DOWN, C.G. *The Manganese Mines of North Wales* (Sheffield: Northern Mine Research Society, British Mining No.14, 1980)

EASTWOOD, T. *See* DEWEY, H. & EASTWOOD, T.

FOSTER–SMITH, J.R. *The Non–Ferrous Mines of Denbighshire* (Skipton: Northern Cavern and Mine Research Society, Individual Survey Series No.5, 1972)

FOSTER–SMITH, J.R. *The Non–Ferrous Mines of Flintshire* (Skipton: Northern Cavern and Mine Research Society, Individual Survey Series No.7, 1974)

FOSTER–SMITH, J.R. *The Mines of Anglesey and Caernarvonshire* (Sheffield: Northern Mine Research Society, British Mining No.4, 1977)

FOSTER–SMITH, J.R. *The Mines of Merioneth* (Sheffield: Northern Mine Research Society, British Mining No.6, 1977)

GEORGE, T.N. *British Regional Geology. North Wales* (Institute of Geological Sciences, H.M.S.O., 1979)

HALL, George William *The Gold Mines of Merioneth or Gweithfeydd aur Meirionydd* (Gloucester: Griffin Publications, 1975)

HARRIS, John R. *The Copper King: A Biography of Thomas Williams of Llanidan* (Liverpool: Liverpool University Press, 1964)

MORRISON, T.A. *Goldmining in Western Merioneth* (Merioneth History and Research Society, 1978)

ROWLANDS, John *Copper Mountain* (Llangefni: Anglesey Antiquarian Society, 1966)

ROWLANDS, John *Copper Mountain* (Llangefni: Anglesey Antiquarian Society, 1. Reprint of 1966 Edition.)

SMITH, B. *Special Reports on the Mineral Resources of G.B. Vol.19. Lead and Zinc Ores of the Carboniferous Rocks of North Wales* (Sheffield: Mining Facsimiles, 1986. Reprint of Geological Survey 1921 Edition.)

SMITH, B. & DEWEY, H. *Special Reports on the Mineral Resources of G.B. Vol.23: Lead and Zinc Ores in the Pre–Carboniferous Rocks of West Shropshire and North Wales* (Sheffield: Mining Facsimiles, 1986. Reprint of Geological Survey 1922 Edition)

THORBURN, J.A. *Talargoch Mine* (Sheffield: Northern Mine Research Society, British Mining No.31, 1986)

WILLIAMS, Christopher J. *The Llandudno Copper Mines* (Sheffield: Northern Mine Research Society, British Mining No.9, 1979)

WILLIAMS, Christopher J. *The Lead Mines of the Alyn Valley* (Flintshire Historical Society, 1980)

WILLIAMS, Christopher J. *Metal Mines of North Wales* (Rhuddlan: Charter Publications, 1980)

WREN, W.J. *The Tanat Valley: Its Railways and Industrial Archaeology* (Newton Abbot: David & Charles, 1967)

Theses

ARMOUR, C. *The Trade of Chester and the State of the Dee Navigation 1600–1800* (University of London PhD Thesis, 1956)

CARR, A.D. *The Mostyn Family and Estate 1200–1642* (University of Wales, Bangor, PhD Thesis, 1976)

HARRIS, J.R. *The Copper Industry in Lancashire and North Wales* (University of Manchester PhD Thesis, 1952)

PRYCE, W.T.R. *The Social and Economic Structure of North East Wales 1750–1890* (Council for National Academic Awards PhD Thesis, 1971)

RHODES, J.N. *The London Lead Company in North Wales, 1693–1872* (University of Leicester PhD Thesis, 1970)

ROBERTSON, J.G. *Some Aspects of Mineral Production in Modern Britain, with Particular Reference to Yorkshire Potash and Merioneth Copper* (University of Hull PhD Thesis, 1973/4)

TEALE, A. *The Economy and Society of North Flintshire, c.1660–1714* (University of Wales, Aberystwyth, MA Thesis, 1980)

TURLEY, J.T. *A Study of the Evolution of the Coal Mining and Iron Industries of North East Denbighshire and Associated Population Changes from the Early Seventeenth Century to the Middle of the Nineteenth Century* (University of Manchester MA Thesis, 1975)

WILLIAMS, C.R. *The Industrialisation of Flintshire in the Nineteenth Century, being an Examination of the Changes and Developments in the Principal Industries from 1815–1914* (University of Wales MA Thesis, 1950)

WILLIAMS, C.R. *A Dissertation on the Industrial Changes and Developments in the County of Flint from 1815 to 1914* (University of Wales, Aberystwyth, MA Thesis, 1952)

Articles

ADAMS, D.R. "Princess Marina Gold Mine, Gwynfynydd, Merionethshire" *British Caver*, Vol.34 (1964), pp.43–46

ANON "A Copper Mine at Amlwch, Anglesea" *British Caver*, Vol.26 (1955), pp.44–45

ANON "The Parc Mine Project" *Mine and Quarry Engineering*, Vol.29 (January 1963), pp.18–27

ANON "Experiment at the Parc Mine" *Mining Magazine*, Vol.108 No.1 (January 1963), pp.26–29

APPLETON, P. "The Park Lead Mines, Minera" *Bulletin of Local Studies*, Vol.3 (1977), pp.15–17

BASSETT, T.M. "The Drwsy Coed Account Book" *Caernarvonshire Record Office Bulletin*, No.3 (1970)

BASSETT, T.M. "A Note on Penrhyn Du" *Transactions of the Caernarvonshire Historical Society*, Vol.XXXII (1971)

BAYLES, Russell "A Brief Survey of Beam Pumping Engines Employed on Lead Mines in Flintshire" *Memoirs of the Northern Cavern and Mine Research Society*, (January 1969), pp.8–14

BAYLES, Russell "Parc Lead Mine, Llanwrst, North Wales" *Memoirs of the Northern Cavern and Mine Research Society*, (October 1969), pp.1–7

BAYLES, Russell "Gilfach Copper Mine" *Memoirs of the Northern Cavern and Mine Research Society*, Vol.2 No.1 (April 1971), pp.20–21

BAYLES, R. "Extracts from the Minute Book of the North Hendre Lead Mining Co. Ltd." *British Mining*, No.11 (1979), pp.50–53

BECK, N.C. "A Brief Account of the Copper Mines of Cwm Dyli, Snowdonia" *Transactions of the Caernarvonshire Historical Society*, Vol.XXXI (1970)

BEVAN–EVANS, M. "Gadlys and Flintshire Lead Mining in the Eighteenth Century. Part 1" *Flintshire Historical Society Journal*, Vol.18 (1960), pp.75–130

BEVAN–EVANS, M. "Gadlys and Flintshire Lead Mining in the Eighteenth Century. Part 2" *Flintshire Historical Society Journal*, Vol.19 (1961), pp.32–60

BEVAN–EVANS, M. "Gadlys and Flintshire Lead Mining in the Eighteenth Century. Part 3" *Flintshire Historical Society Journal*, Vol.20 (1962), pp.58–89

CANNELL, Alfred E. "The Dolgellau Gold Belt" *Memoirs of the Northern Cavern and Mine Research Society*, (August 1964), pp.41–42

CANNELL, Alfred E. & CANNELL, M. "The Llanwrst Mining Area, Caernarvon, North Wales" *Memoirs of the Northern Cavern and Mine Research Society*, (January 1969), pp.76–78

CANNELL, M. *See* CANNELL, Alfred E. & CANNELL, M.

COCKSHUTT, E. "The Parys and Mona Copper Mines" *Transactions of the Anglesey Antiquarian Society* (1960)

COCKSHUTT, E. "The Parys Mountain Copper Mines in the Island of Anglesey" *Archaeologia Cambrensis*, Vol.114 (1965), pp.87–111

COLMAN, Timothy B. & LAFFOLEY, Nicholas d'A. "Britannia or Snowdon Mine" *Bulletin of the Peak District Mines Historical Society*, Vol.9 No.5 (Summer 1986), pp.313–331

DAVIES, Kenneth "The 18th Century Copper and Brass Industries of the Greenfield Valley" *Transactions of the Honourable Society of Cymmrodorian*, (1979), pp.203–232

DAVIES, V.Challinor *See* OWEN, G.W. & DAVIES, V. Challinor

EARP, J.R. "Mineral Veins of the Minera–Maeshafn District of North Wales" *Bulletin of the Geological Survey of Great Britain*, No.14 (1958), pp.44–69

EDWARDS, I "The New British Iron Company" *Transactions of the Denbighshire History Society*, Vol.32 (1983)

HALL, George W. "An Ancient Gold and Copper Mine (Vigra)" *Mining Magazine*, Vol.XCV No.5 (November 1956), pp.277–279

HALL, George W. "Ogafau Gold Mine, Pumpsaint" *Shropshire Mining Club*, Yearbook (1964–5), pp.47–49

HEATHCOTE, J.A. "Unusual Cave Pearls from Minera Mine" *Shropshire Mining Club Journal*, (1975–6), pp.29–32

HOUSTON, William J. "Limestone Mining at Halkyn (and Old Lead-Mines)" *Mine and Quarry Engineering*, Vol.29 (December 1963), pp.514–519

HUGHES, G.B. "Gold in the Welsh Hills" *Country Life*, 2nd October 1969

JACKSON, Peter "Notes on Sygun Mine" *Memoirs of the Northern Cavern and Mine Research Society*, Vol.2 No.3 (September 1973), pp.149–150

JONES, William G. "Prince Edward Mine, Near Trawsfynydd, Merioneth" *Shropshire Mining Club Journal*, (1977), pp.5–6

JONES, William G. "Castell Carndochan Gold Mine and Prince Edward Gold Mine" *British Mining*, No.5 (1977), pp.56–58

JONES, William G. "Llanfair Mines Ltd., Llanfair Talhaiarn, Denbighshire" *British Mining*, No.11 (1979), pp.54–62

JONES, William G. & WILLIES, Lynn "Impressions of Visits to Parc Mine, North Wales" *Bulletin of the Peak District Mines Historical Society*, Vol.6 No.1 (May 1975), pp.47–48

JONES, W. Hugh "A Strike at Talargoch Mine Hundred Years Ago" *Flintshire Historical Society Journal*, Vol.16 (1956), pp.22–30

KELLY, R.S. "Metal Working in North Wales During the Roman Period" *Bulletin of the Board of Celtic Studies*, Vol.XXVII No.1 (1976)

LAFFOLEY, Nicholas d'A. & REX, Anthony J. "Cwm Bychan or Nantmor Mine, North Wales" *Bulletin of the Peak District Mines Historical Society*, Vol.9 No.6 (Winter 1986), pp.387–392

LAFFOLEY, Nicholas d'A *See* COLMAN, Timothy B. & LAFFOLEY, Nicholas d'A

LERRY, George G. "The Industries of Denbighshire from Tudor Times to the Present Day, Pt.II" *Denbighshire Historical Society Transactions*, Vol.7 (1958), pp.38–66

MADOC–JONES, G. "St. David's Mine Area, Vigra, Clogau" *British Mining*, No.1 (1975), pp.63–68

MADOC–JONES, G. "Clogau St. David's Gold Mine, Bontddu, Merionethshire" *British Mining*, No.3 (1976), pp.12–16

MANNING, W.H. "The Dolaucothi Gold Mines" *Antiquity*, Vol.42 (1968), pp.299–302

MICHELL, F.B. "The Dressing of Complex Lead–Zinc Ores (Mill Close and Halkyn)" *Mine and Quarry Engineering*, Vol.12 (November 1946), pp.135–144

MORRISON, T.A. "Gold Mining in Western Merioneth. Part 1" *Journal of the Merioneth Historical and Records Society*, Vol.VII No.1 (1973), pp.28–71

MORRISON, T.A. "Gold Mining in Western Merioneth. Part 2" *Journal of the Merioneth Historical and Records Society*, Vol.VII No.2 (1974), pp.140–187

MORRISON, T.A. "A Brief History of the Merioneth Manganese Industry" *Industrial Archaeology*, Vol.11 No.1 (1974), pp.29–32

OWEN, G.W. & DAVIES, V.Challinor "The Gold Mines of Merioneth" *Journal of the Merioneth History and Records Society*, Vol.IV No.1 (1961), pp.60–71

PATERSON, J.E.A. "Lead and Limestone from North Wales" *Mining Magazine*, Vol.LXXXVII No.5 (November 1952), pp.265–272

PRATT, D. "The Lead Mining Community at Minera in the 14th Century" *Denbighshire Historical Society Transactions*, Vol.11 (1962), pp.28–36

PRATT, D. "Minera: Township of the Mines" *Denbighshire Historical Society Transactions*, Vol.25 (1976), pp.114–154

PRATT, D. "Speculative and Exploratory Lead Mining at Llandegla" *Denbighshire Historical Society Transactions*, Vol.31 (1982), pp.29–46

REES, D.Morgan "Industrial Archaeology in Merioneth" *Journal of the Merioneth History and Records Society*, Vol.V. No.2 (1966), pp.133–146

REES, D.Morgan "Copper Mining in North Wales" *Archaeologia Cambrensis*, (1968), pp.172–197

REX, Anthony J. *See* LAFFOLEY, Nicholas d'A & REX, Anthony J.

RHODES, J.N. "The London (Quaker) Lead Company and the Prestatyn Mines Scandal" *Flintshire Historical Society Publication*, Vol.23 (1967–8), pp.42–53

RHODES, J.N. "Dr. Linden, William Hooson and North Welsh Mining in the Mid 18th Century" *Bulletin of the Peak District Mines Historical Society*, Vol.3 No.5 (May 1968), pp.259–270

RHODES, J.N. "Derbyshire Influences on Lead Mining in North Wales in the 17th and 18th centuries" *Bulletin of the Peak District Mines Historical Society*, Vol.3 No.6 (October 1968), pp.339–352

RHODES, J.N. "The Lead Mills at Mold" *Flintshire Historical Society Journal*, Vol.25 (1971–2), pp.213–30

RICHARDS, Melville "English Miners at Minera" *Denbighshire Historical Society Transactions*, Vol.12 (1963), p.169

ROBEY, John A. "The Parys Mountain Copper Mines and the Amlwch Port, Anglesey" *Staffordshire Industrial Archaeology Society Bulletin*, Vol.2 No.2 (December 1970)

SCHNELLMANN, G.A. "New Operations in the Llanrwst Lead–Zinc District" *Mining Magazine*, Vol.LXXXVI No.6 (June 1952), pp.333–339

VERNON, Robert W. "Gwynfyndd Mine, Merioneth: Its Geology and History" *Shropshire Mining Club Journal*, (1971–2), pp.31–36

WARE, S.Dawson "Non–Ferrous Metal Resources in North Wales" *Mining Magazine*, Vol.LXXXVII No.1 (July 1952), pp.15–20

WEBSTER, G. "The Lead Mining Industry in North Wales in Roman Times" *Flintshire Historical Society Journal*, Vol.13 (1952–3), pp.5–33

WESTON, J.D. "Parys Mountain Copper Mine, Anglesey" *Bulletin of the Peak District Mines Historical Society*, Vol.5 No.2 (October 1972), pp.109–113

WHITTICK, G.Clement "The Earliest Roman Lead Mining on Mendip and in North Wales" *Britannia*, Vol.13 (1982), pp.113–123

WILLIAMS, Christopher J. "The Lead Miners of Flintshire and Denbighshire" *Llafur*, Vol.3 No.1 (1980), pp.87–96

WILLIES, Lynn "A Visit to Parc Mine, North Wales" *Bulletin of the Peak District Mines Historical Society*, Vol.6 No.3 (April 1976), p.140

WILLIES, Lynn *See* JONES, William G. & WILLIES, Lynn

CENTRAL AND SOUTH WALES

Books

ATKINSON, Michael & BABER, Colin *The Growth and Decline of the South Wales Iron Industry 1760–1880: An Industrial History* (Cardiff: University of Wales, 1987)

BABER, Colin *See* ATKINSON, Michael & BABER, Colin

BICK, David E. *The Old Metal Mines of Mid–Wales: Part 1 South of Devil's Bridge* (Newent: The Pound House, 1974)

BICK, David E. *The Old Metal Mines of Mid–Wales: Part 2 Cardiganshire: The Rheidol to Goginan* (Newent: The Pound House, 1975)

BICK, David E. *The Great Metal Mines of Wales: Number One. Dyliffe, West Montgomeryshire* (Newent: The Pound House, 1975)

BICK, David E. *The Old Metal Mines of Mid–Wales: Part 3 North of Goginan* (Newent: The Pound House, 1976)

BICK, David E. *The Old Metal Mines of Mid–Wales: Part 4 West Montgomeryshire* (Newent: The Pound House, 1977)

BICK, David E. *The Old Metal Mines of Mid–Wales: Part 5 Aberdovey, Dinas Mawddwy and Llangynog* (Newent: The Pound House, 1978)

BICK, David E. *Dyliffe: A Famous Welsh Lead Mine* (Newent: Pound House, 1985)

BICK, David E. *Frongoch Lead and Zinc Mine* (Sheffield: Northern Mine Research Society, British Mining No.30, 1986)

BICK, David E. *The Mines of Newent and Ross* (Newent: Pound House, 1987)

BURNLEY, Raymond *See* BURT, Roger, WAITE, Peter & BURNLEY, Raymond

BURT, Roger, WAITE, Peter & BURNLEY, Raymond *The Mines of Cardiganshire* (Exeter: Department of Economic History, University of Exeter, 1985)

ELSAS, Madeleine (Ed.) *Iron in the Making. Dowlais Iron Company Letters, 1782–1860* (Published jointly by Glamorgan County Council and Guest Keen Iron & Steel Co. Ltd, 1960)

FOSTER–SMITH, J.R. *The Mines of Montgomery and Radnorshire* (Sheffield: Northern Mine Research Society, British Mining No.10, 1978)

FOSTER–SMITH, J.R. *The Mines of Cardiganshire* (Sheffield: Northern Mine Research Society, British Mining No.12, 1979)

FOSTER–SMITH, J.R. *The Non–Ferrous Mines of the South Wales Area* (Sheffield: Northern Mine Research Society, British Mining No.18, 1981)

FRANCIS, Absolem *History of the Cardiganshire Mines: From the Earliest Ages and the Authenticated History to 1874, With Their Present Position and Prospect* (Sheffield: Mining Facsimiles, 1987. Reprint of 1875 Edition.)

GEORGE, T.N. *British Regional Geology. South Wales* (Institute of Geological Sciences, H.M.S.O., 1982)

GOUGH, John W. *Sir Hugh Middleton, Entrepreneur and Engineer* (Oxford: Clarendon Press 1964)

HAGUE, Douglas B. *A Guide to the Industrial Archaeology of Mid-Wales* (Association for Industrial Archaeology, 1984)

HALL, George William *Metal Mines of Southern Wales* (Gloucester: John Jennings, 1971)

HALL, George William *A Note on the Decline of Mining in Cardiganshire* (Reprinted from *Caridigion*, 1972)

HUGHES, Simon J.S. *Cardiganshire. Its Mines and Miners* (Ceredigion: Private Publication, 1976)

HUGHES, Simon J.S. *The Cwmystwyth Mines* (Sheffield: Northern Mine Research Society, British Mining No.17, 1981)

JONES, J.A. & MORETON, N.J.M. *The Mines and Minerals of Mid-Wales (North Cardigan and West Montgomery)* (Kegworth: Private Publication, 1977)

JONES, O.T. *Special Reports on the Mineral Resources of Great Britain Vol.20. Lead and Zinc: The Mining District of North Cardiganshire and West Montgomershire* (Sheffield: Mining Facsimiles, 1986. Reprint of 1922 Edition.)

MORETON, N.J.M. *See* JONES, J.A. & MORETON, N.J.M.

PALMER, M. *The Richest in all Wales: The Welsh Potosi or Esgair Hir and Esgair Fraith Lead and Copper Mines of Cardiganshire* (Sheffield: Northern Mine Research Society, British Mining No.22, 1983)

PRICHARD, R.J. *The Rheidol United Mines* (Sheffield: Northern Mines Research Society, British Mining No.27, 1985)

WAITE, Peter *See* BURT, Roger, WAITE, Peter & BURNLEY, Raymond

WILLIAMS, R.Alan *The Old Metal Mines of the Llangynog District, North Powis, Mid-Wales* (Sheffield: Northern Mine Research Society, British Mining No.26, 1985)

Theses

ADDIS, J.P. *The Crawshay Dynasty: A Study in Industrial Organisation and Development 1765–1867* (University of Wales MA Thesis, 1954)

BEYNON, O. *The Lead Mining Industry in Cardiganshire 1700–1830* (University of Wales MA Thesis, 1938)

EVANS, S. *An Examination of Sir Humphrey Mackworth's Industrial Activities, with Special Reference to the Governor and Company of the Mine Adventurers of England* (University of Wales MA Thesis, 1950)

HUMPHREYS, T.M. *Rural Society in Eighteenth Century Montgomeryshire* (University of Wales, Swansea, PhD Thesis, 1982)

INCE, L.C. *The Neath Abbey Iron Company 1792–1886* (University of Bath MSc Thesis, 1978)

JOHN, W.R. *The History of the Growth and Organisation of the Copper Industry of Swansea and District* (University of Wales MA Thesis, 1912)

JONES, J.G. *The Wynn Family and Their Estate of Gwydir: Their Origins, Growth, and Development upto 1674* (University of Wales, Cardiff, PhD Thesis, 1975)

JONES, L. *The Lead Industry in Cardiganshire* (University of Wales MA Thesis, 1915)

MERSHAM, R.R. *The Mining District of Central Wales* (University of Leicester MSc Thesis, 1969)

OWEN, O.P. *Adult and Further Education in Carmarthenshire 1759–1870* (University of Manchester MEd Thesis, 1969/70)

POWELL,J.M. *An Economic Geography of Montgomeryshire in the Nineteenth Century* (University of Liverpool MA Thesis, 1962)

TOOMEY, R.R. *Vivian and Sons 1809-1924: A Study of the Firm in the Copper and Related Industries* (University of Wales, Swansea, PhD, 1980)

WALKER, R.W. *The Trade and Administration of Aberystwyth Harbour 1750-1900* University of Wales, Aberystwyth, MSc Thesis, 1972/3)

Articles

ANON "Bryndyfi Mine" *Shropshire Mining Club Journal*, (1974–5), pp.11–17

BENJAMIN, E.Alwyn "The Enumeration District of Cwm Rheidol, 1861–1871" *Ceredigion*, (1982), pp.128–134

BENJAMIN, E.Alwyn "Melindwr Cardiganshire: The Census of 1841–71" *Ceredigion*, (1983), pp.322–335

BENNETT, J.S. "An Account of a Mine Adventure by John Royle on the Gwydir Estate, 1775–1784" *British Mining*, No.23 (1983), pp.24–28

BICK, David E. "Potosi Mines (Esgair Hir)" *Country Quest*, Vol.12 No.2 (July 1971), pp.25–27

BICK, David E. "Mines of the Ystwyth Valley, Cardiganshire" *Plymouth Mineral and Mining Club Journal*, Vol.4 No.1 (Spring 1973), pp.20–22

BICK, David E. "Remnants of Mining in Cardiganshire before the Nineteenth Century" *Ceredigion*, (1978), pp.355–359

BLAKEY, I.J. *See* JONES, G.D.B., BLAKEY, I.J. & MACPHERSON, E.C.F.

BOON, George C. & WILLIAMS, Colin "The Dolaucothi Drainage Wheel" *Journal of Roman Studies*, Vol.56 (1966), pp.122–127

BOYNS, R.E. "The Bryndyfi Mine" *Ceredigion*, (1977), pp.210–216

BOYNS, Trevor E. "The Mines of Llywernog" *National Library of Wales Journal*, Vol.19 No.4 (1976), pp.430–452

CLAUGHTON, Peter F. "Greenhill Ochre Mine" *Journal of the Friends of the Pembroke Museums*, No.5 (Autumn 1976), p.10

CRITCHLEY, Martin F. *See* SHAW, Richard P. & CRITCHLEY, Martin F.

DAVIES, Hugh "A Gold Mining Legend of Pembrokeshire" *The Quarry Managers Journal,* (December 1948), pp.328–331

DAVIES, Mel. "The Iron, Lead and Copper Mines of South Wales Carboniferous Limestone Outcrops" *British Caver,* Vol.42 (1965), pp.30–35

DAVIES, P.S. "Tragedy at Treginnis (Copper Mine)" *The Pembroke Magazine,* No.39 (November 1985), pp.15–17

EYRE, David "Some Metal Mines of Mid–Wales" *Journal of the Cerberus Spelaeological Society,* Vol.15 No.4 (1985), pp.103–105

HALL, George W. "Van's Nominal Family. A Discourse on the Van Lead Mine, Montgomeryshire" *Shropshire Mining Club,* Yearbook (1965–6), pp.54–58

HALL, George W. "A Note on the Decline of Mining in Cardiganshire" *Ceredigion,* (1972), pp.85–88

HUGHES, Simon J.S. "The Decline of Mining in Cwmystwyth" *Ceredigion,* (1979), pp.419–438

HUGHES, Simon J.S. "The Mines of Talybont: Part 1: From AD 70 to 1800" *Industrial Archaeology,* Vol.16 No.3 (1981), pp.199–212

HUGHES, Simon J.S. "Bwlchglas Mine" *Industrial Archaeology,* Vol.16 No.2 (1981), pp.126–139

HUGHES, Simon J.S. "The Mines of Talybont: Part 2: From 1800 to the Present Day" *Industrial Archaeology,* Vol.16 No.4 (1982), pp.290–307

JENKINS, D.W. "Two Mines: Haffotty and Croesor" *British Caver,* Vol.34 (1964), pp.91–94

JONES, G.D.B. & LEWIS, P.R. "The Roman Gold Mines at Dolaucothi" *Carmarthen County Museum Publication,* No.1 (1971)

JONES, G.D.B., BLAKEY, I.J. & MACPHERSON, E.C.F. "Dolaucothi: The Roman Aqueduct" *Bulletin of the Board of Celtic Studies,* Vol.19 Pt.1 pp.71–84

JONES, G.D.B. *See* LEWIS, P.R. & JONES, G.D.B.

LEWIS, P.R. & JONES, G.D.B. "The Dolaucothi Gold Mines I; The Surface Evidence" *Archaeological Journal,* Vol.49 (1969), pp.244–272

LEWIS, P.R. *See* JONES, G.D.B. & LEWIS, P.R.

LEWIS, W.J. "Some Aspects of Mining in Cardiganshire in the 16th and 17th Centuries" *Caredigion,* (1951), pp.176–192

LEWIS, W.J. "The Cwmsymlog Lead Mine" *Ceredigion,* (1952), pp.27–38

LEWIS, W.J. "A Field Day at Cwmsymlog" *Ceredigion*, (1952), pp.54–55

LEWIS, W.J. "The Anchor Smelting Company, Aberystwyth 1786–92" *Ceredigion*, IV (1961)

LEWIS, W.J. "Lead Mining in Eastern Montgomeryshire" *Montgomeryshire Collections*, Vol.58 (1963–64), pp.114–124

MACPHERSON, E.C.F. *See* JONES, G.D.B., BLAKEY, I.J. & MACPHERSON, E.C.F.

MORRIS, Trevor "The Machynlleth Copper Mine" *Montgomeryshire Collections*, Vol.62 (1971–72), pp.212–216

MORRIS, Trevor "Mining Activity near Newtown" *Montgomeryshire Collections*, Vol.67 (1974), pp.109–116

MORRIS, Trevor & VERNON, Robert "The Van Miners" *Shropshire Mining Club Journal*, (1972–3), pp.36–48

MORRISON, T.A. "Some Notes on the Van Mine, Llanidloes, Montgomery" *Industrial Archaeology*, Vol.8 No.1 (1971), pp.29–51

MORRISON, T.A. "The Initiation of Mining Settlements on the Cardiganshire Orefield" *Industrial Archaeology*, Vol.10 No.2 (1973), pp.161–200

NASH–WILLIAMS, V.E. "The Roman Gold Mine at Dolaucothi" *Bulletin of the Board of Celtic Studies*, Vol.XIV No.1 (November 1950), pp.79–84

NAYLOR, Peter J. "Sir Hugh Middleton: The First Mines Adventurer" *Bulletin of the Peak District Mines Historical Society*, Vol.8 No.1 (June 1981), pp.54–59

NELSON, T.R.H. "Gold Mining in South Wales. Part 1" *Mine and Quarry Engineering*, Vol.9 (January 1944), pp.3–10

NELSON, T.R.H. "Gold Mining in South Wales. Part 2" *Mine and Quarry Engineering*, Vol.9 (February 1944), pp.33–38

NELSON, T.R.H. "Gold Mining in South Wales. Part 3" *Mine and Quarry Engineering*, Vol.9 (March 1944), pp.55–60

POLLINS, H. "The Swansea Canal" *Journal of Transport History*, Vol.1 No.2 (November 1953), pp.135–154

PUGH, Lenan "The Cardiganshire Leadmines" *Planet*, Vol.10 (1972), pp.55–66

REES, R. "The South Wales Copper Smoke Dispute 1833–1895" *Welsh History Review*, Vol.10 No.4 (1981), pp.480–496

ROBERTS, R.O "The Development and Decline of the Copper and Other Non–Ferrous Industries in South Wales" *Transactions of the Honourable Society of Cymmrodorian*, (1956), pp.78–115

ROBERTS, R.O. "The Bank of England, the Company of Copper Miners, and the Cwmavon Works, 1847–1852" *Welsh History Review*, Vol.4 No.3 (1969), pp.219–234

ROBERTS, R.O. "Enterprise and Capital for Non–Ferrous Metal Smelting in Glamorgan 1694–1924" *Journal of Glamorgan History*, Vol.23 (1979), pp.48–82

SHAW, Richard P. "Bwlch Glas Lead Mine, Cardiganshire" *Bulletin of the Peak District Mines Historical Society*, Vol.8 No.3 (Summer 1982), pp.187–192

SHAW, Richard P. & CRITCHLEY, Martin F. "Two Cardiganshire Lead Mines: Caegynon and Rheidol United" *Bulletin of the Peak District Mines Historical Society*, Vol.7 No.2 (October 1978), pp.69–86

THOMAS, B. "Iron Making in Dolgellau" *Journal of the Merioneth History and Record Society*, Vol.IX (1984)

TROTT, R.J. "Llanharry Mine (South Wales)" *Camborne School of Mines Journal*, (1951), pp.51–58

TUCK, J.P. & TUCK, N.W. "Roman Mine, Draethen, Glamorganshire" *Bristol Exploration Club*, Caving Report No.15 (July 1971)

TUCK, N.W. & TUCK, J.P. "Second Interim Report on Roman Mine, Monmouthshire" *British Caver*, (September 1965), pp.1–4

TUCKER, D.Gordon "The Lead Mines of Glamorgan and Gwent" *Morgannwg*, Vol.20 (1976), pp.37–52

TUCKER, D.Gordon "New Light on Llanfyrnach Lead Mine, Pembrokeshire" *British Mining*, No.11 (1979), pp.44–47

TUCKER, D.Gordon *See* TUCKER, Mary & TUCKER, D.Gordon

TUCKER, Mary "Lead Mining in Bishopston" *Gower*, Vol.27 (1976), pp.76–82

TUCKER, Mary "The System of Watercourses to Lead Mines from the River Leri" *Ceredigion*, (1977), pp.217–223

TUCKER, Mary & TUCKER, D.Gordon "The Lead Mines of South East Wales" *Bulletin of the Peak District Mines Historical Society*, Vol.6 No.1 (May 1975), pp.15–27

VERNON, Robert W. *See* MORRIS, Trevor & VERNON, Robert W.

WILLIAMS, Christopher J. "The Lead Mines of the Alyn Valley" *Flintshire Historical Society Journal*, Vol.29 (1979–80), pp.51–87

WILLIAMS, Colin *See* BOON, George C. & WILLIAMS, Colin

LIST OF PERIODICALS CONSULTED

Agricultural History Review

Albion

Amateur Historian

Antiquity

Archaeologia Aeliana

Archaeologia Cambrensis (Journal of the Cambrian Archaeological Association)

Archaeological Association

Archaeological Journal

Britannia

British Caver

British Mining (Journal of the Northern Mine Research Society)

Bulletin of the Association for Industrial Archaeology

Bulletin of the Board of Celtic Studies

Bulletin of the Cleveland and Teesside Local History Society

Bulletin of the Durham City Local History Society

Bulletin of the Geological Survey of Great Britain

Bulletin of the Grampian Spelaeological Group

Bulletin of the Historical Metallurgy Group

Bulletin of Local Studies

Bulletin of the North East Industrial Archaeology Society

Bulletin of the Peak District Mines Historical Society

Business History

Caernarvonshire Record Office Bulletin

Cake and Cockhorse

Camborne School of Mines Journal

Canadian Mining and Metallurgical Bulletin

Carmarthenshire Antiquary

Carmarthen County Museum Publications

Cave Science
Ceredigion (Journal of the Cardiganshire Antiquarian Society)
Chetham Society
Cleveland Industrial Archaeologist
Cornish Archaeology
Cornish Magazine
Country Life
Country Quest
Current Archaeology
Dalesman
Dartmoor Magazine
Denbighshire Historical Society Transactions
Derbyshire Archaeological Journal
Derbyshire Countryside
Derbyshire Miscellany
Descent
Devon and Cornwall Notes and Querries
Devon Historian
Dowty Group Journal
Durham County Local History Society Journal
East Midland Geographer
Economic Geography
Economic History Review
Exmoor Review
Flintshire Historical Society Journal
Geographical Journal
Geographical Magazine
Geography
Geology Teaching
Glasgow Spelaeological Journal
Gower
History Wokshop
Industrial and Commercial Photographer

Industrial Archaeology

Industrial Archaeology Review

Industrial Heritage (Journal of Durham University Industrial Archaeology Group)

Industrial Past

Journal of the Bristol Industrial Archaeology Society

Journal of the Bristol Exploration Club

Journal of the Cerberus Spelaeology Society

Journal of the Chester Archaeological Society

Journal of the Derbyshire Archaeological and Natural History Society

Journal of the Friends of Pembroke Museum

Journal of the Glamorgan History Society

Journal of the Gloucester Society for Industrial Archaeology

Journal of the Halifax Antiquarian Society

Journal of Historical Geography

Journal of the Historical Metallurgy Society

Journal of Industrial Archaeology

Journal of Interdisciplinary Economics

Journal of the Iron and Steel Institute

Journal of the Merioneth Historical and Record Society

Journal of the Northern Pennine Club

Journal of Past and Present Mining Studies (Wigan and District Mining and Technical College)

Journal of Roman Studies

Journal of the Royal Institution of Cornwall

Journal of the Sheffield University Spelaeological Society

Journal of the Trevithick Society

Journal of Transport History

Kingston Geographer

Lady

Lincolnshire Industrial Archaeology Group Journal

Listener

Llafur

Local Historian
Loughborough Museum Services Publications
Manchester School
Manifold Caver
Memoirs of the Northern Cavern and Mine Research Society
Mendip Nature Research Committee Journal
Metallurgia
Midland History
Mine and Quarry Engineering
Mine and Quarry
Mine Explorer (Journal of the Cumbria Amenity Trust)
Mining Magazine
Moldywarps Spelaeological Group Journal
Montgomeryshire Collections
Morgannwg
National Library of Wales Journal
North East Industrial Archaeology Society
North Yorkshire Record Office Journal
Northern History
Old Cornwall
Paedagogica
Past and Present Mining Studies Association Journal
Pembroke Magazine
Planet
Plumbing Trades Journal
Plymouth Caving Club Journal and Newsletter
Plymouth Mineral and Mining Club Journal
Portsmouth Polytechnic Industrial Archaeology Society
Proceedings of the Geologists Association
Proceedings of the Society of Antiquaries of Scotland
Proceedings of the Somerset Archaeological and Natural History Society
Proceedings of the South Wales Institute of Engineers
Proceedings of the Ussher Society

LIST OF PERIODICALS CONSULTED

Quarry Managers Journal
Recusant History
Royal Cornwall Polytechnic Society Annual Report
Ryedale Historian
School Science Review
Scots Magazine
Scottish Archaeological Forum
Sheffield Clarion Ramblers' Booklet
Shropshire Caving and Mining Club Journal
Shropshire Mining Club Journal
Somerset Mines Research Group Journal
Sorby Record
South Eastern Naturalist and Antiquary
South Wales and Monmouth Recreational Society Publications
Southern History
Staffordshire Industrial Archaeology Society Bulletin
Surrey Archaeological Collection
Sussex Industrial History
Tamar Journal
Technology and Culture
Transactions of the Anglesey Antiquarian Society
Transactions of the Bristol and Gloucester Archaeological Society
Transactions of the British Cave Research Association
Transactions of the Caenarvonshire Historical Society
Transactions of the Cave Research Group
Transactions of the Cornish Institute of Engineers
*Transaction of the Cornish Institute of Mining, Mechanical and Metal-
lurgical Engineers*
*Transactions of the Cumberland and Westmorland Antiquarian and Ar-
chaeological Society*
Transactions of the Devonshire Association
*Transactions of the Dumfries and Galloway Natural History and Archae-
ological Society*

Transactions of the Halifax Antiquarian Society

Transactions of the Honourable Society of Cymmrodorian

Transactions of the Institution of Mining and Metallurgy

Transactions of the Newcomen Society

Transactions of the Radnorshire Society

Transactions of the Royal Geological Society of Cornwall

Transactions of the Royal Society of Edinburgh

Transactions of the Scarborough and District Archaeological Society

Transactions of the Teesside Industrial Archaeology Society

Transactions of the Woolhope Naturalist Field Club

Transport History

University of Leeds Spelaeological Association Journal

Welsh History Review

Wheals Magazine (House magazine of South Crofty)

Yorkshire Archaeological Journal

Yorkshire Bulletin of Economic and Social Research

Yorkshire Underground Research Team Journal

Y Cymmrodor